DEATH, SEX, AND FERTILITY
Population Regulation in Preindustrial and Developing Societies

DEATH, SEX, AND FERTILITY

Population Regulation in Preindustrial and Developing Societies

Marvin Harris and Eric B. Ross

Columbia University Press
New York   1987

Library of Congress Cataloging-in-Publication Data

Harris, Marvin, 1927–
    Death, sex, and fertility.

    Bibliography: p.
    Includes index.
        1. Demographic anthropology.   2. Fertility, Human.
    3. Birth control.   I. Ross, Eric B.   II. Title.
    GN33.5.H37   1987   304.6′32   86–18401
    ISBN 0–231–06270–2

Columbia University Press
New York   Guildford, Surrey
Copyright © 1987 Columbia University Press

Printed in the United States of America

Book design by Ken Venezio

Contents

Introduction   1

1.   Population Regulation Among Early Human Foragers   21

2.   Population Regulation and Agricultural Modes of Production   37

3.   Population Regulation and the Rise of the State   73

4.   Population Regulation in the Age of Colonialism   103

5.   Population Regulation and the Development Process   155

References   185

Index   211

DEATH, SEX, AND FERTILITY
Population Regulation in Preindustrial and Developing Societies

Introduction

This book reassesses the balance between mutable cultural factors and more intractable biological processes in the establishment of modes of reproduction among preindustrial and developing societies. We use the expression "mode of reproduction" to denote the interrelated population-regulating activities and "decisions" engaged in either consciously or unconsciously that have the combined effect of raising or lowering rates of population growth.

During the past two decades archeological, historical, and ethnological studies of population phenomena indicate that preindustrial cultural means of regulating population growth exerted a more powerful effect on the balance of mortality and fertility rates than was previously credited. Much evidence indicates that human reproductive patterns are seldom completely at the mercy of sexual and environmental imperatives (Harris 1975:455–459; Caldwell 1977; Nardi 1983), and that preindustrial population rates reflect some form of optimization effort engaged in by individuals and groups, rather than a culturally unregulated surrender to sex, hunger, and death. Among preindustrial populations both age-specific fertility and age-specific mortality could readily be raised or lowered in conformity with optimizing rationalities which maintained or enhanced the well-being of individuals and groups—although seldom with equal or even beneficial results for all.

Infrastructure, Structure, and Superstructure

The research strategy employed in this book is known as cultural materialism. Sociocultural systems are heuristically regarded as having three major sectors: infrastructure, consisting of mode of production and mode of reproduction; structure, or domestic and political economy; and superstructure, or aesthetic, symbolic, philosophical, and religious beliefs and practices. While all three sectors are causally linked to each other, infrastructure is seen as being more powerfully determinative in a probabilistic sense than the structural or superstructural sectors. This is known as the principle of infrastructural determinism. (See Harris 1978 and Ross 1980 for a detailed exposition of the principles and substantive results of the cultural materialist approach.)

In applying this principle to the explanation of demographic phenomena, we commit ourselves to the viewpoint that the primary determinants of different modes of reproduction reside in infrastructure, not in structure or superstructure, as is widely believed. But if mode of reproduction is itself a component of infrastructure, how does the principle of infrastructural determinism apply? We are not prepared to make any categorical assertion that either mode of production or mode of reproduction is dominant over the other. Rather, we propose that both are mutually determinative, causally intertwined in the fabric of human social relations, providing in conjunction the basic demographic, technological, economic, and ecological interface between culture and nature through which the laws of physics, chemistry, biology, and psychology influence the direction of cultural selection and cultural evolution, and thus impart to infrastructure its dominant role.

Before proceeding with a more detailed exposition of what we mean by mode of reproduction, we should indicate that the principle of infrastructural determinism allows for, indeed demands the recognition of, causally powerful but not dominant feedbacks between superstructure and structure upon infrastructure. We insist as firmly as other social scientists that all aspects of sociocultural systems are causally linked to each other but we deny that the links are symmetrical. This qualification emerges from the distinctive comparative and macro-historical-evolutionary perspectives of cultural anthropology and anthropological archaeology and it stands opposed to paradigms in anthropology and other disciplines which ignore the long view.

When sociocultural differences and similarities including demographic variables are examined synchronically, causal relationships rapidly dissolve into an incoherent corpus of middle-range eclectic correlations linking infrastructural, structural, and super-structural components in infinite arrays. It then appears empirically demonstrable that there are no overall asymmetries in the causal nexus. This error cannot be resolved simply by adding short-run time frames. Indeed, dependence on short time frames compounds the problem and leads to the impression that in certain historical moments and societies, structure and/or superstructure dominate infrastructure. For example, in the shortest term, implementation of the Chinese one child per couple governmental population policy has had important demographic effects (although not necessarily only the intended ones). It appears therefore that "politics is in command" (to use a phrase applied to the attempt to increase production during the epoch of the "great leap forward"). Yet in the longer term, it is also evident that the phenomenal growth of China's population during the past century was itself the precondition of the present-day one child policy and, as we would argue, a precondition for the development of China's peculiar agro-managerial "communist" political economy as well.

A similar expansion of time frame exposes the fallacy of "religion in command" as in the case of contemporary Iran. While Shi'ite fundamentalism has profoundly changed the reproductive and productive activities of the Iranian people, the conditions for the overthrow of the Shah were created during the prior colonialist struggle for control over Iran's oil reserves.

As these examples demonstrate, it is easy enough to refute the claim that infrastructure is subordinate to structure and super-structure simply by altering the slice of time during which the relationships among the sectors are examined. But the cultural materialist claim for infrastructural priority is subject to the same refutation. If infrastructural determinism affirms that structural and superstructural features emplaced by infrastructural processes exert a causal influence upon further infrastructural changes—i.e., affirms that causes become effects and effects become causes—then all claims of causal priority are untenable. Our response to this line of reasoning is that the events and transformations of history and prehistory must be read forward, not backward, from the paleolithic to the industrial age. It is a record that has a definite beginning in hunter-gatherer band types of sociocultural systems.

These evolve at definite times and places into sociocultural systems associated with villages, chiefdoms, and states. During these major transformations it can be shown logically and empirically that changes in infrastructure dominate changes in other sectors and that therefore a proper understanding of history and prehistory cannot be achieved by reading arbitrary slices of time, but only by reading forward from the paleolithic or from the junction between major types of social formations.

In general, the preconditions for transitions from bands to villages and from villages to chiefdoms and states are higher levels of productivity and denser and more sedentary populations. These in turn are decisively conditioned by technoeconomic restraints. For example, as we shall see in examining the limited demographic and political potential of the Amazon floodplains later on (chapter 2), no amount of collective political genius could have created in the Amazon the concentrated settlements and high regional densities which are known everywhere else to have preceded the rise of the state (Fried 1967; Sanders and Price 1968; Harris 1977). Human groups in other words cannot arbitrarily and willfully intensify productivity and raise population densities to the levels that make the formation of complex stratified polities possible and probable. If politics or religion were really in command, we should never be able to explain why band organizations persisted for hundreds of thousands of years, villages were rarities until 8000 B.C. and the first states did not make an appearance until a mere 5,000 years ago. One might argue that these dates correspond to the amount of time needed for the maturation of the ideas which were appropriate for the transformations in question, but the fact is that the transformations do not occur everywhere—bands, villages, and agrarian states linger on in some locales to this very day—and it is both their presence or absence in specific places as well as at specific times that needs to be explained. This cannot be done nomothetically without specifying recurrent conditions that are external to structure and superstructure—conditions that can lie nowhere else but among the constants and variables of infrastructure which constitute, as we have said, the interface between culture and nature.

Modes of Reproduction

Modes of reproduction consist of practices which directly or indirectly affect reproductive processes, which, in particular, can modify fertility and mortality rates over a wide range of values according to the optimizing pressures imposed by particular modes of production under given techno-environmental circumstances. It is their tendency, under such pressures, toward a systemic effect that makes us favor the view that such practices may be regarded as the constituents of what we term a "mode of reproduction."

For purposes of clarification, these practices can be grouped into four categories: (a) care and treatment of fetuses, infants, and children; (b) the care and treatment of girls and women (and to a lesser extent of boys and men); (c) lactation frequency and scheduling; and (d) coital frequency and scheduling. A brief discussion of the most important population-regulating practices in each category follows:

Care of Fetuses, Infants, and Children

A subtle gradation leads from mobilization of resources in support of healthy births to indirect and direct abortion. Bearing in mind that intra-uterine death and abortion is "naturally" high—it is estimated up to 25 percent of pregnancies after four weeks (Mac-Cormack 1982:1)—in human females, it is clear that carrying a fetus to term is a process sensitive to varied environmental conditions. Full support of fetuses involves supplementing the diet of pregnant women and reducing their work load. By the same token, apart from miscarriages associated with physiological or genetic abnormality, abortion may be induced indirectly by a wide range of factors, including heavy work and severe nutritional deprivation. This grades into direct abortion where such deprivation or work is avoidable or there is deliberate mechanical trauma (for example, pressure from tight bands) or chemical trauma, caused by the ingestion of toxic substances (Devereux 1967).

Similar subtle gradations lead from the full support of infants to indirect and direct forms of infanticide. Full support of neonates involves nursing at well-nourished breasts, protection from extremes of temperatures, and careful nurturant handling. Indirect infanticide begins with inadequate feeding, withholding of the breast, premature weaning, exposure to extremes of temperature, and careless and indifferent handling especially during illnesses. Direct infanticide involves more or less rapid starvation, dehydration, exposure to the elements, suffocation, and fatal blows to the head.

Scrimshaw (1983) lists seven common forms of infanticidal behavior, only one of which actually involves direct killing:

Deliberate killing
Placing in dangerous situation
Abandonment with chance of survival
"Accidents"
Excessive physical punishments
Lowered biological support
Lowered emotional support

Contrary to the categorizations of scientific vital statistics, there is no sharp behavioral distinction between abortion and infanticide. As Polgar points out:

It may be well for some purposes to treat infanticide and abortion in a single category. The practice of demographers of counting infanticides in both birth rates and death rates, while not including abortions in either, is misleading. The means to prevent the progression from a conception to a live infant practiced by the Yanomama, for one, cannot be easily classified as either abortion or infanticide: they precipitate labor during the sixth or seventh months of gestation and kill the fetus if it shows signs of life after expulsion (Neel 1968). Furthermore, "birth" is often defined socially at a point later than parturition. (1972:206)

Dickemann (1984) has extended this process even further to take into account the fact that it is not only infants who are subject to direct and indirect forms of homicide but children as well. Her suggestion that we rename the category of induced early deaths "feticide-infanticide-pedicide" has considerable merit. It draws attention to the fact that the creation of a new human life does not occur with birth or the fertilization of an ovum by a sperm, but as a result of a continuous process that extends from sexual coupling to several years after birth, with the fate of the emergent individual entirely dependent on the activities of its social companions and guardians, at every point along the way.

It is interesting to note in this regard that from the viewpoints of the participants (emic perspective), the socially sanctioned direct killing of an unwanted infant or child usually takes place before the victim achieves the status of having become human. As Minturn and Stashak (1982) have shown, for example, infanticide usually occurs before the rituals which mark the transition to human status take place. (It should be noted, however, that because demographers do not tend to regard reproduction in biosocial terms, "infanticide is not, strictly speaking, a factor affecting fertility" in their view—Watkins and Van de Walle 1983:14.)

Treatment of Women

Aside from helping to decide the fate of fetus and infant, treatment of women can raise or lower age of menarche, lengthen or reduce the period of adolescent sterility, increase or decrease the frequency of amenorrhea, and hasten or retard perimenopausal fertility decline. Variations in nutritional status are a major source of these effects although their precise influence remains to be determined in particular cases. It is conceded that severe famine-level nutritional deprivations can reduce fertility by 50 percent (Bongaarts 1980:568) but the effects of "mild chronic malnutrition" remain a focus of controversy (Bongaarts 1982). Frisch (1984:184) maintains that a 10–15 percent weight loss "delays menarche and causes amenorrhea." We shall return to this controversy in the next chapter. It should be kept in mind, however, that while the effects of nutritional stress on fertility are debatable, the effects of nutritional stress on the mortality of mother, fetus, and infant are well established. Poor maternal nutritional status increases the risk of premature births and of low birth-weights, both of which increase fetal and infant mortality; poor maternal nutrition also diminishes the quantity, if not the quality of breast milk, which lowers infant survival chances still further (Hamilton et al.

1984:388). In turn, women who become pregnant and who recurrently provide mother's milk from a nutritionally depleted body also have elevated mortality rates (Trussell and Pebley 1984; Jelliffe and Jelliffe 1978; Fedrick and Adelstein 1973). These nutritional effects will all vary in interaction with the amount of psychological and physical stress imposed upon pregnant and lactating women. Female life expectancy in addition can be affected by exposure to toxic body shock techniques of abortion, again in interaction with general nutritional status.

Extreme malnutrition and physical and mental stress may also affect male fecundity by reducing libido and sperm motility (Keys et al. 1950). However, the abundance of sperm as compared with the ova and the female's birthing and nursing physiology render the treatment of females far more important than the treatment of males in modifying fertility. Moreover, higher morbidity and mortality rates among males are readily counterbalanced by the widespread practice of polygyny.

Lactational Frequency and Scheduling

Amenorrhea is a typical accompaniment of breast-feeding. The effect is associated with the production of prolactin, the hormone that regulates mammary activity. Prolactin in turn inhibits the production of the gonadotrophic hormones that regulate the ovulatory cycle (*Nature* 1985). Several biocultural factors appear to control the duration of lactational amenorrhea. To begin with there is the question of the mother's competency as determined by the state of her health and her nutritional status. Additional variables include the intensity of suckling as determined by how rapidly the infant is fed supplemental soft foods, and the scheduling of suckling episodes. While the relative importance of these factors remains controversial (Bongaarts 1980, 1982; Frisch 1984), it is clear that under favorable conditions lactational practices can result in birth spacing intervals of three or more years with a degree of reliability comparable to modern mechanical and chemical contraceptives (Short 1984:36). But one must be on guard against the notion that any social group is free to adjust its fertility rate upwards or downwards merely by intensifying and prolonging lactation. Prolonged lactation cannot take place without suitably nourished mothers (Hamilton, Popkin, and Spicer 1984:9). Moreover, human breast milk is deficient in iron and its use as the sole source of nourishment much beyond six months places infants at risk for anemia. In addition, milk quantity peaks between 3 to 6 months, requiring supplementation by semisolids thereafter (Raphael 1984:204). Finally, demands on mother's labor time may interfere with frequent nursing (p. 203).

Coital Frequency and Scheduling

Coital abstinence can be sustained long enough to influence fertility and delays in the onset of coital behavior can shorten the female's reproductive span (Nag 1983b). The contraceptive effects of lactational amenorrhea can be reinforced by postpartum coital abstinence, while various forms of nonreproductive sex can influence fertility rates with or without being associated with postpartum abstinence. Homosexuality, masturbation, coitus interruptus, and noncoital heterosexual techniques for achieving orgasm can all play a role in regulating fertility. Age at marriage is another important variable whose significance derives from its effect on the scheduling of female participation in reproductive coital sex. Although age at marriage has been emphasized by demographers as the most important factor affecting fertility in European history, it must be remembered that its significance stems entirely from the existence of a taboo on extramarital sex and unwed motherhood. In anthropological perspective, there is little support for Bongaarts' contention that "menarche signals the beginning of potential childbearing but actual reproduction starts at marriage" (1980:566). Even if European parish records convey an accurate picture of the rate of premarital conceptions (which seem unlikely because of their failure to identify out-of-wedlock abortions, and out-of-wedlock infanticides disguised as abortions), reproductive coital sex is by no means universally restricted to married couples. In fact, it is often the case in preindustrial societies (and, indeed, frequently the case in sections of many industrial societies) not that childbearing begins with marriage, but that marriage begins with childbearing (Harris 1985:259–260; Wilmsen 1982:4).

Type of marriage is also relevant to fertility. Polygyny, for example, assures that almost all females will engage in reproductive sex (in the absence of contraception). But polygyny is also effective in prolonging postpartum sexual abstinence and the latter's reinforcing effect on lactational amenorrhea. In addition, polygyny probably results in lower rates of coital intercourse per wife as their husbands grow older (Bongaarts et al. 1984:521–522).

It is clear from this summary that individuals in preindustrial societies possess diverse culturally-patterned means for changing fertility and mortality rates and hence their aggregate demographic destinies. That human modes of reproduction are modifiable through such an array of behaviors does not, of course, mean that the degree of regulation is unlimited. As we have said, population-regulating practices are constrained by reproductive physiology and modes of production which operate within bounds prescribed by biological, technological, economic and environmental conditions. Within such limits, however, observed levels of fertility and mortality can be viewed largely as an outcome of pressures toward minimizing the costs of reproduction and maximizing its benefits. It also bears repeating that the cumulative consequences of fertility-regulating behavior themselves feed back into and condition the mode of production.

Benefits of Child Rearing

Two questions immediately arise: What kinds of costs and benefits enter into the regulatory calculus? And who are the net beneficiaries? The benefits of rearing children certainly include sentimental or affective satisfactions. We assume that humans have a genetically controlled propensity shared with other primates to find infants emotionally appealing and to derive emotional satisfaction from holding and fondling them and from watching and helping them play and learn. As children grow older their respect and love for their parents may also be highly valued. Unfortunately it is impossible to weigh these affective factors—even qualitatively—

against the set of costs and benefits of reproduction discernable in the more "material" aspects of production, domestic life, and political economy. But this admission is not as damaging to our model as it might at first seem. While biologically determined sentimental satisfactions enter into the reproductive calculus, we can assume that all human groups share virtually the same set of relevant genes. We may therefore regard the potential sentimental rewards of reproduction as exercising a constant pressure for birthing and rearing as many children as human physiology permits. It is clear, however, that whatever the precise strength of this pressure, it can be modified by culture so completely as to accommodate extremely antinatal practices resulting in lifetime childlessness for a significant minority if not the majority of men and women. (As among members of celibate orders or today's "yuppie" generation.) Moreover, in view of the constancy of species-given impulses leading to pronatal and child-rearing behavior, the focus of our inquiry necessarily must turn to those variable costs and benefits which sometimes give full reign to human fecundity and sometimes totally suppress it.

Among preindustrial populations the central "material" benefits for rearing children reside in the replacement of deceased or aging producers with younger and more vigorous producers. Fertility and child-rearing are systematically promoted as long as the investment in children results in a net gain for the parental generation (Caldwell 1982, 1983). This gain consists of income, labor, and the care and protection of parents. Another set of material benefits of rearing children relates to their role in marital exchanges and alliances. While incest prohibitions generally deter matings with closest kin, children regularly figure in multigenerational systems of marital exchange. The parental generations of domestic or political groups acquire wives or husbands from each other by, in effect, "mortgaging" unborn children for future exchanges or to consolidate present material advantages. Another value of rearing children relates to the need for individual and group defense. Where internecine threats and/or chronic warfare exist, childless individuals and smaller groups are exposed to greater hazards and possibly higher mortality rates than larger groups. Small groups also are less able to contract marriage-mediated alliances essential for military success (see chapter 2).*

Costs of Child Rearing: Direct and Indirect

Among most preindustrial societies the main child-rearing costs are incurred over a period of five or six years (see chapter 5). Extra calories and nutrients consumed or work foregone during pregnancy and lactation place a considerable burden on domestic budgets. The birth process itself is dangerous for the mother and may result in death or illness and deprivation of her care, affection, and labor power. In addition, considerable effort may be needed to carry infants or toddlers from one place to another. After weaning, however, children in most preindustrial societies rapidly begin to "pay" for themselves. They contribute to the production of their own food, clothing, and housing, and under favorable conditions (discussed later on) they may begin to produce surpluses above their own subsistence needs as early as at six years of age (see Gross 1984 for a comprehensive review). This transition is hastened with successive births since senior siblings and other children assume much of the costs of grooming and caring for their juniors.

It would appear that children are an excellent "bargain" for preindustrial societies insofar as child-rearing costs can be outweighed by the benefits children bestow on the parental generation (especially if we add in affective rewards). The problem, however, is that there are additional costs of an indirect nature

---

*The value of children in exchange or alliance applies to preindustrial and developing societies alike; indeed, royal marriages in Europe functioned in this manner well into the present century, and wealthy families still tend to circulate their offspring within institutional settings—schools primarily—which promote the likelihood of economically and socially favorable marriages. The value of children for defense, on the other hand, has undergone certain fundamental and noteworthy changes. Where offspring in preindustrial populations represented a certain contribution to general community welfare that could positively contribute to average parental welfare, the evolution of class societies created a far less equitable situation. The burdens of fighting were shifted onto the lower social classes and the benefits were monopolized at the top.

which can potentially wipe out all the direct benefits of child-rearing—indeed wipe out the whole society. As fertility and child-rearing rates increase and get translated into population growth, the rising ratio of population to productive resources leads to an accelerating depletion of the environment and declining yields per unit of work effort—unless there is, within a short enough time span, a shift to a more exploitable habitat or to a more efficient or intensive technology.

As we shall see, considerable evidence points to the existence of self-regulating feedbacks between rates of productivity and reproductivity. Depletion-related declines in productivity get more or less rapidly expressed on the level of individual reproductive decision-making, lowering or reversing the cost/benefit balance (or the marginal utility) of additional children and dampening or reversing population growth rates. Throughout prehistory rates of growth were probably checked well before a population's density reached its habitat's carrying capacity under a particular techno-environmental regime, that is, well before miseration and irreversible depletions occurred (Sahlins 1972). This implies that throughout prehistory, population densities and growth rates oscillated within a range compatible with maintaining adequate nutritional standards and moderate work levels.

Control, Consciousness, and Systems

In our view, contemporary demographic approaches suffer from two misconceptions: first, that anything but minimal population regulation exists except when there are conscious policy decisions (Knodel and Van de Walle 1979); and, second, that the main effects of population regulation are achieved through fertility control rather than by mortality or death control. The two misconceptions are interrelated.

The issue of whether or not population is regulated by conscious decisions based upon conscious familial or political policies is in large part rendered problematical by the very nature of observable demographic evidence. We say this because there are no practicable methodologies which can reliably resurrect the actual individual states of consciousness associated with the relevant behavior of persons long dead or even of living people possessing widely different cultural traditions. This is not to deny that conscious decisions based on calculated costs and benefits of rearing children occur among preindustrial (or industrial) societies, but merely to affirm that it is knowledge of aggregate or systematic behavioral effects which is necessary and usually sufficient for understanding different modes of reproduction, as well as other basic aspects of sociocultural evolution. Thus, when most men in a New Guinea society engage in intense and exclusive homosexuality, severely limiting the marital coital rate (see chapter 2), one does not need to know whether or not individuals consciously intend to "control" their wives' fertility rate to conclude that their homosexuality is a population-regulating mechanism.

Accordingly, the "rationality" or "optimizing" tendencies we discern in preindustrial population-regulating systems do not necessarily reside in the consciousness of the individuals whose aggregate behavior constitutes their society's demographic fate— and, indeed, conditions their own. We maintain only that the relationship of births and deaths tends to reflect a biocultural pressure to balance the costs and benefits of reproduction to individuals and/or groups, to minimize the former and maximize the latter. Regardless of whether this "logic" is consciously perceived by individual participants, we may regard it as an aggregate or systemic property of a society's mode of reproduction.

It should not be necessary for us to defend at length the epistemological basis of this claim. Sociocultural systems evolve in conformity with the consequences for individuals and groups who do or do not adopt innovations. We invite those who find it difficult to comprehend how such systems can embody a rational or optimizing calculus in the absence of conscious calculation to examine the occurrence of optimizing relations established through selection-by-consequences in the evolution of species, in the behavior patterns of a single species of organism, and in the behavior of communities of diverse species organized into ecosystems (Skinner 1984). As we shall see in the next section, evidence of conscious intent cannot be made the necessary condition for the existence of either birth or death control, and in fact eventuates in seriously misleading assumptions.

This brings us to the second weakness of contemporary demographic theories, namely the relative neglect of mortality controls as components of modes of reproduction. Preston attributes the "decline of mortality studies" to the presumption that mortality is "outside the policy sphere, since nations will (or at least should) never spend less than the maximum they can afford to promote human health and longevity." Yet, "mortality levels are inevitably a product of social and individual choice made under budget constraints and in the presence of competing alternatives" (1976:x). In our view, the neglect of mortality as a component in modes of reproduction is better seen as a further consequence of the overemphasis on "policy" and conscious decision making, and of an allied tendency to identify population regulation narrowly with modern contraception (Knodel and Van de Walle 1979). While the latter may be a matter of conscious intent, and "birth control" in general is often carried out with conscious design, "death control" (to coin a phrase) may escape notice altogether, if one is not prepared to give priority to behavioral consequences over conscious intent. The tardy recognition of the importance of direct and indirect forms of infanticide in the demographic history of Europe and Asia (as discussed in chapters 3 and 5) reflects the deep-seated conservatism of scholars who are reluctant to confront the lack of correspondence between moral precepts and actual behavior, between intention and deed, not as a footnote but as the main text of history. As we shall see, the same reliance on conscious decision-making confounds the arguments on both sides in the current debate over abortion. As already implied, abortion—feticide—is a form of death control as well as of birth control and it is the unintended rather than the intended effects of suppressing abortion on the rate of infanticide and pedicide that require emphasis— especially in third world and poverty contexts (see chapter 5).

Natural Fertility and Natural Mortality

"Natural fertility" was defined by Henry as fertility which "exists or has existed in the absence of deliberate birth control" (1961:81). Demographers have sought to operationalize the distinction between natural or uncontrolled versus controlled, targeted, or parity-dependent fertility rates on the basis of the shape of age-specific fertility curves. In natural fertility regimes, births are relatively evenly spaced throughout the reproduction span. In controlled fertility regimes, births are clustered at the beginning of the re- productive span and decline rapidly thereafter. Expressed as a percentage of the fertility rate at age 20, the natural age-specific fertility curve is concave, while the controlled age-specific fertility is convex.

The occurrence of these two different types of age-specific fer- tility curves is not in doubt. What needs to be corrected is the interpretation of their significance. First, it is certainly incorrect to posit an equivalence between the concave curve and a lack of birth control. Prolonged lactation controls the number of births by in- creasing the birth interval and yet produces a concave curve (Cash- dan 1985:651). Moreover, if the targeted number of children is very large, birth control through contraception will also produce a con- cave curve (Handwerker 1985:653).

Second, and more important to the thrust of this book, is the unoperationalizable assumption that the existence of a culturally controlled fertility regimen depends upon a deliberate, conscious calculus of an explicitly targeted number of desired offspring. The origin of this assumption lies in ethnocentric and especially in Eurocentric idealizations of the behavior of "progressive" post- demographic transition societies in comparison with the repro- ductive behavior of "backward," pre-demographic transition so- cieties. Only post-demographic transition contracepting societies are viewed as having the capacity to make rational calculations concerning the rearing of optimum numbers of children. Hence, evidence of the use of an array of culturally patterned procedures which demonstrably have the effect of controlling fertility in non- contracepting societies—abortion, abstinence, lactation—is cate- gorically demoted to the status of behavior whose "goal" had nothing to do with fertility control, and which therefore could not be true fertility control in the full noble idealist sense.

We will not repeat here at length our general objections to using intentionality as a mode of identifying cultural practices (see Harris 1979:29–45, 58–59 for a fuller exposition). Most succinctly put, be- havior and intention are often at variance; behavior often satisfies multiple goals; goals are often changed post hoc to justify behavior; contradictory goals exist in the same mind; and it is impossible to identify goals in the minds of the dead. Some of these difficulties can be illustrated with the example of fertility control through long lactation or postpartum abstinence. The expressed goal of most groups is to protect mother and child. Nothing is usually said about limiting fertility (Knodel 1977:220; Page and Lesthaeghe 1981; Cavilli-Sforza 1983:114). But clearly, this mode of protecting mother and child implies that there will be fewer births. To regard postpartum abstinence as an "attempt" to protect mother and child but not as an "attempt" to limit births is to assume a knowledge of thought processes which is thoroughly unwarranted by the available data. As Cashdan has observed,

Even where birth spacing is maintained by long lactation without infanticide or other obvious controls . . . it is not unlikely that the spacing effects of long lactation are recognized and appreciated by the population. . . . As with postpartum abstinence, which is often wrongly assumed to be a taboo practiced without regard for its fertility implications, the distinction between intentional and unintentional controls is not clear-cut. (1985:652)

Defining intentionality may be complicated, moreover, by the way in which conflicting personal, familial, and societal pressures are psychologically reconciled. Thus, since it frequently happens that the value of protecting mother and child is at odds with social demands for cheap children (see chapter 5), it is not unexpected that the adverse effect of the former on fertility would be repressed. In any event, given the impossibility of isolating authentic and unambiguous motives, what must be demonstrated by those who make "goals" the criteria of natural versus controlled fertility is that, as a result of the psychological saliency of the goal of protection over limitation, there is a substantial difference in behavioral outcome. No such demonstration is ever furnished.

Precisely the same issue arises if one turns from birth control to death control. "Overlaying" for example (see chapter 4) was supposedly viewed by European mothers as an accidental rather than deliberate cause of infant deaths. It would be naive in the extreme, however, not to regard overlaying as a culturally controlled component in infant mortality because the goal of the mother was to nurse her child, not to suffocate it.

All this is not to deny that there are important differences between the age-specific fertility curves produced by using modern abortion and contraceptive techniques and dollars-and-cents cost projections and those of preindustrial and prestate societies. But these differences are not a consequence of a supposed lack of "deliberate" birth and death controls among preindustrial populations, but of the absence of efficient means of abortion and contraception, plus the lack of standardized currencies which allow for precise costing.

If the distinction between "natural" and "target" fertility fails in the end as a behaviorally oriented principle, its persistence must be regarded as a reflection of enduring if arbitrary preconceptions about human history, in particular the view that "traditional" societies were characterized by an excess demand for offspring which rendered regulatory techniques unimportant—the essential concept of "natural fertility" (Handwerker in press). Again, it must be said that this arises out of the idealist conviction that "traditional" populations somehow live in a pristine state of nature, where biological processes remain uninfluenced by culture or the kind of rationality that is too often and far too readily equated with the rise of modern capitalist Europe. That such thinking reigned in the heyday of European colonialism hardly ennobles contemporary demographic thought.

Who Benefits?

The problem of describing and predicting (or retrodicting) the quantitative and qualitative features of population-regulating systems would be less formidable if the benefits and costs of rearing children accrued equally to each member of the adult generation. But from remotest antiquity some status roles and groups have probably borne more costs and/or received fewer benefits of child rearing and population regulation than others. Even before the emergence of well-defined castes and classes, sexual hierarchies disproportionately burdened women with the costs both of lowering and raising fertility and mortality rates. The costs of pregnancy, birth, abortion, and lactation are sex-specific as are most other stressful population-regulating mechanisms. To the extent that coercion and exploitation become involved, optimizing pressures must be seen increasingly from the perspective of the politically dominant sex or social stratum. As power differentials increase, the upper and lower strata may in fact develop different or even antagonistic systems of population regulation. In this case, two or more different optimizing rationalities may have to be considered, none of which alone can lead to an understanding of actual population trends. As we shall see, this methodological problem becomes particularly acute with the rise of ancient states and empires for whose ruling classes and peasantries high fertility and population growth had markedly different implications, although the phenomenon was already widespread as well among pre-state peoples in relation to sex-linked inequalities.

Optimal versus Optimizing

The identification of systemic optimizing rationalities in demographic behavior should never be confused with the position known as "panglossian functionalism" (Harris 1967:252). From the above discussion of modes of reproduction that distribute costs and benefits unequally between men and women and among classes and other hierarchical groups, it should be obvious that we do not regard any, much less all, population regulating systems as the best that can be achieved in the best of all possible worlds. Optimizing behavior merely selects for population regulating systems which are as good as or better than feasible alternatives *under the specific infrastructural conditions to which they are a response.* We shall have ample opportunity to demonstrate that "as good as or better than" in preindustrial contexts normally allows for considerable suffering and tragedy, and for the making of reproductive decisions in which infants, children, and mothers pay with their lives.

In the following chapters we shall attempt to survey the changing patterns of human reproductive control through the long course of cultural evolution, from early foraging populations to the appearance of the state and the rise of the capitalist world system.

Although much of our survey is historical and comparative, we believe that the issues raised, even in the course of discussing little-known peoples practicing unusual life styles, are in fact relevant to contemporary demographic processes. The tensions and contradictions that perennially arise between productivity and re-productivity represent a universal feature of human society. To put this issue in historical and comparative perspective may contribute in a positive way toward a future in which human fecundity may be harmoniously reconciled to the most progressive impulses of economic need.

1. Population Regulation Among Early Human Foragers

Although little is directly known about human reproductive behavior during the long span of the Paleolithic period, one fact seems certain: population grew at a very slow overall rate. At the end of several million years of hominid evolution, human beings remained rare creatures with a total worldwide population less than that which can be found today in a single large city such as New York or Moscow (table 1.1).

The basic reason for this slow rate of growth undoubtedly resides in the vulnerability of foraging modes of production to the adverse effects of animal and plant depletions. Hunter-gatherers lack the technology for controlling the rate or distribution of plant and animal reproduction, the hallmarks of domestication, and hence can sustain neither dense population nor prolonged periods of population increase.

Within the bounds set by the limited intensifiability of their

Table 1.1
Rates of Human Population Growth

Period	World population at end of period	Annual growth rate (%) during period
Paleolithic	6,000,000	0.0015
Mesolithic	8,500,000	0.0330
Neolithic	75,000,000	0.1000
Ancient empires (to A.D. 1)	225,000,000	0.5000

Source: Hassan 1978; Spengler 1974.

mode of production, fertility rates among foragers are further conditioned by the need which both sexes confront to walk or even run long distances and to relocate camps and homesites at frequent intervals.

Among foragers, toddlers or nursing infants must be carried thousands of kilometers per year and are therefore reared at intervals which enable their caretakers to escape the cost of more than one such burden at time (Lee 1972; Sussman 1972; Dumond 1975). More significantly, perhaps, foragers must reckon also with the "foregone income" of the burdened child carriers in terms of diminished productivity. This factor seems more important in the light of recent clarifications concerning the division of labor among foragers. Previously, it was widely believed that the dominant activity of foragers was hunting carried out exclusively by mobile males; females were pictured as more sedentary, home-based, and removed from the food quest in order to care for their infants and several children.

The principal implication of the current view that the human line inherited from its apelike ancestors, not a hunting disposition so much as "a generalist-omnivorous foraging strategy" (Zihlman 1983:25) with a preference for animal food (Harris 1986) is that the productive—as opposed to exclusively reproductive—role of women must have been more significant than previously supposed. Even where hunting was concerned, sex role specialization may well have been rather slight, considering that any over-rigid socialization in respect to foraging skills would have been counterproductive in an age when mortality was probably high and hunting in particular was hazardous (Allen et al. 1982). In such circumstances it would have been convenient for both sexes to develop some proficiency in hunting. In this regard, contemporary Eskimo populations are instructive, for it is not uncommon among them for the exigencies of sex ratios to be compensated for precisely in that way. Thus, Briggs has observed:

There is nothing holy to them about the sexual division of labor; neither is there, in their view, anything in the nature of either sex that makes it incapable of doing some of the jobs that the other sex ordinarily does. So if a family is short of daughters, a son—often the eldest son—may be brought up to help his mother. . . . Similarly, if a family has only daughters, a father may decide to bring up one or two daughters as hunters, so that they can help him and also that if anything should happen to him, the family will not be left without a provider. (1974:271)

Having made the point that, among our Paleolithic ancestors, hunting was very likely an activity in which males and females both participated, it remains to note, however, that hunting itself varied in importance according to ecological conditions (being probably more critical in colder zones) and that gathering—in its broadest sense—was more often by default the dominant productive activity. As Tanner and Zihlman have observed:

Although meat is highly valued, in fact women's gathering activities contribute between 60 and 80 percent of the total diet. Among today's remaining gathering-hunting peoples, in all but extremely cold environments gathering is the most dependable food-getting technique, and plant food and small animal protein is the source of a large proportion of daily food intake. Gathering may account for up to 90 percent of diet under some circumstances, and it usually produces over 50 percent. (1976:598)

Such issues have obvious import for understanding the low level of population growth during the Paleolithic period. Handwerker (1983:14–16), Frisch (1978a), and others have made the suggestion that a low fertility rate would have owed much to a high female workload; and, although Handwerker (1983:15) for one tends to assume that such work would largely have entailed child care, the argument is strengthened if adult females engaged in a wide range of subsistence activities whose efficiency would be increased by not rearing another child until the first no longer impeded the mother's mobility.

Physiological Effects of Foraging

Female involvement in foraging activities which require intense physical activity also has a number of significant consequences for reproductive physiology. One is that menarche may be postponed into the late teens and menopause advanced into the early forties (Hamilton, Popkin, and Spicer 1984:6–8). Among the Dobe !Kung, for example, menarche does not occur until a mean of 16.6 years and the average age at first birth is about 19 (Howell 1979:178-179). This does not appear to be a simple result of nutritional status, for

Dobe !Kung women are well nourished from the point of view of protein, minerals, and vitamins. But, their calorie budget is low in relation to their activity level, so that they characteristically present a slender muscular physique with only 20.6 percent of body mass consisting of fat (p. 198). Dobe !Kung women thus resemble Western female athletes or ballet dancers who often have delayed menarche and irregular menstruation (Frisch 1984; Bullen et al. 1985).

The depressing effect on fertility of a foraging life-style is suggested additionally by the observation that !Kung women who have adopted a more sedentary existence at Bantu cattle stations and who consume more grains and milk, reach menarche earlier and have a 30 percent reduction in birth intervals (Howell 1979:210).

Clearly, strenuous physical effort and calorie intake together have a synergistic effect on fertility. The actual processes involved are still unresolved, but seem to depend on hormonal levels which govern the onset of menstruation, its regularity and the resumption of ovulation subsequent to childbirth. Thus, low calorie intake relative to a high level of activity—expressed, for example, as a low percentage of body fat (Frisch and McArthur 1974)—may have an endocrinological effect which, among other things, diminishes fertility by suppressing ovulation (Wilmsen 1982; Graham 1985). Thus, research among the Kalahari San suggests that "anovulatory times may coincide with periods of the year when nutrition is less than optimal" (Van der Walt, Wilmsen, and Jenkins 1978:662).

While the evidence of menstrual dysfunction resulting from athletic activity is fairly strong, there still remains some controversy over the relationship of nutrition and amenorrhea, especially in the postpartum period (Huffman et al. 1978; Bongaarts 1980; Wilmsen 1982). Frisch has suggested "that amenorrhea occurring among poorly nourished lactating women may be a direct effect of their having insufficient body fat" (Huffman et al. 1978). The precise dynamics of lactational amenorrhea remain obscure, however, particularly the role of maternal nutrition. On the other hand, one factor which clearly seems implicated in determining the length of time before ovulation resumes is the duration of breast-feeding (Wishik and Stern 1975). Suckling has been shown to have a direct effect on prolactin levels, which in turn govern ovulation. The extent of the effect probably depends in various ways on the mother's nutritional status, but at present at least what is clear is that breast-feeding plays a major role in prolonging postpartum amenorrhea (Huffman et al. 1978). Thus, among foragers, where weaning foods are scarce, protracted lactation may well have influenced birth spacing.

Spontaneous Abortion Among Foragers

Another important way in which production activities probably influenced reproduction among prehistoric foragers was by affecting the rate of spontaneous abortion. This seems to be a safe conclusion in view of the fact that spontaneous abortion is a mechanism of fertility control which occurs widely in nature in animal species in response to stress. Recent research indicates that abortion is even an important reproductive strategy among angiosperms, or flowering plants (Lovett-Doust and Lovett-Doust 1983:36).

Among humans, abortion is also to some extent an inherent characteristic of reproductive physiology. There is no way to calculate to what degree fetal wastage of this kind may have contributed to low fertility in the human past, but the further back we go into human prehistory, the more we must conclude—on the basis of primate research—that reproductive processes were sensitive to varied forms of stress—both nutritional and social. Thus, Hrdy has noted that in many primate species, there is evidence that abortion and other forms of suppression of reproduction can be induced even by competition among females—competition which presumably is related directly or indirectly to resource availability. As she writes:

In some cases, reproductive inhibition of subordinates can be brought about merely by the presence or seemingly unrelated activities of a dominant female. In other cases, there is overt harassment of the subordinate by the dominant. Among a variety of animals (including such primates as marmosets, tamarins, gelada baboons, talpoin monkeys, and various macaques) the presence of dominant females may be implicated in delays in maturation, inhibition of ovulation, or, in extreme cases, spontaneous abortion by subordinates. . . . The mechanisms of reproductive inhibitions still remain obscure, although experimental work has begun to elucidate the relationships between subordination, social stress and such important components of reproductive physiology as estrogenic hormones. (1981:99)

Again, it is impossible to estimate to what degree such factors would have affected prehistoric human populations. But there is no doubt that the efficiency of human reproduction, and especially of the female reproductive system, was then—as it continues to be—related to diet, workload and psychological stress, all of which affect estrogen levels (Frisch 1978a, 1984).

Some suggestion as to how this may have occurred among early foragers is provided by Wilmsen's work among the Kalahari San. Among these contemporary desert-dwelling people, Wilmsen discovered "a clear cycle of weight fluctuation"—with a maximum weight in the dry season months, June–August, and minimum during the wet season months, December–January (1978:26, 29). Given the short stature and slenderness of the San (Howell 1979:193), such variation tends to have rather important implications for reproductive outcome among a people whose observed fertility is low anyway (p. 198). Thus, Wilmsen also found that there was a marked peak in San births in March and April (32 percent of reported births), which would have meant a peak in conceptions at the time when weights were at their maximum (Wilmsen 1979:20). In contrast, births among San who had access to large amounts of domesticated foods such as milk and maize meal by having established a more sedentary life or contact with neighboring pastoralists and horticulturalists, demonstrated a more even distribution throughout the year.

Thus, quite apart from the question of birth spacing there seems, among foraging San, to be a distinct periodicity in births which is related to diet and its seasonal determinants. Again, an important mediating factor may well be hormonal levels, since Wilmsen found that the hunting-gathering San had significantly lower circulating cholesterol at all sampling periods than did their settled counterparts, while a February (i.e., wet season) sample showed greatly suppressed testosterone and estradiol levels among San females. Thus, Wilmsen concluded: "An intimate relationship between environmental food productivity, ingested diet, responses in the physiological processes of individuals, and consequent metabolic and endocrinal expressions is indicated. These may, in concert, exert controlling effects on reproductive cycles" (1978:31).

It as yet remains uncertain whether the depressed fertility among such San women is attributable to "seasonal suppression of ovulation, implantation failures, or spontaneous abortions of developing embryos" (pp. 31–32). It appears, however, that the latter contributes significantly, for Howell reports that "the known incidence of fetal wastage is about 10% of the number of live births" and considers that the actual incidence is probably "much higher" (1979:138).

Binford and Chasko too have suggested an environmentally linked physiologic effect on hunter-gatherer fertility:

There appears to be a strong relationship between seasonality of conception and an indirect measure of general nutritional state, probably seasonal variations in simple caloric intake. We can expect differences in seasonality and overall subsistence security to vary directly with the magnitude of seasonal variability in both rainfall and solar radiation. Thus depressant effects on realized fertility would vary concomitantly with the increasing magnitude of seasonal oscillations in the gross environment, other things being equal (e.g., storage potential and effectiveness). This means that . . . fertility can be expected to be generally lower in areas more distant from the equator, other things being equal. (1976:135)

Of course, as they caution, other things are rarely likely to be equal; there are countervailing factors, among them the fact that there tends to be an inverse relationship between the extent of female contribution to diet in the form of gathering—which as we have already indicated tends to be more important closer to the equator—and fertility (Brown 1970; Dahlberg 1976).

Induced Abortion: Indirect and Direct

As we have already noted, the distinction between spontaneous and induced abortion is not nearly as sharp as modern forensic and religious notions would have it. Unwanted fetal life may readily become the target of culturally focused pressures, expressed through the self-inflicted or socially enforced mistreatment or neglect of its mother, without any explicit intention of adversely affecting the outcome of pregnancy. Although little is known of the actual incidence of such indirect abortion—not surprising, when one considers the vast number of ways in which it could be expressed—many societies clearly evidence cultural patterns that could readily tend to facilitate the abortion of unwanted fetuses through increments in physiological and psychological stress. Extremes of work load and stress, for example, are reported as inducing abortion among the Yanomamo of the Venezuelan rain forest (Neel 1968). The widespread occurrence of taboos aimed at preventing the consumption of protein-rich foods during gestation (see below) also suggests the likelihood that nutritional stress during hard times, by being directed most frequently or more intensely against pregnant women—at a time of elevated need—could also result in greater fetal wastage.

In the course of their evolutionary development, moreover, humans, in contrast to other animal species, began to assume a certain measure of cultural control over the physiological potential for abortion, acquiring a varied repertoire of means for inducing it with more or less success. But, although Devereux (1967:98), in a study of 350 preindustrial societies, concluded that induced abortion was "an absolutely universal phenomenon," it seems unlikely that either indirect or direct forms of induced abortion constituted a primary means of fertility control during the Paleolithic period. Our remarks here are necessarily purely speculative since there are no data whatsoever on rates of abortion among hunter-gatherers. Nonetheless, the inherent inefficiency and danger of preindustrial forms of abortion lead us to infer that, while the role of spontaneous abortion may have been quite significant in times of environmental or social stress, more reliance would probably have been placed on other means of population regulation (Dickemann 1975:131). As Shorter has aptly noted of traditional abortion techniques, "the least dangerous rarely worked" (1982:178). Such "abortifacients" as preindustrial pharmacoepias usually include have variable efficacy at best and many contain the risk of delivering a toxic shock to the mother which, irrespective of its ability to induce abortion, may kill her in the process (Shorter 1982:179–188). Mechanical means of aborting, such as blows to the abdomen and other forms of physical trauma, entail a similar risk and uncertainty. Indirect methods of inducing abortion, in which malnourished women perform strenuous tasks, are also problematical procedures. They may, for example, rather than eventuating in successful abortion, culminate in a neonate whose physical development has been impaired in utero (Worthington 1979). This, on the other hand, may target such infants for subsequent direct or indirect infanticide—which in many preindustrial societies is rationalized as a means of removing offspring with physical impediments to full social competency (Minturn and Stashak 1982:77).

Infanticide: Direct and Indirect

Along with direct and indirect forms of abortion, early human foragers no doubt had conscious or unconscious recourse to various means of reducing the life chances of neonates. As our remarks above have suggested, however, the distinction between such behavior and what is more typically referred to as abortion is not, in fact, always a clear-cut one (Dickemann 1975:109–110) since the question of when human life commences is usually defined culturally, rather than by parturition alone. Infanticide must often be regarded, like abortion, not as killing but as terminating a *biosocial* gestation process. Among the !Kung, for example, a newborn child traditionally was not recognized as a social being until its mother, having given birth alone, returned with it to the village. If infanticide took place, it usually occurred before such status was bestowed (Howell 1979:120; Shostak 1981:66).

The employment of infanticide, at least, regardless of whether it is associated with induced birth, must have a long history in the hominid line if one may judge from the rest of the animal kingdom and, more specifically, from the primate evidence where it has been reported for langurs, chimpanzees, gorillas, rhesus macaques, etc. (Hrdy 1977:46–47). As Hrdy notes: "Infanticide, either observed or inferred from the disappearance of infants at times when males have usurped new females, has been reported for more than a dozen species of primates. Every major group of primates, including the prosimians, the New and Old World monkeys, apes, and man, is represented" (1977:46).

Perhaps the single most frequent characteristic of such behavior, as this statement intimates, is that it is perpetrated by adult males;

moreover, it is generally directed against the offspring of females with whom they are likely to establish a sexual relationship, when such offspring have been sired by other males (pp. 46–47). Given that such primate females are usually able to ovulate again soon after an infant's death, an argument can be made that such infanticide is a viable reproductive strategy among competitive males. By the same token, females cooperating with such a strategy would—as Hrdy suggests—tend to increase their own reproductive success (pp. 48–49), not least because the other side of the coin of infanticide directed against the offspring of other males is "the tendency among male primates to single out particular infants, watch over them, and even carry or otherwise care for them" when their own paternity seems to be involved (Hrdy 1981:76).

It is extremely difficult to reconstruct the route by which such a general pattern evolved into the more uniquely human one in which infanticide became a major form of fertility/mortality control. But human infanticide exhibits two notable differences: first, where the infanticide reported by Hrdy tends to be fairly infrequent, it is rather common among humans; second, among humans, infanticide seems to be carried out most typically by the mother—but within a cultural context in which such a practice is effectively group-sanctioned (Minturn and Stashak 1982:76). One implication of these differences is that human infanticide has not been culturally selected for its maximization of male reproductive success at the expense of rival males. Rather, among humans, selection is for avoiding the adverse consequences of having too many children (or too many children of a particular sex) in too short an interval. A basic reason for this difference is that non-human primates make a miniscule investment in child rearing compared to humans and receive virtually no material rewards for it, other than perpetuating their genes. For humans, however, the consequences of the decision to rear or not to rear an additional child at a particular moment in time has immediate significance for the whole range of production activities that underwrite individual and group standards of living and which are quantitatively unprecedented among nonhuman species.

Much evidence indicates that among hunter-gatherers rates of infanticide are responsive to fluctuations in resource availability and even to anticipated scarcities (Balicki 1967; Birdsell 1968; Riches 1974). Exactly how such decisions are made remains obscure, but there is no reason to doubt that individuals can "track" their reproductive behavior in relation to fluctuating resource opportunities. As Jochim suggests:

a variety of measures of procurement effort would show changes as the human-resource balance gradually worsened, and these changes in work-load may be the most common means by which population-control measures are linked. Such measures of work might include work hours per day, distance travelled in procurement per day, and frequency of necessary shifts of camp or procurement areas. . . . Another measure of relative resource shortages might be provided by the intensity of competition and frequency of disputes over resources. (1981:182)

It is dubious whether such "indices" would ever have been consciously perceived as necessitating "population control" *per se*, though they had that effect. More likely, females, on whom child care and many crucial productive activities devolved, recognized the threat to the survival of older children and themselves, as well as the increased work load which rearing of a new offspring would have entailed. The local, immediate, and pragmatic nature of such decisions is conveyed by Lorna Marshall's comments on Kalahari !Kung infanticide:

We believe that the meagerness of the resources of food and water puts pressure on the !Kung to keep their population in balance. This, however, does not seem to be the conscious concern of the !Kung when they speak of infanticide. They spoke of the nourishment of the children as the primary reason; they spoke in explicit detail. They want children, all the children they can possibly have, but, they explained, they cannot feed babies that are born too close together. . . . A second grave concern for these nomadic people is the carrying of the children. (1976:166)

It seems likely, therefore, that culturally mediated abortion and infanticide have long been among the most important aspects of human social and demographic life. This consideration puts in doubt many seemingly straightforward references to "natural" fertility and mortality which now seem, more than anything else, to have ensured a persistent underestimation of the rate of human intervention in reproductive outcome—not just in prehistoric but historic times as well. We shall return to this point in a moment.

Female Infanticide

Since the reproductive potential of most sexually reproducing species is determined by the rate of female survivorship (Cavilli-Sforza 1971:670), the most effective method of population control available to Paleolithic communities was direct or indirect female infanticide. Abortion, aside from its other drawbacks which we have already noted, offers no effective control over the gender of offspring, except perhaps in the rare cases where the abortus is actually viable. The greater efficacy of infanticide in this respect is emphasized by the fact that females are targeted in the overwhelming number of ethnographic cases (Dickemann 1975:129). (The way in which this preference is culturally rationalized represents another issue which will be raised in the next chapter.)

Since eyewitness reports of such infanticide is rare, evidence is necessarily indirect, chiefly in the form of data on sex ratios. In a sample of 112 preindustrial societies, for example, Divale and Harris (1976) found evidence for the likely practice of female infanticide prior to contact by European colonial powers, in the form of markedly skewed juvenile (0–15 years) sex ratios ranging as high as 130:100. While these figures do not rule out the possibility that male infanticide was also occurring, they clearly imply that some form, direct or indirect, of female infanticide was probably being practiced in a selective way. On the other hand, the recent suggestion (Chagnon, Flinn, and Melancon 1979) that such ratios might simply reflect a genetic propensity is hardly supported by evidence of such ratios becoming less skewed as a result of new postcontact infrastructural conditions and the decline of warfare, within a time period far too short to permit the necessary genetic change (Harris 1984:196).

It is known that direct and indirect female infanticide was practiced among various Eskimo populations (Balicki 1967; Freeman 1971; Schrire and Steiger 1974), Amerindian hunter-gatherers (Helm 1980) and native Australian hunter-gatherers (Cowlishaw 1978). Birdsell (1968:236–237) estimated that female infanticide rates ranged between 5 percent to 50 percent of all female births in order to maintain a stationary population during the Paleolithic period. Schrire and Steiger (1974:175), utilizing simulation models, subsequently suggested that any rate above 8 percent would lead to genocidal extinction within five hundred years, and on this basis claimed to have "refuted systematic female infanticide as a possible mechanism for controlling population sizes." What they actually demonstrated, however, is the extreme effectiveness of female infanticide as a population control mechanism. Even if rates much above 8 percent could not have been sustained for long periods in small (less than 500) populations, periods of maximum fertility and greater population density would easily accommodate higher rates of female infanticide without leading to extinction. Schrire and Steiger's simulation model errs in assuming that fertility and mortality rates remain constant over many generations. A more realistic assumption is that these rates fluctuated upwards and downwards in relation to local demographic and ecological conditions which raised and lowered benefits and costs. Female infanticide rates in particular could be adjusted accordingly, responding rather rapidly to increases or decreases in reproductive pressure.*

Breast-Feeding Versus Infanticide

Recent evidence supporting the view that prolonged and intense breast-feeding can be an efficient form of fertility control (Nag 1983b) has been used to downgrade the significance of abortion and infanticide among Paleolithic hunter-gatherers. According to Handwerker: "We now have abundant evidence that lactation-induced amenorrhea is a singularly important determinant of birth spacing, that, together with relatively minor misadjustments of coital frequency and timing relative to ovulation, can account for natural fertility levels in the neighborhood of four to six live births" (1983:17).

While breast-feeding may be the most important factor in placing limits on child rearing among the !Kung (Lee 1979), there are objections against regarding their reproductive behavior as represen-

*"Reproductive pressure" refers to adverse cost benefit ratios, as distinct from "population pressure," which usually is taken to mean population growth. Reproductive pressure may increase in the absence of population growth, as a result of depletions and diminishing returns.

tative of Paleolithic hunter-gatherers. The combined effect of !Kung lactation, spontaneous abortions, relatively high infant mortality and nontraditional limiting factors such as gonorrhea-induced sterility, is an average live-birth rate of 4.7 per woman (Howell 1979:123) and an annual compound rate of population increase of .00263—"a growth rate sufficient to double the population approximately every 300 years" (p. 215). Such a rate of increase, as Dumond has argued, "could not have been accommodated for any substantial period of time under stable hunting-gathering conditions" (1975:717). This suggests that no modern hunting-gathering population can really adequately serve as a straightforward model of early human ancestors. The !Kung are the one contemporary group about whose demographic behavior most is known, thanks to the long-term research of Lee (1972), Howell (1979), Harpending (1976), and others, yet they are by no means a traditional foraging population (Schrire 1980; Howell 1979:3–16). There is certainly good reason to think that Pleistocene populations were far more sensitive to resource stress (Hayden in press) and that, consequently, rates of population increase were lower—first, because fetal wastage might have been higher, under such circumstances, than what is reported for the !Kung (see above); second, because resource fluctuations would probably have reinforced the contracepting effect of lactation; and, third, because recourse to both indirect and direct forms of infanticide may also have been more frequent. Female infanticide in particular could have played a crucial role in rectifying demographic imbalances which presented a threat to economic security.

To sum up: by analogy with contemporary foragers, the low average rates of population growth throughout most of prehistory were a consequence of limited food production capacities associated with hunting and gathering as a mode of production. It was achieved by a combination of culturally mediated controls over both birth and death rates. These controls dampened or amplified biological processes such as spontaneous abortion, age-specific mortality, onset of menarche and menopause, and lactational amenorrhea, in conformity with fluctuations in the costs and benefits of rearing children under local technoeconomic and ecological conditions. The notion that during prehistory human foraging populations were regulated solely by "natural" birth and death rates belongs in the intellectual trash heap alongside the idea that humankind once lived in a "state of nature."

2. Population Regulation and Agricultural Modes of Production

The Paleolithic-Neolithic Transitions

By about 12,000 B.P. hunter-collectors had migrated into most corners of the globe and, with this great differentiation of habitat, considerable variation in demographic behavior must have developed as well. As David Harris has written:

By the close of the Pleistocene, when the eustatic rise of sea level associated with deglaciation had brought the world's coastlines approximately to their present configuration, hunter-gatherers had occupied all the continents, except Antarctica, and were subsisting in all major types of physical environments, from the equatorial rain forests to the subarctic tundra. (1981:15–16)

Clearly, different ecological conditions represented different sets of pressures and opportunities which were reflected in diverging modes of production and, as part of these, dissimilar settlement patterns, population densities and economic life in general.

At varying times during the Early Holocene, an important new mode of production began to emerge, utilizing more localized flora and fauna and leading to more sedentary settlement. The causes of this transformation are still a matter of considerable debate, the history of which it is not our purpose to review here. But, on evidence, much of the answer seems to lie in the combined and cumulative effect of climatic change and predation from increasingly proficient hunters (Butzer 1971; Martin 1985), resulting in the development of a "broad spectrum" economy which, in place of the previous focus on large mammalian prey, now rare or near extinction, embraced a more diverse range of subsistence activities, including more reliance on seed and nut collecting, fishing and the hunting of smaller fauna (Hayden in press; Yesner 1983). Such activities tend to be time- and energy-consuming (Hawkes et al. 1982; Hawkes and O'Connell 1981) and, given the increasing evidence that hunter-gatherers tend to optimize energetic efficiency in their dietary strategies (Winterhalder and Smith 1981; E. A. Smith 1983), probably can be assumed to have grown in importance primarily in response to the depletions of the larger species. Such species were intrinsically vulnerable to human predation simply because they reproduce fairly slowly (Ross 1978a). Even without actual human numbers increasing very much, any appreciable development in the technological proficiency of hunting—to which the archaeological record testifies—would have increased the vulnerability of such fauna to overkill.

The demographic aspects of transitional broad spectrum economies are fairly clear-cut. While big game hunting is energetically more efficient than the hunting of small, dispersed species, the transitional period—called the Mesolithic in Europe—was distinguished by an explosive burst of technological innovations (e.g., nets, weirs, fishhooks, canoes, sleds, etc.) which tended to counteract the depletion of larger game.

Much archaeological evidence from both hemispheres corroborates the appearance of larger and more sedentary villages and higher regional population densities in association with broad spectrum subsistence strategies (Price 1983:770; Cohen 1977). A number of suggestions have been made concerning why increased sedentarism translated itself into higher rates of population growth. Binford and Chasko (1976:139), for example, state that, first, increased sedentarism would mean reduced male absenteeism, increased coital frequency, and a greater probability of conception (Handwerker 1983:19); second, greater sedentarism would facilitate increased reliance on plant foods and, with it, the development of ceramic containers in which food could be boiled and substituted for mothers' milk, thus reducing the breast-feeding period and the duration of postpartum amenorrhea. (For some qualifications to this, see below.) As Binford and Chasko write:

Ceramics is commonly added to the archaeological assemblage in the context of sedentarism and is demonstrably associated with a diet characterized by small food packages and the use of stored foods. Although not well understood, the appearance of ceramics, the implied increase in the consumption of boiled foods, and trends in sedentarism are commonly linked. In situations with increased consumption of boiled foods linked to increasing intensification of female labor in food procurement, the depressant effects of the latter might be prevented through increased division of labor with respect to child care. Namely, with boiled foods an elderly woman or man could feed children in the absence of their mothers, therefore obviating the disadvantages of having children closely spaced and of necessity with the mother at all times. Thus, other things being equal, we might expect increased rates of population growth. (1976:138–139)

We would add to this the observation that even if it is the mother who feeds the neonate boiled substitutes for milk, breast-feeding intensity would tend to decline and birth intervals would tend to shorten. We must not, however, lose sight of the fact that Binford and Chasko are here discussing proximate mechanisms governed by more fundamental shifts in the cost/benefits of child rearing. We would therefore emphasize that, on the cost side, sedentarism relaxes the need to transport neonates and toddlers; while on the benefit side, children's labor plays a more important role, especially in tasks such as bleaching, grinding, and pounding of nuts and seeds, in the procurement of molluscs and small fish and game, and in varied house- and child-care activities (Ross 1976; Dufour 1983:349).

It is worth making a special observation here about the importance of children's labor. Up until the time of the emergence of sedentary communities and their "broad spectrum" economies, to judge from recent hunter-gatherer societies, the economic role of children was slight. Although until quite recently little systematic effort had been made even to include children's work in anthropological assessments of production and our comparative perspective therefore tends to be more impressionistic than quantitative, ethnographic evidence generally suggests that children among foraging groups such as the Kalahari San or Mbuti Pygmies make a very small contribution to economic activity. By contrast, among agricultural or pastoral communities, where there exist far more tasks requiring less skill and experience, they may begin to play a useful and even significant role as early as nine or ten years old (Ross 1976; Isacsson 1984). "Broad spectrum" economies thus not only represented the emergence of a more intensive mode of production but a veritable social watershed as the value of children's labor became a powerful new factor among those shaping human modes of reproduction. The full import of this, however, was not to be fulfilled until the dawning of industrial capitalism (see chapter 4).

Demographic Aspects of the Neolithic

The emergence of sedentary agricultural communities took place over a long time period, growing out of the earlier broad spectrum subsistence developments that we have just described. Cohen has summarized the transition to the Neolithic as follows:

[the broad spectrum economy] seems to have resulted repeatedly in the domestication of crops for human use whereby such foods were caused to grow in high densities in the vicinity of human settlements; were altered genetically to grow and to be harvested at human convenience; and were further altered to produce enlarged, and often detoxified and otherwise unprotected edible parts. Simultaneously, however, human habits were domesticated to the convenience of the reproductive cycle of the plants in question. Human groups were forced (or permitted) to be sedentary and work habits were altered to fit the growth cycles of the plants. (1983:3–4)

There were important variations in this general sequence which relate largely to ecological circumstance. Thus, in some regions such as highland Mesoamerica, possibly because of the greater severity of the Pleistocene faunal extinctions, a general absence of domesticable herbivores—such as the sheep and bovines of the Old World—encouraged dependence on small game hunting and a seminomadic settlement pattern long after the development of agriculture (MacNeish 1972; Coe and Flannery 1966); while in the tropical forest coastal lowlands of Veracruz and Guatemala, where riverine resources had already displaced most terrestrial game as a source of dietary protein, a high degree of sedentarism predated agriculture and gave considerable encouragement to its development. In the Middle East, sedentarism based on the domestication of both plants and animals accelerated and intensified all of the demographic effects of sedentarism based on broad spectrum hunter-collector modes of production.

A greater variety of weaning foods became available, further shortening birth intervals; seasonal stress, previously associated with amenorrhea or spontaneous abortion, could now be buffered by stored crops and domesticated animal "food banks"; and the costs of carrying infants and toddlers diminished still further in the context of fully developed village-dwelling styles of life. On the benefit side, the labor contribution of children broadened still further to include tasks such as planting, hoeing, weeding, harvesting, scaring away birds, tending to flocks, etc. Evidence from contemporary nomadic or seminomadic peoples who have adopted a sedentary life-style suggests that infant mortality decreases and fertility increases during the early phase of settlement at least (Roth 1985).

There is no doubt that the spread of agriculture was accompanied by a dramatic rise in the annual rate of population increase— perhaps from some .0015 percent during the Paleolithic period to about 0.1 percent in the Neolithic period (see chapter 1). But, in contrast to earlier views, which tended to perceive the "agricultural revolution" as a persistently and almost unequivocally progressive development (Braidwood 1960), recent research points to the existence of contradictory trends.

Sedentary life based on domesticated foods does not seem to have contributed notably to a decline in overall mortality or an increase in longevity (Hassan 1975:44). Indeed, child mortality may well have increased during the later portions of the Neolithic period. Several reasons can be adduced for this. First, a greater density of population which characterized village life led to an increase in disease, including parasitic and zoonotic infections associated with poor sanitation and animal domestication. Second, with the reduced role of hunting, there was probably a decline in dietary protein, especially where food crops were deficient in this respect. While breast-feeding may have tended to be more protracted in such instances (Whiting 1964), evidence from some contemporary agricultural populations, for example in Bangladesh and West Africa, suggests that the increased demand for women's labor in the fields may have an adverse effect on the scheduling of infant feeding (Chen, Huq, and Souza 1981; Thompson 1977). Third, it is important to note that agricultural economies are frequently typified by periodic food shortages where rainfall is highly seasonal and/or storage facilities are inadequate to cope with shortfalls (Chen, Huq, and Souza 1981). While seasonal deficiencies are expressed in short-term weight loss among adults (Nurse 1975), they often spell elevated mortality among the very young. And, as we shall see later (chapter 5), because scarce foods are more likely to be allocated to male children, it is female offspring who are most often at risk (Lindenbaum 1977; Ross 1983b).

Further evidence for the adverse demographic effects of sedentary agricultural life comes from a recent summary of work in paleopathology. Bearing in mind the necessary cautions involved in generalizing from archaeological sequences from different world areas, each involving its own particular confounding factors, and in comparing studies all of which embrace a host of methodological uncertainties (Buikstra et al. n.d.), Cohen nonetheless feels confident in concluding that "taken as a whole, [they] suggest an overall decline in the quality—and probably in the length—of human life associated with the adoption of agriculture" (1983:25). Thus, on the question of longevity, the majority of studies cited by Cohen (1983) and Cohen and Armelagos (1984) point in a common direction:

Working with relatively good, well-controlled samples (N = 114, 224, 219, respectively) from a single well-defined location, Goodman et al. suggest that there was a progressive decline in life expectancy for all age classes as hunter-gatherers first adopted and then intensified agriculture in Illinois. Buikstra and Cook, from large and well-controlled samples (N = 800 +, 500 +, 336) describe a decline in life expectancy with the adoption of agriculture plus a recovery in life expectancy for adults (but not for children) late in the sequence as agriculture was intensified. . . . Working with more fragmentary and/or scattered data a number of other studies report similar trends. Angel notes a decrease in adult life expectancy from Paleolithic (n = 53) to Mesolithic (N = 120) and Neolithic (N = 106) for males in the Mediterranean. For females he reports an increase in adult life expectancy from Paleolithic (N = 53) to Mesolithic (N = 63) followed by a decline to levels at or below that of the Paleolithic in the Neolithic (N = 200). Kennedy notes that the aggregate pre-agricultural sample from India (N = ± 100) displays higher ages at death than do later agricultural populations. (Cohen 1983:23–24)

It would be of considerable theoretical interest to be able to distinguish between the mortality and longevity rates in the early as compared with the later phases of the Neolithic period, and between regions which possessed and did not possess domesticated animals. The negative effects of starchy plant food diets might not have manifested themselves until local faunal resources were depleted. Moreover, one would expect the rise in mortality consequent upon an intensification of Neolithic modes of food production to be less severe where domesticated animals were available. Unfortunately, the archeological evidence is not sufficiently fine-grained to permit us to draw conclusions about these alternative scenarios.

Nonetheless, there is considerable agreement that while the Neolithic economy led to population increase, it did so in ways that were not clearly manifested in improved quality of life at the level of the individual where the adverse effects of greater settlement densities and a decline in dietary sources of quality protein, animal fats, and iron are widely observed. The lesson here is equally pertinent to all subsequent cultural evolution: changes in modes of production which lead to an absolute increase in population do not necessarily entail any improvement in average standard of living. Large increases in population numbers or density are compatible with falling standards of living.

If we further inject at this point the question of "who benefits?" the results of Neolithic demographic trends may have been even more contradictory. It has been argued, as we have seen, that a foreshortened period between successive births would have taken place as the combined workload of subsistence tasks and carrying children declined; thus, women could have—energetically—afforded to have more young children around at a given time. But this does not take into account the other costs of rearing more children at shorter intervals—costs which women are more likely to assume than men. As Carol Ember has written:

Worldwide cross-cultural data suggest that mother's child-care work probably increases with more children. Summarizing data from Barry and Paxson (1971) on 186 societies, Weisner and Galimore (1977:170) find that mothers almost always provide more than half the care of infants (in early childhood, though, caretakers are usually not the mother). Thus, if mothers are the principal caretakers of infants, a shorter birth interval must surely increase child care responsibilities for the mother. (1983:296)

Furthermore, closely spaced multiple pregnancies and births increase the discomforting and life-threatening aspects of the birth process, costs of which, if shared at all, are shared only indirectly by males. These considerations link up with a widely held view that women in agricultural societies enjoyed a less favorable gender role status than is true of women among band organized hunter-gatherers (Leacock 1978). Males have often derived greater advantages than women from rearing more children, directing their labor, and using them in marital exchanges. It would not be surprising, therefore, if elements of compulsion and exploitation lay behind the contradiction between Neolithic population growth and declining standards of living.

Variations in Post-Neolithic Modes of Production and Reproduction

Although one can recognize certain general patterns and trends in the worldwide emergence of agriculture, the potential for the evolution of agricultural economies was not everywhere the same and the degree of intensification of domesticated food production showed marked variation. We hold that these variations in turn account for major differences in the value of rearing additional children, and as a consequence, new modes of reproduction characterized by differences in the size of settlements, regional population densities, sex and age specific mortality rates, and other demographic effects. These new modes of reproduction in their turn contributed to the appearance of other modes of production associated with the rise of complex stratified political-economic systems, each again, in turn, with its own asymmetric division of child-rearing costs and benefits.

Pastoralism

Thus, in some regions—usually arid grasslands where rainfall was too irregular or periodic drought occurred—animal husbandry based on ruminants took greater precedence over plant production. In such circumstances, chiefly in Asia, the Circum-Mediterranean and East Africa, diet typically consisted largely of animal by-products, including cheese, milk, and blood, with relatively small inputs of meat as few animals were actually slaughtered. Such pastoralist populations practiced cultivation in varying degrees according to the marginality of their environment (Gulliver 1955; Dyson-Hudson and Dyson-Hudson 1969), which also determined the scope of their annual movements in pursuit of pasturage for their herds (Barth 1961). Most pastoralists, however, maintained some kind of relations with neighboring agricultural communities, obtaining some or all plant food through trade or raids (Salzman 1971; Schneider 1957; Khazanov 1984; Cole 1975; Barth 1961).

But, from the viewpoint of population dynamics, judging from recent studies of contemporary pastoralists, it was essentially the exigencies of herd management against a background of uncertain climatic variation which was most influential in preventing either excessive rates of population increase or any significant density of settlement. Herd sizes were constrained by unpredictable drought; but, even in good years, the normal conditions of semi-arid grasslands with low carrying capacity tended to retard the maturation and calving rate of animals (Moran 1979:227), which in turn affected human numbers in various ways. As Moran suggests, for example, reviewing Sato's work (1977) among the Rendille camel herders of northern Kenya, there would have been a tendency among such pastoralist groups for human reproductive patterns and fertility-related behavior in general to develop a certain necessary synchronization with the reproductive potential of their animals. Thus,

Age-sets are formed every fourteen years in Rendille society, a figure that approximates the generational span of a camel (that is, 13.87 years). These age-sets serve to create a close generational association between Rendille and their camels. Increases in human population match almost exactly the increases in camel herd size. Because camels have slow reproductive rates, the population institutes a variety of social mechanisms to slow down human population increases. Celibacy for males between ages twelve and thirty-one is required and only 50 percent of these males will be able to afford the brideprice that must be paid in the form of camels. Their enforced celibacy is probably the most important population control mechanism among the Rendille. (1979:230–231)

For reasons stated previously, however, we doubt that the polygynous Rendille depended primarily on male celibacy to equilibrate camel and human numbers.

There is also reason to assume that pastoral populations in many regions had another demographic option, when their numbers began to strain the resources of their economy: spillage of their excess into sedentary life—a process that sometimes took place through peaceful integration, at other periods by conquest. Compared to such sedentary communities, pastoral existence was comparatively healthy, and it seems that it has often been the sedentarization of pastoralists which has replenished the population of neighboring villages and towns with their higher mortality. By the same token, as Barth for one has suggested, without this process it is questionable whether nomadic pastoral economies could have survived (1961:126).

Among the Basseri of the Fars Province of Iran, when camel numbers rise to the point where they strain grazing capacity, the animals begin to suffer from poorer health, diminished fertility and increased susceptibility to disease. As these reduce their numbers, herders left with too few animals to maintain their pastoralist livelihood tend to settle in nearby towns. As Barth observes: "Because of the pattern of economic organization, animal epidemics thus serve as a control not only on the size of the animal population, but also on the human nomad population of the area" (1961:126).

Slash-and-Burn Agriculture

Elsewhere, where soil and rainfall conditions permitted, agriculture became more fully developed. Yet, as Meggers (1954) and others have noted, even where agriculture evolved, the potential for its elaboration and for the emergence of a full-fledged sedentary life-style was clearly not everywhere the same. Frequently, for example, agriculture began in an extensive form, known as slash-and-burn, which, while human densities remained relatively low, allowed land to be used for a short time and then left fallow for a longer period while the forest regenerated.* In temperate zones, however, forest regeneration is slower than in tropical regions where primary productivity tends to be considerably higher because of high rainfall, a longer growing season, and the high amount of solar radiation (Moran 1979:250; Little and Morren 1976:10). As a result, in temperate zones, one is more likely to witness a shortening of fallow period and a concomitant fall in soil fertility—both of which, in turn, encourage a faster centrifugal population movement. Such a factor may explain the relatively rapid spread of agriculture out of the Middle East and into Europe. Thus, while one of the earliest Neolithic towns, Jericho, dates to 10,000 B.P., farming communities were also being established in Greece by 8500 B.P. and, over the next one thousand years, spread well up the Danube River Valley.† Equally, as in the Middle East, deforestation not only stimulated outward migration, but impelled the resident population to develop more intensive agricultural methods, which were themselves associated with denser, more stable population centers.

Root Crops Versus Grains

In tropical forest regions, on the other hand, the likelihood is that it was less the nature of slash-and-burn agriculture per se than the quality of the crops which became prominent that tended to limit human density and numbers. It is notable, for example, that in temperate zones it was principally various wild species of herbaceous plants—cereals and legumes—which were elaborated into

---

*It should be noted, however, that recent studies suggest that many slash-and-burn agriculturalists probably continue to take an active involvement in "abandoned" fields, "including planting and protection as well as utilization of certain useful wild plants that appear at various stages of fallow succession" (Denevan et al. In press:2).

†Similar rapid spread of agriculture from both dependent and independent centers of domestication throughout vast regions of Africa, Asia, and the New World occurred at approximately the same time.

staple crops. This was the case in Europe, much of Asia, highland Mesoamerica, and the Andes. In tropical forests, on the other hand, it was chiefly tubers and starchy tree crops (manioc, yams, sweet potatoes, taro, bananas/plantains, sago, etc.) that dominated agricultural economies. While one hesitates to oversimplify the contrast between these two distinctive foci, certain obvious differences help to explain the general course of demographic and cultural processes in tropical forested regions. Herbaceous plants (including major "grains" such as wheat, barley, maize, etc.) which evolved protein-rich seeds as a means of storing nutrients for reproductive purposes despite periods of low temperature or moisture, have a tremendous versatility. Thus, as David Harris has noted, "They have been exploited as staple foods in all the inhabited continents and in most types of terrestrial ecosystems, particularly in the temperate zone of cold winters; in the summer-dry, or Mediterranean, sub-tropics; and in the semi-arid and sub-humid tropics of long dry season, the semidesert and savanna zones" (1981:16).

Such plants are probably least suited to tropical rain forests, not simply for climatic reasons, but also because they require relatively fertile soils in order to produce their nutrient-rich seeds which, in other regions, provide human populations with a valuable source of essential amino acids. There is doubt, however, whether the generally poor soils of the lowland tropics can sustain satisfactory or secure yields of such plants. Thus, as Johnson has recently reported for the Machiguenga Indians of the Peruvian montaña, maize output—despite considerable effort involved in planting—is decidedly variable: "Many seeds are planted in each hole, but usually only two or three sprout and grow to maturity. Of these, all three may grow tall and yield many healthy ears, but perhaps only one or two will yield, and sometimes none bear seed. Furthermore, whole areas of a garden may have maize plants that grow well enough, but produce no seed" (1983:46).

Such difficulties might have been tentatively dealt with by greater labor investments—for example, more intensive weeding—but this was not likely to occur when root-crop cultivation, combined with wild game, provided an energetically less costly alternative as a source of an adequate diet. (Indeed, the burden of weeding is frequently cited as a principle reason for field abandonment; cf. Denevan et al. in press; Carneiro 1983:103–104.) On the other hand, dependence on hunting to provide most necessary amino acids—while root-crops, which are notoriously deficient in these, offered a rich source of calories—could only succeed as a long-term strategy where population densities, and hence predation pressure, remained relatively low. The demographic and cultural consequences of such an economy are, thus, profound; as David Harris has written:

[It] has a lower potential for supporting large clustered human populations and for expanding into new habitats than do such nutritionally self-sufficient agricultural systems as developed in Mesoamerica and the Andean highlands. The latter are more capable of both intensification and expansion, and it is therefore not surprising that they sustained urban civilizations and expansive empires in marked contrast to the much sparser and less socially differentiated populations of eastern South America. (1981:26)

Nor is it surprising, as Whiting (1964) has shown, that there is a significant statistical correlation between societies dependent on root crops and long postpartum sex taboos—a relationship which, as he explained, tends to be associated with longer periods of nursing, as a means of preventing infant protein deficiency disease. In light of what is now known about the relationship between prolonged lactation and postpartum amenorrhea, we would add that the nutritional deficiencies of root crops severely limited population growth in fairly direct ways, quite apart from any indirect association with postpartum constraints on sexual activity within marriage. Providing rather inadequate weaning food, they encouraged more protracted breast-feeding which thus played an enhanced role in dampening fertility. In contrast, populations with protein-rich cereal foods—which also happen to be more likely to possess animals that provide milk (Textor 1967; Ember 1983:296)—offered the opportunity for earlier use of supplementary protein-rich foods in the infant diet, thus reducing the lactation period and releasing previous physiological constraints on fertility.

Since cereal-based modes of production tended to develop higher degrees of agricultural intensification, there was also pressure on adult women to increase their productivity simultaneously with an increase in their reproductivity. As Ember has suggested from her cross-cultural analysis, intensive agriculture—which is to say, largely agriculture based on cereals and pulses—imposes quite notable work loads on adult females. It does not so much add new burdens to agricultural work per se, compared to what one finds in less intensive conditions (Ember 1983:288–289), but substantially increases domestic labor associated primarily with food preparation and other household tasks related to increased sedentarism (pp. 288–291). These data point to a considerable further deterioration in female status that probably emerged during the Neolithic, and reinforces our previous comments about the increasing role of gender-based exploitation that accompanied the development of agricultural modes of production, with their attendant rise in population.

Table 2.1
Work-Time Comparisons: Simple Agricultural and Intensive Agricultural Cases

Simple Agriculturalists	Total Women's Worktime	Outside Women's Worktime	Inside Women's Worktime
	(hours per day per 7-day week)		
Machiguenga (Amazon)	7.40	3.90	3.50
Kayapo (N. Brazil)	4.90	3.80	1.10
Bemba (N. Zimbabwe)	6.00	—	—
Genieri (Gambia)	—	6.60	—
Ihangiro (Tanzania)	8.50	4.40	4.10
Mean	6.70	4.68	2.90
Intensive Agriculturalists			
Tenia Mayo (Mexico)	9.00	2.00	7.00
Kali Loro (Java)	11.00	5.90	5.20
Le Levron (Switz.)	9.40	5.00	4.40
German Swiss	11.81	4.54	7.27
Nepal villagers	12.40	7.25	5.15
Kabupaten (Java)	—	1.20	—
Medieres (Switz).	13.65	5.90	7.75
German peasants	8.30	3.90	4.40
Mean	10.81	4.46	5.88

Source: Minge-Klevana 1980:281; Ember 1983:289.

Tropical Forest Systems: The Amazon Basin

Tropical forests are themselves by no means uniform and in limited areas have revealed a potential for considerable elaboration of sedentary life based on intensive agriculture, even while exploiting nondomesticated animals. In Amazonia, such development occurred, for the most part, not in the vast inland forests which constitute as much as 98 percent of the whole region (Meggers 1971:14; Denevan 1976:214), but along the narrow floodplains (*varzeas*) of the major alluvial rivers where not only was soil exceptionally fertile but wildlife—especially aquatic and semiaquatic fauna—was unusually abundant (Ross 1978a, 1978b:195–197). Because such riverine resources provided a productive and stable alternative to forest hunting and promoted a high degree of sedentarism, they also tended—as Carneiro (1968) and others have observed—to promote greater commitment to agricultural activity. Population densities also tended to be higher in such areas. Denevan, for one, contrasts an estimated aboriginal density for the low interfluvial forest of 0.2 persons per square kilometer with over fifty times that for the Amazon floodplain (1970), while there is evidence, both historically and archaeologically, that pre-European settlements had evolved to at least a chiefdom-level of politico-economic organization, in marked contrast to the band-level societies that generally characterized the Amazonian interior.

Despite the higher densities of population achieved along the Amazonian floodplains as compared with the interior, economic productivity in this habitat was in turn severely limited compared with other great river valleys (e.g., Nile, Tigris-Euphrates, Indus, Ganges, Yangtzee, Hwa Ho, etc.) which from early in the Neolithic reached high population densities and were thereafter the locales for the emergence of the world's earliest states and empires. It is instructive to examine the particularities of the Amazonian situation in order to guard against the facile conclusion that the relationship between productivity and reproductivity has been governed more by chance or arbitrary "cultural" factors than by the intensifiability of various modes of production and the associated cost and benefits of greater or lesser fertility in specific material circumstances.

Amazonian floodplains present some formidable environmental hazards, including a marked seasonality of river levels which made the time of high water a season of relative scarcity. Faunal populations decline drastically along the Amazon during this (rainy) period as fish swim inland with floodwaters, birds migrate, and turtles, which lay their eggs in prodigious numbers on river beaches during the dry season, disappear. In a recent study by Stocks (1983:246), for example, among the Cocamilla Indians of the Huallaga River floodplain in eastern Peru, the effect of this ecological periodicity is quite marked: "Fish intake drops from 17.2% to 4.3% of the total weight of food consumed. Thus, there is a relative and consciously perceived strain on subsistence when the peak flood season comes from March to May and again in November" (1983:246).

In addition to such drops in faunal productivity along the floodplain during the high water period, the threat of unpredictable flooding is greater in the Amazon as compared with other major river valley systems. This unpredictability is largely due to the fact that Amazon floods are the cumulative result of the rise and fall of so many tributaries over a vast distance, with some originating north of the equator and others to the south, that seasonal conditions dictating their respective flood patterns vary considerably. Manioc, the staple root crop of Amazonia, appears to be especially vulnerable to the effects of flooding. Bolian (1971) reports that among the riverine Tukuna manioc rots after ten or twelve days of submergence. In addition to its vulnerability to floods, manioc benefits comparatively little from being planted on rich alluvial soils. These circumstances help to explain why native Amazonian riverine populations adopted maize as soon as it became available. Indeed, Roosevelt (1977:3) has argued that the "alluvial soils of the floodplain regions would have been essentially irrelevant to the cultivation of manioc" in pre-contact times, a view which reinforces the earlier argument that the chief ecological merit of the Amazonian flood plains was their abundance of animal foods rich in protein, fats, iron and vitamins. But these resources were not abundant during the rainy season, as we have noted.

Whatever strategies might have been devised prior to the introduction of maize to cope with such seasonal scarcity, it is doubtful that they could have sustained a large sedentary population through the lean months; thus, despite the high productivity of the dry season, demographic adjustment must have been primarily to the period of most problematical output. The eventual adoption in alluvial zones of maize, as it spread into the Amazon basin, provided a critical nutritional bridge across the rainy season which made possible a higher productive and reproductive potential (Roosevelt 1980).

It is probable as well that the evolution of floodplain agriculture subsequently entailed a rather complex system of intensive labor management. The reasons are apparent:

During the period of low water, all foods are simultaneously at peak abundance and must be gathered in sufficient quantity not only to satisfy immediate daily needs but to accumulate a surplus for consumption during the months of reduced productivity. The most efficient way to cope with such a situation is to split the labor force and allocate to each group a specific type of activity. Furthermore, agricultural operations on the varzea must be systematically organized because of the time limitations imposed by the regime of the river. If planting is delayed too long, the crop will not mature before inundation; if planting is done too soon, seeds or cuttings may rot before they sprout. Timing is even more critical when two harvests are programmed, as they were in the case of maize. (Meggers 1971:141)

Thus, maize not only helped circumvent some of the ecological constraints of the flood season on demographic development; it is likely that by the nature of its complex labor demands, it was in itself a further stimulus to population growth. Yet, in the end, the immensity and unpredictability of flooding arrested the process of population growth and sociopolitical evolution at levels that were quickly surpassed in other major river valley systems. Villages along the mainstream of the Amazon grew to two or three thousand inhabitants, a magnitude greater than that of the interfluvial settlements, but a magnitude smaller than that of the early riverine city-states that evolved in more favorable habitats.

Demographic Consequences of
Hunting-Dependent Agriculture

Among the consequences of agriculture and increased sedentarism were greater social complexity, new problems of resource scarcity, and attendant pressures toward overt competition among individuals and eventually among different social and economic groupings. Here again, one can see evidence of certain important distinctions that emerged as agricultural intensification evolved to varying degrees—distinctions, from the perspective of the present discussion, that had a profound demographic dimension.

As we have noted, the need for many cultivators to maintain a commitment to hunting in order to obtain the protein and other nutrients not provided by agriculture tended to curtail the rate of increase among such populations more than among cereal-producing groups.

Most of our insight into this issue comes from contemporary villages of non-cereal-producing hunter-agriculturalists occupying tropical forest regions. As we have noted at several other junctures, such groups can never be regarded as survivals of prehistoric populations. All of them have been to some extent affected by diseases, trade, and other outside influences over many hundreds of years and most decisively since the dawn of the age of European expansion (Wolf 1982). Yet, there is much to be gained by making judicious inferences.

Despite the prejudgment that it was "preposterous" to suppose that a scarcity of animal foods in the habitat subjected low-density tropical forest hunter-agriculturalists to reproductive stress (Chagnon 1974:76), it is now firmly established that such societies are indeed limited by this factor (Hames and Vickers 1983; Harris 1984; Ross 1978a; Gross 1975, 1982). It is important to clarify the nature of this limitation: if one examines the energetic structure of tropical forest ecosystems, it is evident that—with the principal exception of the river floodplains—they provide relatively little opportunity for large concentrations of animal biomass, particularly on the forest floor where vegetation is meagre; in contrast, reflecting the concentration of most plant biomass in overstory stems and leaves (Golley et al. 1969:694), the largest proportion of mammalian species tends to be aboreal—a trait particularly dramatic in the tropical forests of Amazonia (Ross 1978a:2). As a result, large terrestrial mammals tend to be sparse while arboreal animal life, though more abundant, presents such particular logistical problems that many species are widely disregarded as food sources altogether.

In the Amazon, for example, the greatest single concentration of vertebrate biomass may be represented by sloths, animals so cryptic that most Amerindian hunters dismiss them as a food resource (Eisenberg et al. 1972:871; Montgomery and Sunquist 1975:90; Davis 1945:291; Ross 1978a:11).

Contemporary ethnographic research demonstrates that tropical forest hunters can, where animal populations have not been severely overpredated, manage to harvest perfectly adequate supplies of game; but, there is a necessary trade-off: to do so, their settlements tend to be small, highly mobile and schismatic, prone to fissioning as social strains, which appear to be associated with declining yields, generate insupportable internal antagonisms (Ross 1978b:31; see below). Most importantly, population density, such as presently found in the Amazonian hinterland, is usually quite low—rarely more than one person per square mile—primarily as the result of fertility/mortality controls of various forms and of a tendency for population groupings to be dispersed and distanced from one another by recurrent feuds and warfare, which seem to be primed by a variety of behaviors which are directly or indirectly related to diminishing returns in hunting (Harris 1984).

Warfare as a Component in Population Regulation

Warfare in prestate societies does not in itself have great demographic consequences, and it is not entirely correct to regard it as a direct mechanism of fertility/mortality control per se. (We regard it as an aspect of structure rather than infrastructure.) Rarely, for example, does it anywhere seem to affect female mortality to an extent that would seriously depress population growth over the long run (Polgar 1972:207; Livingstone 1968). On the other hand, when viewed as a pattern of behavior that is closely related to questions of resource availability, it seems to be implicated in the emergence or perpetuation of cultural practices which do, in fact, curtail fertility and increase mortality, especially through infanticide biased against female offspring. Before discussing this relationship in more detail, the reader must be alerted to the absolutely crucial distinction between the demographic consequences of warfare in band and village societies and warfare in state and imperial contexts. In the former, as we shall see in a moment, warfare often helps to restrain population growth; in the latter it is part of a political-economic system which is predicated on territorial and demographic expansion. We shall examine the latter relationship in the next chapter.

We have already alluded to the widespread occurrence of direct or indirect female infanticide as a population-regulating mechanism among hunter-collectors. As Divale and Harris (1976) have shown, there is a striking correlation between the use of this mechanism—evidenced by high male juvenile sex ratios—and the practice of warfare among prestate populations in general. The interpretation of this correlation between warfare and female infanticide given by Divale and Harris is that warfare carried out with muscle-powered weaponry decisively alters the cost/benefits of rearing female as opposed to male offspring (Hamilton 1982:134) and is further connected with the development of exaggerated masculine values which provide ideological support for culling female neonates (including live-born, late pregnancy aborted fetuses).

This of course is not to say that female infanticide occurs only in the presence of warfare or necessarily varies with it in intensity. Under certain technoeconomic conditions, the more robust nature of male anatomy may place a premium on rearing males for hunting quite apart from the life-and-death urgency of rearing them for combat. This seems especially true for arctic and boreal hunters where the margin between success and failure in the hunt is very thin and, where, at the same time, a scarcity of collectible plants means that women do not occupy the role of harvesting calories which are elsewhere the mainstay of most prestate societies.

While there is reason to believe that the significance of adult female labor has a strong general effect upon the incidence of female infanticide (see chapters 4 and 5), a special demographic problem of tropical forest village agriculturalists is that, though the productive and reproductive contribution of women tends to be highly valued, high rates of population increase would readily eventuate in declining yields—especially of animal prey. It is with regard to such societies that the Divale-Harris seems to present a plausible explanation of how the temptation to raise daughters might be mitigated. According to the cross-cultural evidence, drawn in fact from preindustrial populations inhabiting a great diversity of habitats, warfare seems to play a cardinal role in maintaining a high mortality rate among female neonates and children (table 2.2).

Table 2.2
Sex Ratios and Preindustrial Warfare

	Young Males per 100 Females
Warfare present	128
Stopped 5–25 years before census	113
Stopped over 25 years before census	109

Source: Divale and Harris 1976.

One effect of the interconnection of warfare and female infanticide is that communities may increase their relative proportion of hunter-warriors (whose numbers are eventually reduced in war, however) who, in turn, often seek to capture adult females from other villages. This, in part, explains why emic rationales for warfare often attribute them to competition over women. From a processual viewpoint, however, what is happening is that communities are regulating the pressure they put on local resources through female infanticide, without necessarily having to forego the productive benefits of adult females. In this way, female infanticide, motivated by a preference for male warriors, and warfare, by a scarcity of women, propel one another and animate a system in which population increase is moderated yet productive activity is ensured.

The Yanomamo: A Case Study

Thus, although warfare is not purposefully conducted toward population control, its occurrence in low density prestate societies may have been recurrently selected for because of its link to population regulation through direct and indirect female infanticide. An example of how this may occur is provided by recent ethnographic research among the Yanomamo Indians of the upper Orinoco. Chagnon (1973:138) reported juvenile sex ratio in eleven Yanomamo villages in an intensive warfare zone as 157:100; but in twelve villages where warfare was less intense (Chagnon 1974:129), the ratio was 121:100 (Chagnon 1968:139). Two villages reported on by Lizot (1977) show an even more marked correlation between warfare intensity and juvenile sex ratios: 260:100 versus 77:100. Recently Good (personal communication) recorded the following juvenile sex ratios for eleven previously uncensused villages for ages 0–4 as: 100:100; 700:100; 333:100; 237:100; 700:100; 500:100; 108:100; 193:100; 200:100; 237:100; 83:100.

The most traditional Yanomamo live in "villages ranging in size from 40 to 250 people,* with most . . . located in the deep forest and away from large navigable rivers" (Hames 1983:33). In such interfluvial zones, not much more than 7 to 9 percent of animal protein can be derived from fishing (Ross 1976; Good, pers. com.); this and the extremely low protein content of their staple plantains necessarily mean that an adequate provision of amino acids—and of other critical nutrients such as fat and iron—depends on an active hunting schedule. The obvious labor investment in agriculture (Chagnon 1968), however, implies a considerable degree of sedentarism. While plantains, being perennials and having leaves which shade out weedy growth around their stems, require substantially less attention than root-crops such as manioc (which must be regularly weeded and replanted after harvesting) and thus permit greater community mobility, the Yanomamo nonetheless must spend much of the year in and around their home villages in order to protect and exploit their gardens which guarantee them the calorie supply which subsidizes other activities such as hunting.

Even small communities (25 to 50 persons) in Amazonia, especially where fishing productivity is low and greater attention must therefore be paid to hunting, can severely deplete game supplies a year or two after a settlement is first established (Carneiro 1968:245; Ross 1978a). Recent research demonstrates how dramatic this decline can be, both in terms of actual output and in relative efficiency (Vickers 1983). The problem of game depletions is par-

---

*Again "traditional" is a relative concept. The most isolated Yanomamo communities cultivate a nonindigenous crop, the plantain, employ machetes, introduced into their territory by missionaries, and are exposed to malaria, which is sufficiently new as still to be epidemic in character.

ticularly acute for the Yanomamo when their villages grow to over 100 to 150 people. Typically, as the size of settlement increases, large game animals—tapir, peccaries, deer—decline rather rapidly, with small prey—birds, rodents, smaller monkeys, etc.—showing less appreciable effect (Ross 1978a:5–6). But, anywhere between 65 and 80 percent of Yanomamo meat by weight is derived from just three species: tapir, white-lipped peccary, and collared peccary (Lizot 1979:151; Good, pers. com.), all of which can only be regularly pursued by what has been described as "deep-forest hunting" (Chagnon and Hames 1979:911).

It has been shown that while these few animals constitute a disproportionate share of total weight, they are, in fact, not harvested at a commensurate frequency, collectively representing 20 to 30 percent of all animals killed, in spite of systematic efforts to extend hunts into less routinely exploited reaches of the forest. The ensuing irregularity of meat intake levels, which seems to be characterized by a few peaks and long intervening periods of marginal consumption (Ross 1979:153–154), imposes considerable stress on the fabric of Yanomamo village life as different sectors of the community begin to feel the effects of low hunting returns. In particular, frictions develop as a result of inequalities in game distribution (Ross 1978:31), and these in turn build to the point where the village actually fissions, reducing the size of distribution networks and increasing individual shares. Good has compared distribution patterns of meat in pre- and post-fission stages (table 2.3).

It is important to bear in mind that among the Yanomamo, as in many such populations, game is distributed among adult males; in particular among the Yanomamo, the actual size of a received portion varies considerably (Good n.d.:23) and depends to a large extent on a man's social status. Since this is closely related to hunting skills, poor hunters and their families tend to suffer doubly as far as meat acquisition is concerned, but to a greater extent as communities enlarge. Moreover, because men who receive meat then allocate it to their wives, children and unmarried sisters, poor hunters may be tempted as yields decline to withhold an increasing amount for their own consumption and additional pressure is brought to bear on their dependents.

Table 2.3
Pre-Fission (village population = 115)

Animal	No. of distributions recorded	Average cooked wgt. per piece	Number of adult men	Number of men omitted
Tapir	5	0.91	38	2
White-lipped peccary	15	0.34	24	7
Collared peccary	11	0.27	24	6

Post-Fission (village population = 41)

Animal	No. of distributions recorded	Average cooked wgt. per piece	Number of adult men	Number of men omitted
Tapir	3	1.57	11	0
White-lipped peccary	10	0.62	11	0
Collared peccary	9	0.41	11	0

Source: Good n.d.:23.

This, in turn, has subtle but important demographic consequences. Most Yanomamo have been reported to be "in good physical condition" (Chagnon and Hames 1979:911), but this may mean simply that the healthy survive: James Neel, who participated in an interdisciplinary biomedical survey of the Yanomamo, has, for example, commented that the Yanomamo evidence a relatively high mortality rate in their reproductive years. For men this is manifestly due to warfare, but in respect to women it has not been satisfactorily explained (1977:163). Yet, figures on mortality by gender suggest that females may succumb disproportionately to disease (Chagnon 1974:160), perhaps reflecting their generally inferior social and nutritional state. If so, it points to an important means of "tracking" rates of infanticide to environmental stress: as hunting yields fall, women tend to regard a neonate as direct competition with their own or their older children's increasingly problematical animal food supply and their resolve not to bear the costs of rearing additional children is strengthened. Since husbands eagerly await the benefits of additional future warriors, un-wanted female infants suffer the brunt of this "tracking." Chagnon's data further suggest that headmen—who enjoy greater access to game and other food than non-headmen, reflecting the relationship of game distribution to status—have offspring with a sex ratio indicative of a significantly lower rate of female infanticide (1979).

The likelihood is that a similar variation in the frequency of infanticide could be found to correspond to male status in general. As we shall see, at higher levels of agricultural intensification, such status differences between males play an increasingly important role in reproductive behavior, but with the important provision—important from the point of view of the debate concerning the sociobiological principle of reproductive success—that higher ranking males do not always outproduce lower ranking ones.

Yanomamo villages formed out of fissioning tend to remain as closely situated allies (among other things, they still share a common investment in nearby gardens) but have acquired the advantage of distributing meat among fewer families. Remaining on more or less friendly terms also permits them to conjoin forces for defense, a necessary consideration since fissioning has reduced their individual forces. But, at the same time, such village splits do not necessarily reduce the need to pursue game regularly in distant regions, until or unless they actually diminish local density. The result is that most competition tends to be generated among more widely separated communities (Chagnon and Hames 1979:912), with the hostilities generated in the process being largely responsible for the creation of uninhabited tracts of forest—no-man's lands—where predation is precarious and irregular, but, therefore, unusually productive (J. Ross 1980).

Thus, viewed systemically, while warfare creates and maintains such zones in which major game species may be buffered against excessive hunting, it is the periodic efforts of rival groups to exploit such productive areas which, in turn, contributes so much to the perpetuation of hostilities (Hickerson 1962). Without attempting periodically to tap such resources, Yanomamo settlements could probably not grow as large as they do but, at the same time, it is their size which so rapidly depletes local game supplies and re-inforces the pressure to pursue prized mammalian prey in buffer zones.

A comment on the representativeness of the Yanomamo's population-regulating system: it should not be concluded that the extremely high rates of warfare and female infanticide reported for the Yanomamo are typical of tropical forest groups (or even of the Yanomamo since these traits vary as we have seen from village to village). It is generally agreed (Hames 1983:425) that the Yanomamo population is expanding as a consequence of moving into habitats that were previously dominated by other ethnic groups whose extinction or migration has left behind a demographic vacuum. It is reasonable to suppose that both the warfare and infanticide would be reduced after villages space themselves more evenly throughout the habitat and the high levels of infanticide succeed in lowering population growth to rates more characteristic of long-term inhabitants rather than of an essentially pioneering population. Unfortunately, such predictions will never be tested because the Yanomamo are rapidly being subjected to intense outside forces, including missionaries and multinational development of parts of their region.

The Role of Animal Domesticants

As Carneiro effectively demonstrated over two decades ago (1960, 1961), the cultivation of root crops is capable of meeting the energetic requirements of quite large settlements (>1,000). The principal problem, as we have seen, is the deficiency in other critical nutrients characteristic of such diets* and the need to supplement them with animal foods, thereby making demographic growth dependent on the biobehavioral characteristics of prey species. In some instances, however, the depletion of feral species provided the impetus for shifts to new modes of production which relied on the husbandry of domesticated species as the principal source of animals. This was the case in New Guinea where root-crop

---

*We refer to diets which have neither milk or milk products, or eggs, or significant quantities of domesticated animals.

agriculture proved capable of sustaining far greater human densities than those found in the more extensive Amazonian forests.

Watson (1965) has argued that the dense populations of the central highlands of New Guinea (100+ persons/km²) developed only during the last 300 years as a consequence of the introduction of the sweet potato. While there is still considerable debate on this point (Morren 1977), there is no doubt that the village societies of highland New Guinea demonstrate a dramatic association of dense human settlements and commitment to the cultivation of this particular starchy tuber (Clarke 1966; Brookfield and Brown 1963). But, equally important is a correlation with the raising of domesticated pigs. Recent efforts to clarify the evolutionary relationship of these variables—population growth, agricultural intensification and pig husbandry—in New Guinea have much to contribute to our overall understanding of cultural and demographic developments at various times and places in the Neolithic, particularly the transition from hunting to animal domestication, to compensate for hunter-induced depletions and dependence on high calorie, low protein crops. In highland New Guinea, the sweet potato is not simply the basis of intensive agriculture, but of pig rearing as well. The latter represents one of the few large-animal sources of quality protein in an environment where forests have given way to grassland, with a concomitant and severe decline in wildlife (Clarke 1966; Sorenson 1972).

According to Watson, prior to the introduction of the sweet potato, the cultural features of the Central Highlands were much like what one may still find in the lower montane rainforest today, among such groups as the Miyanmin, for example, who practice slash-and-burn agriculture, hunt, and engage in only the most casual form of pig husbandry. Rather, it is the wild pig—which predates sweet potatoes in New Guinea for many thousands of years (Little and Morren 1976:72)—which predominates in their hunting-oriented economy (p. 76).

In the absence of adequate archeological evidence, it is difficult to discern the precise relationship of factors which promoted the rise in highland population densities. Watson attributes this phenomenon, which he describes as rapid, to the sweet potato, which had a greater agricultural and ecological potential than earlier crops such as taro, and seems to provide more productive fodder for pigs (1965:299). Morren (1977), on the other hand, has tended to emphasize the increasing role of pigs, as hunting declined, in stimulating greater agricultural intensification. What is clear, however, from comparative research among contemporary populations of the New Guinea highlands, is that pig raising, sweet potato cultivation, and population density have all generally helped to carry one another to higher levels, against a background of increasing environmental depletion, represented by deforestation, the spread of grassland and the decline of prey species (Lindenbaum 1979:24).

In examining four communities in upland New Guinea, one in the central highlands proper and three others in mountainous country to the north, William Clarke (1966) was able to show how agricultural intensification went hand in hand with higher population densities; but that there was also greater degradation which, in turn, tended to induce further labor intensification, including that invested in pig husbandry. This was able to sustain continued population growth but at some cost to average standard of living (table 2.4).

Clarke suggests that agricultural intensification (including pig husbandry) was able to sustain continued population growth—a level of 300 persons per square mile (116/km^2) with no arable land left was reached among the Enga, for example (Meggitt 1977)—but at increasing costs, including losses in dietary quality (and, he might have added, in lives, as warfare grew more intense and frequent). Thus, he corroborates an argument which we have made earlier about the price of population growth during the Neolithic:

The variety of the food supply is impoverished. The protein-rich leaves of forest trees and ferns become scarce. Game diminishes. Sweet potatoes become increasingly important at the expense of yams and taro—a change that not only increases monotony but may also decrease the nutritive value of the diet by lessening the complexity of the amino acid combination. Also, if there is a conversion of forest to grass, the work needed to cultivate grassland is long and tedious compared with the excitement and irregularity of clearing forest. Moreover, because the output of food per hour decreases, the increase in total production within the territory can hardly be said to be economic growth (1966:357–358).

Table 2.4

A Comparison of Agricultural and Demographic
Conditions in Four New Guinea Communities

	Nduimba Basin	*Kompiai*	*Upper Kaironk Valley*	*Batainabura*
Approximate population density (sq. mi.)	30 (11.1/km²)	75 (12/km²)	relatively high	relatively high
Harvest intensity	low	med-high	high	high
Garden preparation	incomplete clearing and burning of forest	incomplete clearing and burning of forest; rudimentary terracing	grass cultivated and burned; rudimentary terracing and irrigation	grass cultivated and burned; soil turned, worked and mounded; some drainage ditches
Grassland use for cultivation	never	very rare	common	common
Fallow	15–18 mos., 1 harvest	15–20 mos., 1 harvest	15–30 mos., 1–2 harvests	several years; several harvests
Labor/input yield	low	low	relatively high	relatively high

Source: Clarke 1966:350.

At the highest levels of intensification, it is arguable if pig husbandry in New Guinea actually contributes as much to human dietary needs as wild pigs and other feral species contribute to less intensive systems. The consumption of pork is characteristically associated with ritual occasions which are concentrated within a fairly short time-span. But, pig husbandry plays other roles which in turn have demographic consequences. For example, gifts of meat solidify alliances among communities; and warfare—success in which depends on such alliances—is a major route to securing additional garden land. Moreover, to some extent, the raising of pigs serves as a complex ecological regulator. First, it "banks" a considerable proportion of agricultural output which otherwise would surely be transformed into more people. Pigs, however, have the advantage that, at some point, they may be easily slaughtered to provide meat, to secure allies, and to reduce ecological pressures. Second, as Rappaport has suggested (1983), the rearing of pigs serves to schedule the occupation of garden lands acquired in warfare. As such land tends to have been intensively cultivated, it requires fallowing before it can be productively employed by a victorious community. The length of the fallow period is determined by the amount of time it takes to build up pig herds to a size considered adequate for ritual sacrifices to ancestral spirits, but it is also effectively determined by the toleration by adult women of the increasing work required to care for such pigs. When this reaches its limits, the pig feast takes place, the new gardens begin to be cultivated, and war breaks out anew. The overall result in some cases may be that a balance is struck between the intensive use of old gardens and the ecological processes needed to restore them to productive use. But, these mechanisms seem not to be effective in the long run (Buchbinder and Rappaport 1976).

Coital Abstinence and Reproductive Pressure

There is little doubt that agricultural intensification produces severe strains on both environment and social system alike, even though cultural mechanisms may evolve to cope with and minimize the costs of such stress. One consequence in highland New Guinea was a deepening antagonism between men and women and the institutionalization of elaborate forms of male homosexuality.

To understand this, it must be recognized that homosexual behavior is part of a general mammalian capacity for considerable flexibility in sexual response (Ford and Beach 1970); and one that has been observed in a variety of primate species (Hrdy 1981:170). What seems apparent in the case of humans is that the outward form that such responses take depends significantly on cultural conditioning.

That homosexuality may be accepted, encouraged, or rejected

according to cultural context is amply demonstrated by history (Harris, M. 1981:103–104; 109–111; Boswell 1980); and that such variations in sentiment may correspond to deeper societal features related to demographic trends is suggested by cross-cultural comparisons. Werner (1979), for example, divided a sample of 39 preindustrial societies into pro- and antinatalist groups and found that male homosexuality was frowned upon or punished for all individuals in 75 percent of the former but permitted or encouraged for some people in 60 percent of the latter. Despite this suggestive result, it should be emphasized that there is no theoretical reason why homosexuality should always vary directly with reproductive pressure since homosexuality is not incompatible with frequent heterosexual coitus. We need to know if and to what extent homosexuality occurs as the exclusive or nearly exclusive form of sexual intercourse in order to demonstrate its relationship to reproductive pressures. Unfortunately, such data have seldom been recorded.

In this connection, it is interesting to note that in the New Guinea highlands where, as we have just seen, arable land was scarce and animal food resources were severely limited, male homosexuality in conjunction with extremes of heterosexual coital abstinence has been noted by several ethnographers. The ideological justification for such abstinence and for homosexual indulgence has been described for the Etoro (Kelly 1976): it was believed that each man had only a limited supply of semen and that when the supply was exhausted, he died. While coitus between husband and wife was deemed necessary in order to prevent the population from becoming too small, sex was taboo between married couples for over 200 days per year. Males regarded wives who wanted to break the taboo as witches. To complicate matters, the supply of semen was not something that a man was born with; semen could only be acquired from another male and Etoro boys got their supply having oral intercourse with older men.

Reproductive Pressure, Pollution, and Witchcraft

The ideological associations of such behavior suggest that it is an extension of a more general phenomenon of male hostility toward women. As such, it may not actually require an accompanying shift toward such endemic homosexuality to exert a dampening effect on fertility.

Such antipathy seems to be relatively rare among low-density hunter gatherers, emerging most conspicuously with the intensification of horticulture and accompanying environmental stress. One common manifestation is the belief that women are polluting—a view which, carried to its extreme, not only rationalizes homosexuality as found in New Guinea but also underlies a belief in witchcraft.

The notion that women are polluting has an obvious implication for fertility since it typically derives its rationale from the significance attached to menstrual blood. Among foragers such as the !Kung, however, both the ideological and behavioral ramifications of menstruation appear to be relatively slight. (Of course, !Kung women do not menstruate very frequently as a result of lactational amenorrhea.) According to Martin and Voorhies, "Although there are certain prohibitions against women's touching men's arrows, especially while menstruating, and to engaging in sex during the height of the menstrual flow, these prohibitions do not extend to sleeping beside each other at the same time. . . . Women are not considered a threat to the ability of !Kung men to maintain their male identities and functions" (1975:239–240).

In the densely populated valleys of the New Guinea Highlands, on the other hand, women are characteristically regarded as polluting in the extreme. Among the Hagen, for example, the sexual organs—male and female—are regarded as "bad," as is sexual intercourse, the frequency of which is therefore discouraged. Women are considered threatening to men in varied respects, but especially in regard to menstrual blood, which is believed to have great supernatural power, to be dangerous in the extreme, and to be capable of poisoning men if absorbed or ingested even in imperceptible amounts (pp. 269–272). In this way, the concept of pollution, so strongly associated with women (Lindenbaum 1979:131–132), vitalizes the notion of witchcraft, of which they are regarded as the principal practitioners.

The belief in witchcraft seems to have a distinct relationship to environmental stress and among some New Guinea groups may have contributed to population regulation with or without any association with heterosexual coital abstinence. Among some, such as the Hewa, it has been estimated that within a two-year period as many as 30 female witches were accused and killed. Even when accusations do not eventuate in death, they may lead to banishment and deprivation of strategic resources. Thus, "Hewa witches, said to be women or weak old men . . . are those that society most consistently deprives of animal protein" (p. 133). From a cross-cultural perspective, there is evidence that suspicions of witchcraft increase in proportion to the level of dissension and frustration within a community (Mair 1969; Nadel 1952), either of which, of course, can have many causes. But, where such stress can be associated with depletions or rapid population growth, witchcraft accusations, as in the New Guinea Highlands, are often primarily directed against women and in a way which may not simply curtail fertility but put their very lives at risk. This brings us back once more to the question of who benefits from population growth among agriculturalists and who bears the costs.

Distribution of the Costs of Intensification

In this context, we should again take note of recurrent dietary differences between men and women; in most such instances, these differences seem to disadvantage the latter, often involving restrictions on access to high quality animal foods (Rosenberg 1980). Our presumption is that such deprivation affects female mortality and fertility, though there is rarely adequate data to substantiate this for prestate societies. Nor has there been any systematic effort to ascertain whether dietary inequalities between the sexes correspond cross-culturally to marked resource scarcity. Nonetheless, there are some interesting suggestions that this would prove to be the case. We have already seen, for example, how declines in hunting-yield among Amazonian societies are more likely to translate into nutritional stress for women than for men—a situation which we suggested may, in turn, influence infanticide rates. Another illustration is found in Lindenbaum's work among the Fore of montane New Guinea, cultivators whose exploitation of game had gradually given way to pig husbandry in the wake of population-induced environmental change. But pork was not equitably distributed—with surprising consequences. As Lindenbaum writes:

> Population increases in the region and the conversion to the sweet potato as a dietary staple . . . appear to have led to the progressive removal of forest and animal life, to cultivation methods involving more complete tillage of the soil, and to the keeping of domestic pig herds, which compensate for the loss of wild protein. As the forests' protein sources became depleted, Fore men met their needs by claiming prior right in pork, while women adopted human flesh as their supplemental *habus*, a Malanesian pidgin term meaning "meat" or "small game." (1979:24)

Some evidence of sex-associated dietary variation can be found among hunter-gatherer populations (Harris 1978:127; Jelliffe et al. 1962:909; Rosenberg 1980:184–185). In general, however, food distribution among foraging groups seems to have reflected the pervasive "reciprocity of the sexual division of labor" (Leacock 1981:149; Lee 1982) and thus to have been relatively egalitarian. Some indication of sex-differentiated consumption is also reported among pastoralists, among whom men may appropriate a larger proportion of blood or meat (Dyson-Hudson 1970:103). But, in general, differentiation according to gender in access to strategic resources seems largely to have evolved with the development of sedentary agricultural life, higher population densities, and the growing complexity of economic organization required to manage intensive forms of resource utilization and distribution.

We have already suggested that one characteristic of this trend was a more pronounced separation of domestic economic activity and what one might refer to as public forms of production, with women increasingly subjected to increased labor demands in the form of domestic provisioning, food processing, and child care (Ember 1983). The other side of this coin is that men gained more control over the disposition of household production, while women's position became ever more contingent on the public status of their husband or male kin and more bound up with the reproduction of the labor supply (Leacock 1981), to which end their own material condition was frequently subordinated.

The consistency with which this subordination has been expressed in terms of diet is, in fact, a quite remarkable feature of the ethnographic record—to the extent that we may reasonably assume that it has been a long-standing cultural component of intensive economies of various kinds, ranging from agriculturalists to modern industrial capitalism (Harrison 1983:332; Roberts 1971:84).

To arrive at a satisfactory understanding of how such pressures were allowed to bear on women is no easy matter. But, it is clear that the common parental interests of men and women have long been complicated by divergent social priorities reflecting their different status in the social system as a whole—a divergence which entails the biological as well as economic exploitation by men of the women closest to them, and which bears a powerful similarity to relations between classes. We shall return to this issue in chapter 5.

3. Population Regulation and the Rise of the State

Pristine States and Population

The state in its earliest manifestations was the political and economic outcome of a complex evolutionary feedback involving reproductive pressure, intensified agricultural production (especially of grains), increased social stratification, militarism, and territorial expansion. Earlier voluntary systems of communal redistribution and provisioning had developed, with intensive grain production and harvest surpluses, into systems where storage, redistribution, and trade were dominated by "big men"; in some cases, these had in time given way to even more productive, but coercive economies characterized by taxation and labor conscription, enforced by bureaucratic theocratic-police-military specialists. Taxes and forced labor were invested in public works, especially canals, roads, and storehouses, which led to further intensification of the production base. Population increased further, responding to more favorable cost/benefit child-rearing ratios and density soon surpassed all previous levels.

The political-military-theocratic authority and power of the ruling class increased commensurately. Adjacent territories could now be conquered and their defeated armies and peasantries incorporated into the state-controlled labor forces as peasants, serfs, and slaves. (Band and village warfare in contrast did not result in territorial and manpower expansion.) The larger the territory, the greater the population and the tax and labor base, the more powerful the military-bureaucratic-theological ruling class, the greater the orbit of conquest. Hence, the earliest states moved inexorably from incipient formations that were barely distinguishable from large chieftaincies, to empires, in conformity with the natural and cultural opportunities of their distinctive habitats.

One can safely assume that, to the extent that the earliest or "pristine" states (e.g., pre-dynastic India, China, Southeast Asia, Mesoamerica, and Peru) had conscious state-formulated population policies, they were strongly pronatalist, in keeping with the expansionist dynamic of their economic systems. The demand of military campaigns, for example, through which centralized authority was able to achieve hegemony over neighboring populations, meant that, in order to extend the power-base of the state, a substantial proportion of its core labor supply had to be diverted from agricultural production to warfare. This and the demand for warriors, and eventually the support of a permanent specialist force of trained fighters, compelled further intensification of production and made greater demands on the reproductive potential of the peasantry. The momentum of state expansion tended to encourage the development of its ideological counterpart: it was in the interest of the ruling class that state institutions, secular and/or religious, induce the peasantry to "be fruitful and multiply"—and, initially, at least, this positive advocacy may have been readily compatible with improvements in peasant living standards. Thus, in regions such as the eastern Mediterranean during the late bronze age, evidence suggests that there was a gain of one to three years in female longevity and of up to six years for males (Angel 1972; 1975).

In the long run, however, it would be wise to assume that, as in any class-based system, just as economic interests diverged between rulers and ruled, between peasants and urban-dwellers, so reproductive interests varied. Thus, caught between state demands, embodied in corvée, taxation, conscription, etc., and local ecological imperatives of production, peasants could virtually never have manifested reproductive careers that unfailingly reflected imperial injunctions, any more than their behavior in other spheres could be regarded as a direct translation of state ideology (Mitchell 1980).

Interestingly, the rates of increase attributed to early states are not markedly different from those attributed to the Neolithic, ranging in the vicinity of .04 percent to .13 percent per annum; but,

Table 3.1
Ancient State Population Growth Rates

	Percent/yr.	*Period of Estimate*
Mesopotamia	.07	Early dynastic
Egypt	.05	3000 B.C.–150 B.C.
Aegean	.04–.15	Neolithic–Early Bronze
Mesoamerica	.13–.39	1200 B.C.–A.D. 1520

Source: After Hassan 1981:234.

spurts of growth as high as 1.0 percent were possible for short periods (Hassan 1981:234). These spurts are prominent in the archaeological record in connection with the growth of urban centers during regional transitions from chieftain-level to state-level polities. Once the state and/or a capital city formed, further population growth was often achieved by centripetal immigration, which raised local densities but left regional densities unaffected (p. 250).

It is important to point out that increases in the populations within the orbits of state and imperial control were not dependent on an excess of births over deaths. States and empires grew as much by conquest and incorporation of defeated peoples as by indigenous population growth. Moreover, there were frequent shifts in political fortunes, with new centers replacing old as a result of environmental depletions involving, variously or in some combination, anthropogenic problems such as deforestation or river silting, which might result from overintensive agriculture (Sanders, Santley, and Parsons 1979), or natural processes, such as flooding, severe climatic change, or tectonic uplift, phenomena which could dramatically transform the nature and distribution of agricultural resources (Mosley 1983).

Equally, the rise of urban concentrations which have been characteristic of state formations presented unprecedented conditions for density-dependent diseases to flourish. As we have noted earlier, the transition to sedentary economies had already created new opportunities for disease transmission; these intensified with the emergence of city states and administrative and urban centers, establishing a pattern that would persist in Europe well into the last century and in many underdeveloped countries today: the replenishment of the population of high mortality urban areas through immigration from their healthier surrounding hinterlands (Polgar 1972:205; Wrigley 1969). The diseases that urban living conditions favored—and this seems to apply both to the New World and the Old (Storey 1985:532–533)—were, for the most part, the result of chronic problems of poor sanitation, crowding, and food shortage, with the general demographic effect of high juvenile mortality (p. 532). But, we can also assume that such problems worsened and disease manifested a special virulence in times of economic and ecological stress. Thus, while the slope of the population growth curve during the period of the early states and empires may not have been very different from the main trend during the Neolithic, massive oscillations became commonplace.

Mature and Secondary States

While peasant living standards may have risen during the initial period of state formation, the general level of welfare over the long term rose and fell according to a variety of idiosyncratic or systemic factors, with one fairly constant feature being the contrast between the living standards of members of different classes. Thus, a striking characteristic of the skeletal remains of ancient state populations is the difference in stature and in other osteological indicators found in high and low status burials. In the domain of the Maya state in the Yucatan peninsula, for example, where elaborate urban-ceremonial centers reached their zenith between A.D. 300 and 900, the advance of political centralization coincided with a notable decline in average male stature—by about 7.6 cm. (3 inches) over roughly that same period at Tikal, the largest Mayan city center. More important, as an index of the class structure of Mayan society, at the end of this period males who received high status burials were 7.0 cm. taller on average than lower class males (Haviland 1967).* Yet, there is reason to believe that the Mayan economy was never characterized by the extremes of power and

---

*That this kind of contrast has been a persistent feature of state formations is suggested by statistics from England where, by the end of the nineteenth century, 12-year-old boys in private schools were on average five inches (11 cm) taller than those in local authority or council schools (Howe 1972:181).

privilege that were typical of other early—and later—states (Vogt and Cancian 1970).

Such trends, which marked the careers of mature ancient states and empires and "secondary states" (those which arose subsequently and within a geopolitical context in which preexistent states were at least one important factor in their own development), point up the inevitable contradiction between the interest of a ruling class in further intensification and the burden, both economic and biological, which such interests imposed on those whose labor in the end sustained the state infrastructure. The demographic consequences may be read in the historical and archaeological record, where the populations of diverse state systems around the world evidence something less than a steady progressive advance. Thus, both India and China, according to Clark (1967:75–76) "experienced long periods of stationary or declining population." India, for example, had an estimated 100–140 million people in the second century B.C. during the reign of the Emperor Asoka; by the year A.D. 1000 it was as low as 48 million; it rose again in the fifteenth century during the Mogul empire's early phase, but suffered substantial decline again in the late seventeenth and eighteenth centuries, a time of considerable civil disorder. In Egypt, the population of the Nile Valley quadrupled between 4000 B.C. and 2500 B.C., remained stationary for the next 1,000 years, rose to a new peak in 1250 B.C. and had fallen back to Old Kingdom levels by the time of the Greek and Roman conquests. Under the Romans, it rose to new heights but settled back by A.D. 500 to what it had been 3,000 years earlier (Butzer and Freeman 1976). Between A.D. 2 and A.D. 742, China's overall population ranged from 48 to 58 million. In the Hwa Ho River heartland of the Han Dynasty, population fluctuated sharply from 35 million in A.D. 2 to 25 million in A.D. 140 to 31 million in 509, and 23 million in 742 (Bielenstein 1947).

The complexity of causes underlying such population declines and long passages of negligible growth should not be minimized; but, two general observations can be made. First, the toll of taxation and increasingly onerous labor demands by the state sharpened class divisions and eventuated in periodic agrarian rebellions and general political upheavals (Needham 1969:112, 254) which were costly in life, economic productivity and social cohesion. Second, peasant families often defied the pronatalist policies which ruling classes sought to impose upon them and, for their own immediate material survival, practiced a variety of population-regulating behaviors including adjustments in the care and treatment of infants, children, and females, lactation frequency and scheduling, and altered coital frequency and scheduling including changes in the age of marriage. And in all likelihood, many of the physiological mechanisms of fertility control that we have referred to earlier came into play here as well, wherever severe malnutrition or chronic undernutrition existed. But it is impossible even to speculate about the exact mix of these factors among the various peasant populations of antiquity and their role in specific episodes of population expansion or contraction.

Pronatalist Policy in European Antiquity

An ideal of early empires from China to Rome was the large family. In Sung China, for example, large extended families were referred to as "righteous gates," and the emperor's officials issued testimonials of merit and exempted them from labor conscription. One such family was said to have 700 members who dined together, minus children, under one roof (M. Cohen 1976:227).

The Romans evinced a similar enthusiasm and rewarded outstanding examples of familial size with triumphal processions to the Capitol, one of which (described by the Elder Pliny) featured a freedman, his 8 children, 27 grandchildren, and 18 great-grandchildren (Wilkinson 1979:23). Official Roman policy was highly pronatalist (Strangeland 1966:29). Their word for ordinary people, *proletarii*, meant "breeders." In 131 BC. the censor Metellus Macedonius made a speech to the Senate, "On Increasing Offspring," in which he recommended making marriage compulsory. In the next century, the famous orator Cicero warned Julius Caesar of the need to encourage reproduction. Caesar, in turn, according to Strangeland (1966:31), "prohibited women of twenty-four who were unmarried and childless from wearing precious metals and jewels and from using litters, and he rewarded those who had large families." His successor, Augustus, introduced legislation penalizing celibates and childless couples and bestowing privileges upon those who had three or more children (Wilkinson 1979:29). The thrust of such laws seems to have been directed largely at the patrician class (Strangeland 1966:33), perhaps partly influenced by the perennial fear among ruling classes of being deluged demographically by their subjects (at the same time that they rely upon the latter's reproductive potential); but, whatever the precise target, a long succession of warnings and statutes testifies both to a preoccupation and to the failure to achieve any practical effect. Nonetheless, the ideal of the Roman state was to stimulate population.

Officially, the city states of ancient Greece were as pronatalist as Rome. Sparta, for example, enacted severe penalties for celibacy (Strangeland 1966:21). Pericles, in his funeral oration of 430 B.C., called upon the bereaved parents of Athens to breed more sons to replace those who had died in the war with Sparta, and husband-sharing was introduced as an emergency measure to bolster fertility in the aftermath of the Sicilian defeat in 413 B.C. (Wilkinson 1979:21ff.).

Anti-Natalist Behavior in Ancient Greece and Rome

From an early date, however, there were strong ideological currents that ran contrary to Greek state policy. This is not surprising, given the highly restricted resource base to which the Greek city states were confined. Aristotle, for example, was more concerned about overpopulation than underpopulation. He considered that failure to control population growth could lead to poverty, crime and rebellion and was among the first to propose that there was an optimum population level to be achieved and maintained. Plato, too, linked excessive numbers of offspring with poverty and war. In the *Republic*, he advocated the abolition of marriage and state regulation of intercourse among the "guardian" class, although his prescription for the subservient classes remains in doubt (Wilkinson 1979:19ff.). It is interesting to note as well that Phillip of Macedon, father of Alexander the Great, had been urged by the Athenian Isocrates to conquer Persia as an outlet for Greece's surplus and rebellious population.

If official policy or even public opinion was equivocal, there is little doubt that the Romans and the Greeks frequently *behaved* as if large families were undesirable. Both the ruling and subordinate classes employed an impressive array of fertility/mortality mechanisms to defend themselves against the adverse consequences of having to rear too many children. Infanticide, for example, appears to have been an important means of population regulation and a practice condoned by virtually all the most illustrious thinkers in both Rome and Greece until the fourth century A.D. (De Mause 1974:26). In the *Laws*, for example, Plato has his guardians "not bring to light" or "dispose of" unwanted children, and in the *Republic* infanticide is treated as a normal prerogative of parents.

A decided bias against females was evident as well. Females in general were kept on diets less nourishing than those reserved for men and boys, and had a life span from five to ten years shorter than males. As in many prestate societies, there was also a marked bias against females in the practice of infanticide. A popular Greek saying was: "Everyone, even if poor, raises a son, but even if rich, exposes a daughter " At Delphi in the second century B.C., only 1 percent of 600 families reared more than one daughter, but families with several sons were common—a situation that does not seem to have been unusual (Wilkinson 1979; De Mause 1974:28).

Turning to Rome during the Republic, we find the well-known provision that the *paterfamilias* had an absolute legal right to determine whether any infant should be reared. Attempts at abortion must also have been common enough, judging by the varied methods recorded, including insertion of needles, malnutrition, purgatives, diuretics, emetics, pessaries, acidic potions, punching, lifting heavy weights, jumping, and riding in a cart along bumpy roads (Wilkinson 1979:37). There seems, however, to have been more reluctance to induce abortion than to practice infanticide, probably because the sex of the fetus could not be ascertained in advance of birth, as well as because of considerable risk to the mother—as its prohibition in the Hippocratic oath suggests. In Rome, the sale of abortifacients was illegal and there was considerable criticism of women who attempted abortions. Yet, no one seems to have expected the lower class to give them up (pp. 38–39).

Homosexuality

The Greek concern with fertility/mortality control suggests that the prevalence of male homosexuality in European antiquity had a demographic basis which has hitherto been ignored by classical scholars. There are a few indications of homosexuality in Homer and other pre-classic sources associated with the transition from chieftancies to states. It becomes ubiquitous, however, in the writings of the seventh and sixth centuries B.C. in association with the maturation and consolidation of the city-state. Like the homosexuality of New Guinea highlanders, Greek homosexuality involved the notion that the educational process was facilitated through sexual relations between senior and junior males (Dover 1978:202). Greek males were also often separated from their wives—although as a result of military service and travel rather than taboos—and women were held in low esteem by men. These conditions correspond rather closely to those which promote the toleration or advocacy of homosexuality among prestate, antinatalist societies (see chapter 2).

The history of homosexuality in Rome is also instructive in this regard. During the rapid ascendancy of Rome when the city itself grew from a large town based on "a simple near-subsistence economy" in the early third century B.C. to an imperial capital with an estimated population of about 1 million by the end of the last century B.C. (Hopkins 1978:2, 19), the state was effectively transformed into an expansionist war machine which drew an increasingly high percentage of the population into military service. As Hopkins writes: "If the evidence on army size and citizen population is anywhere near right, then a very large proportion (say over half) of Roman citizens regularly served in the army for seven years in the early second century B.C. By the reign of Augustus, the army was thoroughly professionalized, but an average of twenty years' service still required the enlistment of about one fifth of seventeen-year-old citizens" (1978:35).

This insatiable demand for warriors provides some understanding of the infrastructural support for Roman pronatalism and negative views of homosexuality. Thus, Greek homosexuality was explicitly ridiculed, while soldiers were forbidden to use each other as sexual partners and the death penalty was prescribed for homosexual relations between free-born men and boys (Wilkinson 1979:136).

But, there were contradictory currents as well and, much like the Greeks, the Romans seem generally to have acknowledged that homosexuality and heterosexuality were not mutually exclusive (Boswell 1980:73). Thus, in civilian life, homosexual relations were not regarded as incompatible with married life or a career of procreative sexuality. Moreover, under the empire (officially established in 31 B.C.), a process of conquest and greater political integration profoundly altered the nature of Roman society, which in the long run was to lead to greater tolerance of homosexual behavior. Foreign treasure, the product of distant wars, provided the Roman elite with great wealth which they invested in Italian land, largely confiscated from the peasantry. Their new estates were provided with labor by enslaved war captives. By the end of the first century B.C., of a population in Italy of 6 million, about one-third was probably slaves (Hopkins 1978:102)—while a high proportion of displaced peasants was conscripted into the Roman army. With the increasing professionalization of the army, however, more and more peasants poured into Rome; though provisioned with free wheat, their threat to political stability could nonetheless not be easily nullified. The pressures generated by their numbers and poverty combined with the inefficiency of slave-based agriculture did much to shift general attitudes toward a more antinatalist stance.* By the height of the empire, in fact, homosexuality was widely tolerated (Boswell 1980:62–73).

How commonly it was practiced among the masses is problematical, and what contribution it made to demographic trends, relative, for example, to infanticide, remains speculative. But, considerable evidence suggests that it was fairly common among the Roman elite, among whom fertility was in decline by the second century A.D. While the causes of this decline were varied and are not yet entirely clear, one suggestion is that wealthy families recognized that high fertility, combined with the prevailing pattern

*Compare this with the similar development of antinatalism among landlords in nineteenth-century Ireland as they cleared land of peasants in order to create large cattle farms, as described later.

of partible inheritance, high dowries, and a social order in which political influence depended on vast expenditures, threatened the perpetuation of a family's fortune (Hopkins 1983:89). As a consequence, both infanticide and homosexuality became fairly common among the rich (Hopkins 1983:225; Boswell 1980). This may also help to explain the Augustan laws on marriage—for, as much as it may have been in the interest of the Roman aristocracy to limit family size, it was undoubtedly in the emperor's interest to increase family size to prevent any threatening concentrations of wealth among potential political opponents (Hopkins 1983:98). Thus, from Augustus onward, disabilities were imposed on the unmarried and childless: "The unmarried were forbidden to inherit property; fathers were given preferential treatment in the allocation of public offices; and matrons were awarded the rights to wear distinctive costumes. . . . In addition, family allowances were given for children, and abrogating a traditional paternal right, infanticide was made a capital offense" (Abernathy 1979:109). But despite these measures, prostitution, homosexuality and other nonreproductive forms of sex increased, the average age of marriage increased, and both abortion and infanticide became more prevalent (p. 110).

It was not until the third century, with the Roman empire slowly disintegrating and army generals in control of civil authority, making and breaking emperors, that pronatalist forces seem to have gained the ascendancy. As Langer has noted: "The later Roman Empire apparently suffered from progressive depopulation, due to devastating epidemics, recurrent famines and general disorder. Under the circumstances there was clearly no need to limit population growth. On the contrary, increased fertility was desired" (1974:355). Homosexuality for example came increasingly under official attack by the late third century (Boswell 1980:711). By A.D. 318, under the Emperor Constantine, infanticide was declared a crime, though it was not regarded as murder or punished by death until much later in the century (Langer 1974:355; De Mause 1974:28).

This trend, which owed much to the deteriorating condition of the Roman empire, was undoubtedly encouraged outside the sphere of state policy by the transformation of the economic and social order within much of its western reaches. There the centuries-old influence of Rome was giving way to an encroaching Germanic tribal economy, a process which would eventually give birth to Western European feudalism by the tenth century (Anderson 1974). Long before this, however, the relaxation of imperial rule and the resurgence of frontier conditions encouraged a less restrictive pattern of fertility than in earlier times when a high proportion of agricultural labor had been derived from imported slaves.

Early Christianity

It was against this background that Christianity developed as the official religion of the empire. As Boswell has shown, its doctrines were not intrinsically adverse even to homosexuality (1980:92–117); while its views against contraception, most notably expressed by St. Augustine, were never pronounced with formal authority until comparatively late in the Middle Ages (Noonan 1966:231). The standard interpretation of church doctrine, rather, was at any given historical moment a reflection of prevailing social and economic currents and the needs of the Church and its political allies relative to them.

Like Buddhism and Hinduism with which it shared many common roots, Christianity spread through a world of aristocratic privilege and hedonism juxtaposed with mass hunger and servitude. In this setting, not surprisingly, it expressed contradictory values. On the one hand, there was a certain antinatalist disposition. Thus, Christ, like Buddha and the Hindu saints, condemned the indulgence of carnal appetites. The Pauline letters advocate virginity and chastity over sexuality; sex was permissible only in marriage, but even then, continence was regarded as a virtue: "It is good for a man not to touch a woman . . . I say therefore to the unmarried and widows, it is good for them if they abide even as I. But if they cannot contain, let them marry: for it is better to marry than to burn. . . . But this I say, brethren, the time is short: it remaineth, that they who have wives be as though they had none" (I Corinthians 7:1–9, 29).

At the council of Elvira (A.D. 306) chastity was made a condition of priesthood and shortly thereafter, Constantine, the first Chris-

tian emperor, proclaimed celibacy to be a holy state and disman-
tled the laws which had favored marriage and subsidized
reproduction (but not those which prohibited infanticide and abortion). These measures complemented a common early Christian
belief that the world was full and that there was no need to pro-
create further while awaiting the imminent return of the Messiah.

The Rise of Christian Pronatalism

Given that early Christianity was an inchoate and often contradictory movement (Pagels 1979), however, such views coexisted with
more pronatalist views. These began to gain the upper hand with
the interpenetration of the Church and the structures of the Roman
state. Thus, while St. Augustine (354–430) believed that human
procreation was necessary to increase the number of citizens in
the heavenly City of God, it can scarcely be a coincidence that his
concern over increasing the number of human souls corresponds
in time, as we have seen, to what is generally regarded as a period
of marked population decline throughout the Western dominions
of the Roman empire (UN 1973:16ff.). Pronatalism thereafter became a constant feature of Catholic population policy and of Christian population policy in general, until the late industrial era.

One need not invoke depopulation, however, to understand the
ascendancy of a pronatalist position within the Christian church.
The earliest mode of propagation of the faith was almost exclusively through proselytization and conversion; but, with increasing
success and institutionalization, it came to rely more upon ascrip-
tive and descent-like principles of membership, a tendency served
by the encouragement of large families. It should, of course, also
be noted that the institutionalization of the Church meant an increasing role in the wider economy. Through the ensuing Middle
Ages, as it came to play a major part as landowner, it found additional reason to encourage reproduction among the peasant class
(Goody 1983).

While official policy in Europe tended to be pronatalist through
most of the Middle Ages, Church teaching on marriage and procreation was, again, often contradictory. The medieval Church, for
example, was responsible for drastically reducing the range of per-

missible marriages—banning unions between a deceased man's wife and his brother (the levirate) or between a deceased wife's husband and her sister (the sororate), as well as marriage between stepchildren, cross and parallel cousins, and all "close relatives." It also banned divorce, polygymy, and concubinage. All of these restrictions have antinatalist implications and if strictly obeyed would have depressed fertility. According to Goody (1983), these measures become intelligible in the light of the Church's interest in increasing the volume of donations by propertied men and women who lacked male heirs and who would therefore be likely to will their estates to the Church, which in fact did become Europe's largest landowner. We suggest that celibacy among the priesthood and holy orders can also be seen as functionally related to the economic interests of the Church, since it prevented the devolution of wealth to heirs outside of the corporation.

Other compromises with antinatal practices may represent the Church's accommodation to defensive measures employed by couples and unwed mothers aimed at reducing the number of unwanted children. Thus, it was only from the early thirteenth century onward that contraception was actually condemned, while abortion up to "quickening"—approximately the sixteenth to eighteenth week of pregnancy when fetal movements are first felt by the mother—was generally accepted well into the nineteenth century (Noonan 1966:231).

Demographic Theology in the Middle Ages

The formalization of Church doctrine on procreation that was characterized by Thomas Aquinas in the mid-thirteenth century bore an interesting relationship to developments in Western Europe at that time, which again suggests the influence of economic and social conditions on theological doctrine. Most notably, this was a period of great revival in population and of a reemergence of centralized political authorities. After a long epoch of relative stagnation, Western European population—along with agricultural production (which was characterized during this period by a series of important technological innovations [Duby 1974; White 1964;

Slicher Van Bath 1963])—evidenced a broad pattern of expansion. The twin phenomena of population increase and agricultural development seem undoubtedly linked, but precisely what triggered their advance is difficult to say. Certainly a powerful argument can be made that it owes much to a commercial revival and "an increasing percolation of money into the self-sufficiency of manorial economy" (Dobb 1963:37), both of which were themselves closely associated with changing relations between Europe and regions beyond. What is clear, however, is that agriculture entered a phase of unprecedented productivity, which featured both intensification of activity on old lands and what Duby has described as "a regular conquest" of previously uncultivated lands, including forest, marshland, and pasture (1972:198). The picture one has of the thirteenth century is of a classic frontier demand for labor, favoring larger families.

This population expansion meant cheaper labor and this, combined with rising rents, caused considerable wealth to flow to feudal landlords, including the Church. It subsidized dramatic urban growth (P. Anderson 1974:190; Power 1932:723), helped to sustain the development of trade, and provided the means to erect the great Gothic cathedrals whose construction began during this era as well. Given the relationship between rising population, agricultural expansion and the prosperity of the Church, to which such edifices testified, it is hardly surprising that this was also the time when a prominent ecclesiastical figure such as Aquinas emerged to emphasize a view of procreation as a natural good (Noonan 1966:245).

Economic expansion seems to have begun to overextend itself, however, toward the late thirteenth century. As Duby has observed: "It seems that all the lands susceptible of being profitably worked with renewed techniques had by then been brought into production" (1972:199). There are suggestions that labor productivity began to fall, while at the same time the peasantry was subjected to onerous feudal demands and pressure from increasing land subdivision (Pounds 1973:311). Thus, the grandeur of Gothic architecture obscured the fact that it was paid for by the growing misery of the peasant class (Pounds 1973:312).

The Late Feudal Pattern of Fertility Control

The established view among modern demographers is that the most important means employed by Europeans to regulate population growth in conformity with economic prospects was to vary the age of marriage (R. Smith 1981; Wrigley and Schofield 1981).

We do not doubt that variation in age at marriage played a part in regulating fertility throughout much of Europe as well as elsewhere. During the post-Roman population depression, for example, age of marriage as low as twelve years for females and fourteen for boys are reported (Glass 1940; Wrigley 1969). Marriage age seems to have been low in the early Middle Ages and higher later on (Coale 1975:348–349). On a finer time scale, rapid responses in marriage rates have been detected in relation to population and repopulation, as in Tuscany where the female age of marriage varied from 16 before the onslaught of the great epidemics of the fourteenth century to 15 at the beginning of the fifteenth century. By the late fifteenth century, the age of marriage was back up to 21 years (Herlihy 1977:152). Hajnal (1965) associates a distinctive pattern of late marriage in Western Europe with the beginnings of capitalism in the sixteenth century.

Age at marriage, however, regulated population growth only because it was embedded in a distinctive complex of sexual taboos, marital exchanges, family organization, wealth inheritance, celibate orders, and infant death control. A later age at marriage reduced female fertility, for example, only to the extent that pregnancy and child rearing outside of wedlock were preventable in any significant degree. In fact, toleration of illegitimacy was highly variable, both through time and according to the value of heritable property. Thus, in southern France in the fourteenth century, while the possibility of an illegitimate child might cause considerable anxiety to the nobility, for most people "the moral and social status of bastards . . . presented them with problems which were not completely insoluble" (Le Roy Ladurie 1978:174–175). That the onus of bastardy was not an effective deterrent to sexual activity through much of the population is suggested by evidence from England, where "the expected age for a woman to produce a child outside marriage was very much the same as the age which she would produce her first child within marriage" (Laslett 1980:55). Obviously a certain proportion of illicit pregnancies occurred where marriage was already contemplated (Levine and Wrightson 1980). But, there is, of course, also a possibility that, rather than the stigma of illegitimacy necessarily reducing the birthrate, it meant that extramarital pregnancy was in many cases an inducement to marriage. In the end, the extent to which marriage actually regulated fertility is confounded by the likelihood that many illicit offspring were never officially registered (Laslett 1977:108–110) and that illegitimacy rates were higher than they appear.

What it is important to bear in mind, therefore, is that the official value placed on marriage and legitimacy cannot be directly equated with actual patterns of sexual unions or procreation any more than a formal doctrine on contraception or abortion could be taken as a credible measure of fertility-regulation in practice. Again, age at marriage confers little immediate insight for that reason on fertility-related behavior within marriage. As Noonan (1966:230) notes: "Within marriage, the same economic motives that prompted postponement of marrying would have been present to stimulate contraceptive practice. Again, with such motives at work, and a means like coitus interruptus available, we cannot suppose that all married couples would have followed the law of the Church" (1966:230).

This kind of discrepancy between doctrine and practice which, as we have already said, is apt to prevail in any state society, is hardly difficult to understand if one recognizes that the ruling class, in Europe as elsewhere, endorsed a system which favored procreation by seeking to conjoin sex and marriage, but which otherwise offered little or no subsidy to the marital economy. Far from it, while the full costs of child rearing were endured by parents, most of the substantive benefits of a large labor reserve accrued to their rulers through taxation, conscription, corvée, and other forms of economic extraction. For the peasant, it was often the case that, as Le Roy Ladurie has commented, "to marry and have children was at least to risk ruin" (1978:182).

Infant Mortality Control: Europe

No description of preindustrial Euro-Asian population regulation can avoid a frank and open discussion of the importance of infant death control.

Reviews by Langer (1974) and Kellum (1974) show that direct or indirect infanticide was practiced continuously in Europe from Greco-Roman times to the nineteenth century. But, since infanticide was a crime in Christian Europe (although it was difficult to prove), it tended, as with abortion, to become more well-concealed—particularly in the case of illegitimate births—and indirect forms tended to emerge. Several of these became institutionalized, in the sense that they occurred according to a set formula and were not regarded as homicide by practitioners or the authorities. The first was "overlaying," whereby mothers rolled over in their sleep and suffocated the infants nursing at their sides. So prevalent did this become in medieval Europe that laws were passed attempting to prohibit mothers and infants from sleeping in the same bed (Langer 1974:356). But such laws could obviously not be enforced; and since homicidal intent could rarely be proved, a conviction for overlaying was punishable only by public denunciation and penitence in the form of a bread and water diet.

The second form involved the institution of sending a new infant to a "wet nurse." During the late medieval period, upper-class townswomen sought to be relieved of the burden of caring for and nursing their infants by turning them over to women who made a living from breast-feeding other people's children. As preference frequently was given to a wet nurse whose own child had died shortly after birth and who therefore would not have to divide her milk between two infants, "the demand for wet nurses caused poor countrywomen to destroy their own offspring" (Dickemann 1979:353). Their charges fared little better, however, and the mortality rate among infants sent off to wet nurses was notoriously high; yet, parents who had lost one child in this way often had little apparent hesitation in risking another (De Mause 1974). Nor were the well-to-do the only ones to engage in this practice. Even poorer families sought the service of wet nurses; and children born out of wedlock to servant girls who performed the role of concubine in their employer's household were routinely placed with country wet nurses who, again, regarded themselves as under little obligation to preserve the child's life (Trexler 1973a).

Perhaps one of the most popular indirect forms of infanticide was simply abandonment. This was already such a common practice that as early as 787 an asylum was established in Milan exclusively to care for abandoned infants (De Mause 1974:29). Over the following centuries many such foundling homes, both public and charitable, grew up in Europe, gathering in large numbers of babies which of necessity were then farmed out to country wet nurses whose self-interest was best served by a rapid turnover of the infants in their care. Ironically, then, these institutions which had arisen to counter the tide of abandonment and high infant mortality in the end had much the same effect; foundlings had a short life expectancy (Langer 1974:356; Trexler 1973b). Even at a later period, in the eighteenth century, for example, of the 15,000 admissions to London's first foundling hospital only 4,400 survived beyond childhood (Langer 1972:96–98).

But, of course, unwanted infants were destroyed by many other, more direct means as well: they were drugged to death, buried alive, or simply not fed. The incidence of such activities was obviously troubling to civil authorities, who from time to time sought to employ the force of the law. Thus, in 1624, the English Parliament passed an act "to prevent the murdering of bastard children" which required any single woman who hid her pregnancy and whose child was subsequently found dead to assume the burden of proof on the question of whether it had been born dead (McLaren 1984:130–131). Such a law was apparently wholly ineffectual, however, for the sympathy of juries invariably tended to lean toward the accused, from whom almost any word of explanation was sufficient. This is as good an indication as any of the light in which popular opinion viewed the practice of infanticide. Nor is there any reason to believe that infanticide did not persist into more recent times as something more than the occasional event. As late as the eighteenth century "it was not an uncommon spectacle to see the corpses of infants lying in the streets or on the dunghills of London and other large cities" (Langer 1972:98). And early in the nineteenth century "there is no doubt . . . the infant mortality rates were inflated by the deaths of babies ill-fed and often ill-used by those in whose care they were left by their mothers" (Pinchbeck and Hewitt 1973:405).

It is necessary to add, however, that allegations of infanticide or even of poor child-rearing practices among the poor must always be regarded with caution in the light of the tendency for well-to-do observers to moralize about the life-ways of those less well provisioned than themselves. The effect of their comments was frequently to make it seem that intentional depravity prevailed over the cumulative systemic effects of endemic poverty, a view which was convenient to the degree that it evinced social concern without requiring any commitment to substantive economic change.

An important but unresolved issue is the extent to which females were more often the victims of direct and indirect forms of European infanticide than males. Abnormally high sex ratios have been reported for medieval Britain during the fourteenth century, for scattered towns in France and Germany during the eighth and ninth centuries, for peasants farming monastery lands in eighth- and ninth-century France and Italy, and for fifteenth-century Florence, but it is difficult to separate out the effects of infanticide from the underreporting of females and the differential rural-urban migration pattern of the sexes (Dickemann 1979:350–354).

The Failure of Pronatalism in Europe

As we noted earlier, Western Europe in the twelfth to fourteenth centuries had experienced dramatic population growth—estimated at about 60 to 65 percent (Pounds 1973:310; Russell, J. C. 1972). By 1300, however, there were signs that environmental depletion, particularly of forestland, was straining the feudal economy and that various population controls were slowing down the rate of population increase (p. 40). Increasing nutritional stress on the peasantry probably contributed as well to the general susceptibility of the population to disease and laid the basis for the devastation of the years of the Black Death in 1347–1351 and 1385 (Dobbs 1963:48–49). (It is likely as well that the preceding two centuries of rapid urban growth and of the intensification of town life had also put a higher proportion of the population at risk.) The general effect across Europe was a catastrophic loss of population (Russell 1972:41). In England, where the demographic crash of the four-teenth and fifteenth centuries has been best studied, it dropped from about five million in 1300 to half that in 1450 (Hatcher 1977:71). Thereafter, it took approximately two hundred years—from 1450 to 1650—for the population of England to reach its mid-fourteenth-century high point and no substantial increments be-yond that level occurred until after 1750. For Europe as a whole, the rate of increase over the period 1500–1700 was only about 40 percent (Mols 1974:39).

Hatcher, while admitting a relationship between living stan-dards and population growth, argues that both the crash and the low rate of increase thereafter were primarily a consequence of the high mortality inflicted by the Plague and other epidemic diseases. Of special theoretical interest, however, is his contention that the sustained depression in England's rate of population growth was associated with a relatively high standard of living during the fif-teenth and early sixteenth centuries—a standard of living which he attributes to the persistence of "very high death rates which stopped the population from recovering" (p. 73). Hatcher bases his claim for a relatively high standard of living on the real wage rates of England's craftsmen which during the period 1400–1550 were almost double what they were before and after (p. 71). We would add Braudel's description of Europeans, including ordinary people, during this same period as enjoying a diet so rich in animal foods that it made Europe seem carnivorous by comparison with other centers of civilization (1973:127ff.; Glamann 1974:467–468).

At first sight, it appears contradictory to claim that both living standards and mortality were high, but there is a simple resolu-tion. To judge from modern-day high birthrate/high mortality so-cieties, 35 to 40 percent of all deaths were likely to have occurred among infants and children aged 0–5 (Gwatkin and Brandel 1982:58). This seems to have been more or less the pattern in the fifteenth and sixteenth centuries—and one which extended into the succeeding centuries during a time of worsening economic conditions (Mols 1974:69–71).

There is no doubt that periodic epidemics played a role here.

But, as we have seen, a significant portion of infant and child mortality probably also was induced by direct and indirect forms of neonate and infant death control. We interpret this as part of an attempt by subordinate classes to adjust their child-rearing responsibilities to the generally smaller farms and guild-limited wage labor opportunities of late medieval society (Dobb 1963:224–230). In essence, then, this is exactly the same paradox of the high rates of infanticide among healthy, vigorous, well-fed hunter-gatherers and hunter-agriculturalists discussed in chapter 2: a high standard of living that was contingent on optimizing family size to meet prevailing economic conditions.

The success of this strategy was tentative and relatively short-lived however. By the latter half of the sixteenth century economic and social changes of such great proportions were underway that the regulation of fertility was hardly enough to maintain a decent standard of living among the vast majority of people.

Reproductive Pressures and the Fear of Witches

The demographic trends of the thirteenth to the early seventeenth century suggest an additional dimension to the question of fertility in an important shift in attitudes toward women. As we saw earlier in examining the agricultural populations of the New Guinea Highlands, environmental pressures and attendant scarcities tended to generate considerable male antagonism toward women, culminating in accusations of witchcraft. A similar kind of development can be discerned in the European historical record.

The economic expansion of the late eleventh to the thirteenth centuries which served as the backdrop for the development of the views of Aquinas and others on the merits of population increase was also accompanied by an elevation in the image of women (J. C. Russell 1972:45). This was the time of the elaboration of the cult of the Virgin Mary and of courtly romance. And while there is little concrete evidence that the actual treatment of women in general, except perhaps of those of the upper class, was ameliorated (J. B. Russell 1972:280), it is important that the prevailing image of womanhood was decidedly positive.

In contrast, some time toward the sixteenth century things took a different turn. It is the beginning of a period that marks a critical and turbulent transitional era in Europe between late feudalism and the capitalist epoch, during which time rural populations in particular were subjected to severe economic and social pressures. It was an era of mercantile expansion overseas and the first real assertion by the European bourgeoisie of its claims to economic and political authority at home. In England, one sign was the increased pace of the commercialization of agriculture. This was marked by new enclosures and the wholesale dispossession of peasants—with consequences which Thomas More immortalized in *Utopia* when he wrote of "shepe that were wont to be so meke and tame, and so small eaters [that] now, as I hear say, be become so great devourers and so wylde that they eat up and swallow downe the very men themselves" (quoted in Morton 1979:167). The clearing of the land in turn created an army of the unemployed (Morton 1979:165–168) who were brutally penalized for begging and petty theft on the one hand and for failure to work on the other (Dobb 1963:225, 233–234; Morton 1979:169). As in England, so in Flanders, France, and Germany "the sixteenth century was one of acute destitution and a redundant army of labourers, as it was also a century of falling real wages" (Dobb 1963:234). It was a time of peasant revolts and the formative years of the European proletariat.

It is difficult to be precise about demographic trends during this period. Sella (1974) speaks of an impressive upswing, Mols variously describes the century as one of "demographic expansion" (1974:39) and a time of "a certain increase" (p. 78), while Schofield writes of "a sustained rise in population . . . with rates of growth of between 0.5 and 1.0 percent per annum" (1983:70). What is certain is that by the latter end of the sixteenth century the relatively high standard of living of the fifteenth and early sixteenth centuries gave way to scarcity and famine. Minchinton observes:

If food budgets from the sixteenth century are compared with those of the seventeenth, an unmistakable decline appears. The average decrease in per capita food consumption has been estimated at one-third. And the general trend was punctuated by years of abundant harvest and years of famine. In England, from whence had come reports of how well people fed in the early sixteenth century, come complaints that the poor now had to eat black bread. In 1590–1 famine occurred in Italy, Spain and parts of France. (1974:117)

One concomitant development was that, from the late fifteenth century onwards, people seem to have become more receptive to the idea of witchcraft (J. B. Russell 1972:233). There was an explosion of literature on the subject, including the classic inquisitorial work *Malleus Maleficarum*, "The Hammer of Witches," which was published in 1486 with a preface by Pope Innocent VIII. Thus, although a belief in witches had a long history in Europe, the dawning of the sixteenth century heralded a new virulence which can only be explained in terms of the overall disruption of the European social order. And, as societal dislocation intensified, so too did the persecution of witches, with most witchcraft trials occurring in the last third of the century (Lea 1957). In England, for example, where the first statute against witchcraft was passed in 1542, there were terrible famines in 1587–88, 1597–98, and 1623 (Appleby 1978:95) and "the most severe fluctuations in food prices occurred in the period 1596/97 to 1597/98 when the national death rates were also considerably above trend" (Schofield 1983:88). Not surprisingly, the climax of witch persecutions came during the 1580s and 1590s as well (Smith 1984:207–208).

It is easy enough to see how Church and State made a general use of witchhunts to dampen political opposition. But, we must also not overlook the notorious fact that, in almost every district of Europe, the victims of witchcraft accusations were disproportionately women. To take a locality at random, in Eichstätt, Germany, from 1603 to late August 1627, 122 people were executed for witchcraft, of whom only 9 were men (Lea 1957:1129). There thus seems little doubt that, in one community after another, the tensions and conflicts of the time were translated into a great wave of misogyny (the *Malleus* contains assorted rantings against women). Above all, this centered on a barely disguised fear of female sexuality (thus, prepubertal females were generally not among its victims) (J. B. Russell 1972:283–284).

This is not to say that there was necessarily a conscious perception of excessive population. On the contrary, various statutes against witchcraft that were passed by the English Parliament in

1542, 1563, and 1604 actually expressed fears of witches causing infertility (McLaren 1984:39); in a similar vein, a notable group among victims of witchcraft accusations were the midwives who often doubled as abortionists (p. 98). This is all evidence of certain pronatalist tendencies at the national and local levels. On the other hand, there is a widespread pattern of women accused of being witches being charged with copulating with the devil and assorted incubi (J. B. Russell 1972:232–237; Lea 1957)—suggesting perhaps a pervasive fear of a malevolent or destructive fertility at work. Thus, the witch craze of the sixteenth century seems to ride a wave of social contradictions, reflecting no doubt the conflicting interests of the rulers and the ruled, with the latter seeking to limit fertility and the former to stimulate it. In the end, however, there is no doubt that the witchcraft persecutions contributed to a curtailing of European fertility as much as any great epidemic. At least one historian of the period describes the witchcraft persecutions after 1500 as "blood-baths" (J. B. Russell 1972:335); the number of women who actually died is difficult to estimate but it may well have exceeded half a million (Harris 1974).

Infant Mortality Control: Asia

There is no doubt that direct and indirect infanticide was practiced in India, China, Japan and other preindustrial states, as well as in Europe. Moreover, the evidence indicates that females were more often the target than males. Sex ratios in nineteenth-century India and China are too high to be accounted for by the underreporting of females. In parts of northern India, for example, early nineteenth-century censuses reveal childhood sex ratios of over 400:100 among certain castes in Gujarat; 300:100 in the Northern Provinces; and 119:100 in the Punjab. Some castes were reported not to rear daughters at all (Dickemann 1979:328ff.).

As for imperial China:

nineteenth-century surveys report childhood sex ratios up to 430:105 . . . as late as the 1870s. . . . Highest frequencies of infanticide among the peasantry occurred when there was greatest rural poverty and tenancy, especially in the lower Yangtzee Valley, Amoy, and Fukien. In these areas women seldom allowed more than two daughters to live. . . . 40 postparous Swatow women . . . had destroyed 28 daughters out of 183 male and 175 female live births; other combined small postparous samples from various regions totaled 160 women who had borne 631 sons and 538 daughters; 360 sons (60 percent) had survived to ten years of age, but only 205 daughters (ca. 38 percent). No male children had ever been destroyed, but 158 daughters had admittedly been killed. . . . Nineteenth-century surveys of Amoy give average rates of removal of 30–40 percent of female livebirths for the province as a whole, village frequencies ranging from 10–80 percent. (p. 341)

Infanticide was also widely practiced in Japan, again with indications of a bias against females, in spite of the fact that, since the 1600s and through much of the eighteenth century, government policy was decidedly pronatalist and included material inducements to reward parents for additional children (Hanley 1977:176). Dickemann (1975:128) has estimated a late Tokugawa infanticide rate of 10 to 25 percent of all livebirths. Village level studies show that child sex ratios of 140:100 were not uncommon and that the sex ratios of the last children in families was especially high:

There is support in the literature on Tokugawa Japan for the conclusion that women tended to keep only male children at the margin, making the decision whether not to keep the child immediately after it was born . . . families in some communities were laughed at and marked if they had more than three children, and thus it became customary to raise only two boys and one girl. Killing a baby at birth was so prevalent that it became the custom not to congratulate a family on the birth of a child until it was learned whether or not the child was to be raised. If the answer was negative, nothing was said; if positive, the usual congratulations and gifts were offered. (Hanley 1977:182)

It is interesting to note that Hanley associates the small size of the Japanese family and the slow rate of population growth during the Tokugawa period with a rising standard of living. Thus, as in the case of Europe between 1450 and 1650, the use of infant death control, delayed marriage, and other population regulation mechanisms in preindustrial Japan can be viewed as an active attempt to optimize family size in relation to the costs and benefits of rearing children, rather than as a passive reaction to cultural and natural conditions.

Indeed, recent studies suggest that the control over family size and composition achieved by the practice of infanticide in eighteenth- to nineteenth-century rural Japan was as closely calculated, widespread, and effective for family planning as contraception in contemporary industrial societies. For example, about one third of all couples in two study villages reported on by G. W. Skinner (1985) destroyed their firstborn. Male firstborn were more likely to be destroyed than female firstborn if the mother and father were young. The rationale for this was that daughters helped to rear sons, but sons did not help to rear daughters. A young couple could afford to risk waiting for a male heir (destroying subsequent daughters), but an older couple could not risk delay and therefore was less likely to destroy firstborn sons and more likely to destroy firstborn daughters. In addition, daughter-first strategies were more likely to be followed by wealthier couples than poorer ones. Wealthier couples had more children; hence, they were less likely to miss out on a male heir. Moreover, wealthier couples left without a male heir could adopt a son-in-law.

The practice of general infanticide in Europe, India, China, and Japan was at least as common, if not more common among the privileged castes and classes as among the peasantry. Among the peasantry, optimum family size was a function primarily of the marginal utility of additional labor in relation to a fixed or diminishing size of landholdings. The child-rearing calculus of very wealthy families, however, was not based on labor costs and benefits but on the benefits of maintaining concentrated holdings in land and other forms of wealth. The logic was similar, but the "currency" and amounts were different—and the pay-off such that the well-to-do often took the lead, in Japan as in other times and places (Schneider and Schneider n.d.), in adopting innovations in fertility control. In this regard, we take issue with Dickemann, who interprets the prevalence of female infanticide among traditional Euro-Asian elites, coupled with hypergyny and concubinage, as a sociobiological strategy aimed at maximizing the reproductive success of high-ranking males. It seems clear, however, that neither the peasantry nor the elite were raising as many babies—male or female—as they were biologically capable of doing (Vining 1985), precisely because they were weighing the costs as well as the benefits of offspring under the specific conditions imposed by their social rank and their life prospects.

Infant Mortality Control and the
Demographic Transition

Our reason for stressing the role of infant mortality control is not that we believe it was the most important form of population regulation in preindustrial states, but that its recognition opens up a new perspective on some puzzling features of demographic transition theory. Demographers, for example, have long been puzzled by the fact that the late eighteenth-century upturn in European population (Wilson and Parker 1977)—especially marked in England—was associated with a drop in mortality which preceded the main advances in medicine and public hygiene by at least fifty years (McKeown 1979; Tranter 1981:213–215). The explanation frequently given is that food became more abundant and more mouths could be fed. As we shall see in the next chapter, however, there is little evidence that the industrial revolution as a whole, let alone its early years, was marked by notable dietary or other improvements in general welfare. (Indeed, an argument could be made that more people were just fed on less.) A more plausible explanation for the early decline in mortality, which was most dramatic among infants (Tranter 1981:212), is that it was produced by a relaxation of infant mortality controls and by more careful nurturance in response to a new balance of child-rearing costs and benefits brought on by the shift to wage labor and industrial employment (Boserup 1981:122; Coontz 1957:166ff.). With the expansion of factories, shops, mines, mills, transport, and other industrial capitalist enterprises, wage labor opportunities for children increased (Birdsall 1983); children became relatively more valuable and infanticide, direct and indirect, yielded—though never entirely—to more positive nurturance.

This may also help to clarify a paradox at the heart of demographic transition theory: that Europe experienced an explosive rise in population precisely at a time when, demographers have argued, Europeans were beginning consciously to control their fertility. (The positing of a more conscious, more deliberate form of fertility regulation has not, in fact, proven to be a particularly parsimonious explanation of a period of unprecedented population growth.) There is less apt, however, to be any such paradox once it is acknowledged that, as we have endeavored to demonstrate, fertility control, conscious or not, did not arrive late on the scene of human history, and that infant mortality control has played a strategic role in effecting such control. What was new were the emergent material conditions, in particular, the magnitude of the incentive which industrial capitalism in the late eighteenth and early nineteenth centuries presented for the relaxation of behaviors which had heightened the risk of infant and child mortality.

This is not to say that the overall living standards of the multi-child family necessarily improved, but simply that wage-earner parents who reared more children were better off than those who reared fewer children under the existing conditions. Indeed, it seems likely that for the children themselves, life was more "mean and brutish" than ever. It was apparently common for a child to be fed at near starvation level until such time as it was necessary to fatten it up to go out and seek work (Rudd 1982). As Boserup remarks: "It is difficult to reconcile workdays of 12–16 hours for miserable wages in the new factories with the theory that the main cause of declining mortality was better resistance to disease due to improved nutrition. Apart from famine years, the ancestors of these people probably had better nutrition in the Middle Ages, when mortality was high, than in the eighteenth century when it began to decline" (1981:118).

The implicit warning here is that the use of infant mortality controls to reduce child-rearing costs cannot be taken as an index of miseration, nor can an increase in child rearing be taken as an index of melioration.

Another derivative point is that the relaxation of infant mortality controls, i.e., a diminution of direct and indirect infanticide, is likely to show up in demographic tables not only as a decrease in mortality but as an increase in fertility as well. Live births previously regarded as spontaneous abortions or stillborn and never registered would, under a more nurturant behavioral regime, actually be registered as live births and would distort the rate of fertility change in a upward direction. These artifacts must also be taken into account in comparing pretransitional vital rates in Europe with those in other regions where live births were not registered even if death occurred weeks after birth. In Tokugawa

Japan, for example, mean death rates for villages ranged between 20 and 23 per 1,000, and birthrates ranged between 18.5 and 26— far below pretransitional rates in Europe. But, the shortest lifespan reported was three weeks (Hanley 1977:169–170), implying that even shorter-lived infants who were not to be reared were never recorded as either a birth or a death.

One would expect therefore that in any situation where controllable infant deaths are an important component of population regulation, a transition to higher levels of nurturance (with a consequent decline in mortality) would tend to be accompanied by an apparent rise or continued high level of fertility which was in large part an artifact of the birth registration process. In the case of the late eighteenth-century upswing in English population, the failure to regard infant mortality control as a prominent feature of preindustrial demographic systems may help to explain the position recently taken by Lee and Schofield (1981:31–32) who maintain that new estimates by the Cambridge Group assign a dominant role to a rise in fertility rather than to a fall in mortality (Tranter 1981:212–213). The same faulty perception of fertility/mortality data may be implicated in the classic view of the European demographic transition where an apparent lag between a drop in mortality and a decline in fertility has often been attributed to the irrational inertia of custom.

4. Population Regulation in the Age of Colonialism

Historical Processes and the Demographic Transition

With the age of European capitalist expansion, the economic and demographic development of Europe and the rest of the world became inseparably linked. This observation seems self-evident, yet is rarely given due consideration. Thus, it remains to a very large extent a formidable component of Western intellectual folklore that the economic development of Western Europe since the late seventeenth century (encompassing the period called "the Industrial Revolution") was largely the product of the ascendancy of a new consciousness, a heightened "rationality," that was especially conducive to capitalist growth and to a regime of low fertility and low mortality—the "demographic transition." This view in turn coincides with the assumption that non-European civilizations lacked that particular attitude which was a necessary impetus to, if not precondition for, modern capitalist society (G. Marshall 1980:20–26; for a recent work on this general theme, see May 1981) and for its associated demographic regime. We would merely point out in passing that by 1500, there was a definite manifestation of characteristically capitalist economic and social forces, not in Europe alone, but in India and China as well. That capitalism never matured as a purely indigenous development in these civilizations has several explanations, the least instructive of which is the Weberian notion that they lacked a proper capitalist spirit. To begin with, there is the difference in the environmental basis of the agrarian systems found in Asia and in Western Europe (M. Harris 1979:169ff.). Second, and more self-evident, the historical crisis produced by colonialism rendered local political and economic interests subordinate to those of Europe and in many ways coopted and deflected their development.

In any event, it is precisely against the backdrop of imperialist expansion that the rise of modern capitalism and its associated demography in Europe must be viewed. The rise of European capitalism was not, as the Weberian view would have it, the indigenous product of a peculiarly European *Zeitgeist*. To get to the heart of the matter, it was to a critical degree the result of the establishment of lucrative overseas mercantile dependencies whose natural resources and human labor could be looted and exploited.

The Weberian view of historical processes underlies much of the attempt to explain the European demographic transition. Thus, as we have shown, predemographic transition populations are considered to have been characterized by "natural" or "uncontrolled" fertility, with the transition itself heralded as the advent of "controlled" fertility (Tilly 1978:3). Wrigley, for example, has described this as a change from "unconscious rationality" to "conscious rationality" and roughly equates the rise of the latter with modernization and a general trend toward economic maximizing—that is, toward the general behavioral orientation associated with the rise of capitalism. Indeed, as in the Weberian view of the origins of European capitalism, the kind of rationality associated with the demographic transition is suggested by Wrigley and others to have developed "largely as a consequence of the diffusion of new ideologies" (Tilly 1978:44), among which the "Protestant ethic" seems to be regarded as preeminent. As a result, somehow, control of fertility is said to have shifted from being a function of customary institutions to being a matter of calculated individual choice (p. 148). In a related vein, Stone (1977:239–259) associates the transition with the emergence in the seventeenth century of what he terms "affective individualism," which, in turn, and in a peculiarly abstruse way, he attributes to the emergence of a new personality type particularly conducive to pleasure-seeking in economic and social activities.

Such views are largely contradicted by the considerable evidence presented in previous chapters that control over human fertility/mortality has been exercised at least since the Pleistocene. As previously stated, the suggestion that *conscious* recognition of the nature of such an effort is relatively late in human history (Knodel and Van de Walle 1979) seems hardly the most salient point. The fact is that we can seldom infer the degree of consciousness associated with the use of the extensive array of preindustrial fertility/mortality controls. Hence, it would be very difficult to prove that the effectiveness of such controls is a function of consciousness in general, let alone of capitalist consciousness in particular.

England: The Demographic Rewards of Colonialism

Between 1770 and 1820, England experienced a rate of population growth that was at once dramatic and without parallel elsewhere in Western Europe. No one would suggest that the causes were simple or self-evident, especially in the light of the persistent debate which has surrounded this phenomenon in the historical and demographic literature (Wrigley and Schofield 1981:213–215). Yet, somehow one cannot escape the surmise that much discussion of this issue has been misdirected—and, in turn, complicated—by attempting to comprehend these demographic trends without serious regard for their relationship to the social and economic changes wrought by England's overseas enterprises during this general period.

As Andre Gunder Frank has written: "The central fact is that the worldwide historical expansion of mercantile, industrial, and monopoly capitalism brought all humanity on this particular globe into a *single* social system. This system has always functioned, and still functions, so as to generate socioeconomic development for the few while simultaneously causing degenerative change without development for the many" (1970:68). It was the nature of this global system that vast numbers of people around the world were relegated to a new condition of subservience to the process of capital accumulation taking place in Western Europe—a process which depended crucially upon a transformation of the traditional labor and property relations in colonialized regions which reoriented them to the production of commodities for European consumption (Wolf 1969:279–280, 1982). The demographic dimensions of this upheaval cannot be minimized. In some instances (one thinks of the impact of the Spanish in the Caribbean) the result was catastrophic: virtual extinction as a result of strange diseases and brutal labor demands to enrich the coffers of European monarchies and merchant bankers (Cook and Borah 1971). Elsewhere, indigenous populations were more studiously and self-consciously conserved, their life-ways manipulated or reconstructed so that native labor, instead of being exterminated, might pay steady dividends.

In the end, this infamous pattern—production of wealth abroad and its accumulation, through the varied channels of mercantile endeavor, at home—inevitably had its own profound demographic consequences for England. Some of these will be examined below. For the moment, what is important is to emphasize that, as colonies and colonizers were linked by the demands of profit and as each, in its special way, suffered the corrosive effects of capitalist production, both became parts of a *single* demographic system. It is for that reason that we argue that, behind the rise in English population in the late eighteenth and early nineteenth century, lay inescapably the lucrative if unpleasant realities of European colonialism.

England, up until the middle of the eighteenth century, was still largely a rural economy. Despite initial steps toward a modern manufacturing technology, industry remained generally confined to the old cottage system. Where new machinery was beginning to be introduced, it was not yet liberated by use of coal and steam, but remained tied to upland streams and waterfalls.

The apparent barrier to the eventual explosive rise of new industry and the factory system has been ascribed to various factors, but an essential one was that of capital accumulation. From the end of the seventeenth century, capital accumulated from overseas ventures, increasing dramatically, as foreign commerce doubled between 1700 and 1780 (Mathias 1969:98). The great transformation that took place in the English economy during this period can be seen in the reorientation in the direction of trade: "When the eighteenth century opened 78 per cent of British exports were going to Europe; in 1800 only 45 per cent. On the import side the same is true: over 50 per cent of imports came from Europe in 1700; by 1800 this had fallen to 31 per cent" (p. 100).

What were some of the demographic implications of these developments? England's trade, from the middle of the eighteenth century onward, was inextricably linked to the process of industrialization, for which, indeed, it provided the essential stimulus. New colonies represented a market that was comparatively unlimited, in contrast to that at home. They therefore created an unprecedented demand for manufactured goods (for which they often provided the requisite raw materials as well) and, in turn, for the labor power to produce them. For various reasons it was in the textile sector that these connections were most forcefully established (Mathias 1969:105).

The connection between colonization, the demand for labor, and population growth can be shown by examining the history of the cotton industry. Well into the eighteenth century, English textile production was dominated by a rural woolen industry, based primarily on domestic supplies of yarn and therefore well integrated into the agricultural economy by which some two-thirds of the English population still lived. The revolutionary transition of textile production to town-centered industry was predicated, not on wool, but cotton—for reasons intimately associated with English colonialist fortunes in the Caribbean, Africa, and Asia.

The ascendancy of cotton, however, was initially retarded by the woolen manufacturers and by competition from cheap, attractive cotton goods imported from India. At the end of the eighteenth century Parliament began to curtail the import of Indian cottons, and with a long succession of acts eventually decimated Indian cotton manufacturing (Morton 1979:337; Dutt 1940:124ff.). It was, in part, in reaction against the competition of Indian cottons that English textile manufacturing was impelled along new avenues of invention. But its actual improvement and intensification depended most of all on access to investment capital. Here the new colonies played a crucial and pivotal role. Just as they provided the land and labor for plantation production of cotton (and, hence for the production of textile fiber on an unprecedented scale) so they also became the principal source of the capital needed for industrialization. The watershed was reached in 1757, with the battle of Plassey, which marked a definitive phase in the British conquest of India. According to Brooks Adams, "very soon after

Plassey, the Bengal plunder began to arrive in London, and the effect seems to have been instantaneous; for all the authorities agree that the 'industrial revolution' . . . began with the year 1760" (quoted in Baran 1957:146).

India, of course, was not the sole source of the wealth which poured into England in the second half of the eighteenth century. There was also the slave trade and the Atlantic "triangular" trade of which it was an integral and cardinal part. The Americas were the principal market for African slaves, and the Treaty of Utrecht, which ended the War of the Spanish Succession in 1712, ceded monopoly control of the slave trade in Spanish America to England. This had several important consequences. First, it diverted much of Spain's New World wealth into English hands, reducing the former in the process to the status of a trading colony (Glamann 1974:450). Second, it opened the way to the unfettered expansion of English interests in the West Indies (Morton 1979:297), a region which was to provide some of the most vital raw materials, including sugar, tobacco, and eventually cotton, and to become a major market for English manufactures as well.

The tropical colonies gave England tremendous leverage in European commerce and provided a crucial link in the emergence in the last half of the eighteenth century of a global mercantile system that provided the effective underpinning for English domestic industrialization. As Deane describes this complex network:

> Weapons, hardware, spirits from Britain, and calicoes from India were shipped to west Africa and exchanged for slaves, ivory, and gold. The slaves were sold in the West Indies for sugar, dyestuffs, mahogany, logwood, tobacco, and raw cotton. The gold and ivory were shipped to the East and Near East for teas, silks, calicoes, coffee, and spices. The tropical goods were sold in Europe for Baltic timber, hemp, pitch, and tar (all essential naval stores), Swedish and Russian iron; and, in the fourth quarter of the century, they paid for the foreign grain which was vital when the harvest failed and which was regularly required in most years even when the harvest did not fail. (1979:55)

The impact of this lucrative system was most dramatically witnessed in the rapid growth of such port cities in England as Liverpool and Bristol. Such towns grew rapidly in the second half of the eighteenth century as a combined result of their dominance over the commerce in slaves and their important role in the sale of manufactures to the West Indies (Aikin 1968). As they did, many of their successful merchants invested their burgeoning profits in textiles and other industries, which were then on the lookout for new sources of capital (Mathias 1969:105).

As the colonialist system took firm root, as plantations replaced subsistence agriculture in regions such as India and the Caribbean, the supply of cotton, like many other raw materials, grew enormously and fell precipitously in price. The price of cotton, for example, dropped from £0.1 in the 1780s to £0.05 in the 1820s (and was halved again by the 1840s) (Brown 1974:87). This, together with the capital accumulated from colonial plunder and trade, provided a tremendous impetus for English industrial expansion. This, it was soon to be seen, created an enormous appetite for a growing reserve of domestic labor.

The Labor Value of Women and Children

The general pattern of industrial expansion in England had a profound effect upon population growth as evidenced in an increase in the annual growth rate from 0.48 in 1745 to 1.35 by 1800 (Wrigley

Table 4.1
Relationship Between the Development of Cotton Imports and Population Growth

	Retained Imports of Raw Cotton (million pounds)		Annual Growth Rates, England and Wales
1725–34	1.79		
		1735	
1735–44	2.83	1740	0.21%
		1745	0.48
1745–54	2.57	1750	0.75
		1755	0.51
1755–64	4.03	1760	0.42
		1765	0.54
1765–74	7.36	1770	0.89
		1775	0.88
1775–84	24.45	1780	0.69
		1785	1.21
1785–94	42.92	1790	1.16

Source: Wilson and Lenman 1977:121; Wrigley and Schofield 1981:213.

and Schofield 1981:2.3). This was associated with a tendency toward earlier marriage and a notable decline in infant and child mortality (tables 4.2 and 4.3). One result of these trends was that the English population in general became "relatively young"—to the extent that by 1826, 1.5 percent was comprised of infants and 39.6 percent by all children under the age of 16 (Wrigley and Schofield 1981).

We suggested at the end of the previous chapter that a major factor in this demographic trend was the increasing labor value of children and the effect on mortality control. It is not too difficult to see as well that the growing proportion of children within the general population was bound to reinforce this, as industry inevitably came to regard them as a most significant reserve of labor.

The industrial revolution, of course, hardly introduced the idea of employing children. We have seen earlier how an increase in the labor value of children was associated with previous epochs of economic intensification, for example, the Neolithic, and there is ample evidence that children played a fairly significant part in the domestic economy of Western Europe in the preindustrial period. But, the last decades of the eighteenth century saw children

Table 4.2
Simple Means of Infant and Child Mortality Rates in
Twelve English Parishes (per 1,000 live births)

	1700–1749		1750–1799	
	M	F	M	F
0–1	168	148	135	122
1–4	97	95	87	87
5–9	38	44	31	30
0–9	277	263	235	222

Source: Wrigley and Schofield 1981:249.

Table 4.3
Mean Age at Marriage in Twelve English Parishes

	1700–1749	1750–1799	1800–1849
Male	27.5	26.4	25.3
Female	26.2	24.9	23.4

Source: Wrigley and Schofield 1981:255.

beginning to acquire an unprecedented role. Children in work-houses, which proliferated in England during this period (Morton 1979:342), were frequently taught to spin or weave and "were later transported in thousands to the mills of Lancashire, where, being entirely defenseless, they formed the ideal human material for the cotton masters" (p. 342). But, quite apart from this particular feature of the workhouse system, children's contribution to the household became generally as crucial to the well-being of low-paid parents as their labor was to the profits of the industrialists who employed them. In some instances, it was the parents who were most eager to bring their children with them into the mills—a carry-over, as Mathias notes, from the pre-factory system of production based on the domestic unit (1969:202)—but, as often it was the case that parents could not obtain poor relief unless they sent their children to work (Morton 1979:344). Then, with more and more improvement in mechanization, fewer adult skills were required in factory employment. "Machinery was soon developed to the point at which few men were needed and widespread unemployment among them was often accompanied by the over-working and intense exploitation of women and especially of children" (p. 344). One of the largest and most detailed surveys of the working class districts of Liverpool in the early 1840s shows that a third of male laborers were totally unemployed while over a quarter worked three days or fewer. Even for males with a specific craft, full employment was rarely achieved by more than one-half at any point in time (Finch 1842:30).

Given that, even in a "normal" year, a fifth of the population in a mill town might exist at or below the subsistence level, it was inevitable that all the production resources of a family would eventually be called upon to contribute to the domestic economy. Thus, by 1833, in a sample of 48,645 workers at various industrial establishments in the counties of Lancashire and Cheshire, 41 percent were under 18 years of age, while 22 percent were under 14 (Collier 1964:68). In 1843, the Children's Employment Commission reported an age and sex distribution of employees in calico print works in Lancashire, Cheshire, and Derbyshire (table 4.4). Of 565 children from this sample, taken at random, nearly two-thirds were found to have begun work before the age of nine. Seventeen

Table 4.4
Age and Sex Distribution of Employees in Calico Print
Works in Lancashire, Cheshire, and Derbyshire

	Male	*Female*	*Total*
Adults (21+)	8,620	484	9,104 (46%)
Young persons (13–18)	4,147	995	5,142 (26%)
Children (under 13)	3,616	2,030	5,646 (28%)

Source: Hutchins and Harrison 1966:124.

years later, a sample of 500 operatives in a Lancashire cotton mill found that 31 percent were children (Chadwick 1862:47).

Women, too, had become a major source of industrial labor. Thus, by 1860, in a cotton town such as Preston, men over 18 constituted just under a third of the total labor force. Some 26 percent of all wives living with their husbands worked—just over half of them in factories. In the Lancashire towns of Blackburn and Oldham, 24 percent and 45.5 percent respectively of women operatives were married, according to the census figures for 1851 (M. Anderson 1971:73).

If the growing utilization of child labor helps explain the general intensification of reproductive effort which marked the late eighteenth and early nineteenth centuries, the increasing role of women must be seen as a major factor as well, to the extent that it gave an added incentive, against a background of economic uncertainty, to marriage. Thus, ironically, at the very time that Thomas Malthus (see below) was preaching the "economic rationalities" of delayed marriage and sexual continence within marriage, the need to marry, at least among the working class, was mounting. (Accounts of working-class life make a forceful impression of the extent to which, in spite of an apparent dearth of emotional attachments, couples in nineteenth-century England remained together primarily as a functioning economic unit based on compelling practical necessity.)

Malthus, it must be said, had correctly perceived that there was a positive feedback between population increase and the diminishing price of labor: while the size of an individual family might be directly proportional to its economic security, on a wider scale the more the size of the total work force increased (particularly in the days before widespread trade unionism), the more difficult it became for any given family to subsist on the income provided by the male head of the family (Levine 1977).

To that social contradiction must be added another: that, after the early 1800s, a general rise in population growth was paralleled by increasing mortality among the working class, especially in the urban districts. Despite the demand for child labor by the factory system, which we have argued encouraged parents to place greater emphasis upon positive nurturance, the adverse systemic effects of capitalist intensification were too great. They not only stimulated a higher birth rate, but also produced a dramatic escalation in childhood mortality.

The Growth of England's Urban Centers

Since the rise of urban concentrations in the Neolithic, large towns and cities have tended to exhibit excess mortality compared to more rural, less densely inhabited regions. In the late seventeenth century, William Petty had written of London that it "would in time decrease quite away, were it not supplied out of the country" (in Wilson and Lenman 1977:119). By the end of the eighteenth century, England was witnessing an explosion of urban growth (table 4.5) which fed off the countryside and quite belied the rising death rates within the cities themselves.

Together with industrialization, this rapid growth of English towns and cities was one of the great social phenomena of the age. But, as we have intimated, it would be nothing short of grotesque to imply that urban population growth was brought on by improvements in living conditions. On the contrary, urban growth was the product of the powerful economic changes which steadily drew workers into new centers of production. This demographic shift was accommodated by the construction of overcrowded and unhealthy warren-like habitations (Treble 1971:168–170) which represented anything but improved living conditions for the multitudes of workers who were forced to live in them.

In the early seventeen hundreds Daniel Defoe had observed that

Table 4.5
Population Growth in Selected Cities in the
County of Lancashire

	1801	*1821*	*1841*	*1861*	*% increase 1801–61*
Manchester & Salford	94,876	161,763	311,269	460,018	384.9
Liverpool	82,295	138,354	286,487	443,874	439.4
Oldham	21,677	38,201	60,451	94,337	335.2
Blackburn	11,980	21,940	36,629	63,337	426.9
Wigan	10,989	17,716	25,517	37,657	242.7
Burnley	3,918	8,242	14,224	28,789	634.8

Source: Chadwick 1862:14.

"there is no town in England, London excepted, that can equal Liverpool for the fineness of the streets, and beauty of the buildings" (quoted in Marriner 1953:109). Between 1720 and 1772, the population of Liverpool, largely as a result of a commercial prosperity which rested on its involvement in the African slave trade (Aikin 1968), had jumped from 10,446 to over 60,000. But, by 1794, there were already almost 1,200 persons impoverished enough to have to seek sanctuary in the city's workhouse, where more than a quarter were employed as "cotton pickers" while the merchants of Liverpool made their fortunes out of Caribbean plantations and investments in Lancashire textile mills. As the decades went by, speculators and profiteers transformed the face of the city: as the ruling class moved progressively further from the old center, the latter was redeveloped into a dense, unsanitary realm where more than one-eighth of the population dwelled in dank, sunless cellars that encouraged a variety of diseases, from cholera to typhus (Treble 1971:168). In the worst parts of the city, such as the central ward of Vauxhall, almost 57 percent of the residents lived in cellars and in notorious courts where houses had been built so tightly together, utilizing every spare bit of space, that little light or fresh air ever reached the crowded tenants (Shimmin 1864). In such districts, the result of urban industrial development was a population density of over 700 persons per acre (Taylor 1974:45), a feature of inner city working-class existence which was directly implicated in the high incidence of disease—most especially that of tuberculosis, one of the great endemic killers among the Victorian poor.

Urban Mortality

These inhospitable conditions were more or less characteristic of all of England's cities (Engels 1958) and persisted well past the middle of the nineteenth century. They serve to remind us that the prosperity of the industrial elite during this period owed as much to its treatment of cheap labor at home as it did to colonial exploitation abroad, and that one of the apparent foundations upon which industrial growth was erected was the dire poverty in which so much of the working class was compelled to live by low wages and the insecure or erratic employment opportunities which characterized industrial capitalism.

From a demographic viewpoint, therefore, it should come as no great surprise that, despite the fact that England's population as a whole was rising at between 0.5 and 1.0 percent per annum, mortality rates in the urban centers were climbing as well, especially, as we have said, among the young. In Liverpool, one of the most "prosperous" cities of the period, between 50 and 60 percent of all deaths occurred among children under five (Parker and Sanderson 1871:56). The mortality trends in the textile town of Preston, Lancashire, may be regarded as fairly typical (table 4.6). One con-

Table 4.6
Mortality Trends in Preston, Lancashire, 1783–1841

	Average Age of Death	% Deaths >5	% Deaths <5	Town Population
1783	31.7	70.7	29.3	c. 6,000
1791	28.6	55.1	44.9	c. 8,000
1801	23.3	55.6	44.4	11,887
1811	20.0	48.7	51.3	17,065
1821	19.0	43.4	56.6	24,575
1831	23.4	67.8	32.2	33,112
1841	19.5	46.6	53.4	50,131

Source: House of Commons 1845:357.

sequence is that, where, earlier, industrialization had been responsible for a steady increase in the proportion of the population in the 0–4 age category, by about 1826 this trend had peaked (Wrigley and Schofield 1981:216)—though the demand for child labor was far from abating.

Such data also reinforce the observation made earlier that the dramatic urban growth witnessed during those years were maintained by a steady immigration from more rural areas and cannot be taken as evidence of economic prosperity. This is confirmed by various surveys from the period. One, of Vauxhall ward in Liverpool in 1842, revealed, for example, that of 4,979 families interviewed only 1,326 (27 percent) were actually native to the city (Finch 1842:13). According to the 1841 census for Liverpool as a whole, of 286,487 persons only 157,748 (55 percent) had been born in Lancashire; 64,192 had been born in other English counties, 11,088 in Scotland, and 49,639 in Ireland (House of Commons 1845). In many of the textile towns in Lancashire, as Anderson's work (1971) has shown, as much as 50 percent of the population was apt to have been born elsewhere. That the factory centers had such power to attract population despite the living and working conditions which typified them is a measure of the economic upheaval of the early decades of the nineteenth century, of the social and demographic effects of the increasing centralization of production which such towns represented and, in the end, of the waning of the older land-based political and social system. On the other hand, it is precisely those conditions which the working class faced in the midst of those industrial centers, whether they were born there or had migrated to them, which demonstrate most cogently that the rewards of English colonialism were equivocal at best for them.

Class and Demographic Transition

Any attempt to explain the relation between industrialization and reproduction in England has to deal with the fact that national fertility rates reached their peak in about 1815 shortly after real wage rates reached their lowest point (R. Smith 1981:597). Thereafter, the fertility rate continued to fall for the rest of the century (except for the period from the mid-1840s to the 1870s), even though wage rates measured in terms of purchasing power continued to rise. (This is not to say that wages were sufficient to avoid continued miseration and poverty—they did not regain the level which had existed in 1750 until the 1840s.) It is easier to account for the continuing decline in fertility later in the century (say the 1870s) since by that time children had ceased to be important sources of household income and the costs of rearing them had greatly increased as a result of the introduction of compulsory education and the enforcement of laws prohibiting child labor.

But why did the fertility rate reverse itself as early as 1815 when child labor laws were as yet rudimentary and unenforced? Part of the answer we feel lies in the increasingly adverse costs which pregnancy and child rearing entailed for the female proletariat. During the initial phases of industrialization, high fertility was compatible with high rates of female participation in manufacturing enterprises through various kinds of "putting out" and cottage industries. As the scene of female labor shifted from the house and local workshop to the factory, a contradiction developed between women's roles as producers and reproducers. Child rearing and mother's wage employment outside of the home were mutually antagonistic, especially in view of the fact that younger children were themselves caught up in the wage process and therefore could not be used to nurture their siblings. (A similar contradiction accounts for the sharp fall in fertility rates in the United States after 1957 when married women were forced to choose between having children and earning money outside the home.)

Suffice to say, the new industrial system could not long endure without solving the contradiction which it had created between production and reproduction. On the one hand, factory production sought to avail itself of child and female labor at rates that were consistently less than adult males would have commanded for the same work. At the same time, it was the inadequacy of wages for male workers that compelled working-class families to maximize their earning power through the work effort of women and children. Thus, by maximizing their profits, the industrialists threatened the reproduction and hence the employability of the very class upon which those profits depended. This was assuredly one of the reasons that witnesses before the commissioners of child labor in 1833 argued against limiting the employment of children lest it compel more mothers to seek work in factories (Pinchbeck and Hewitt 1973:405).

Such an intractable contradiction cannot be said to have been solved even yet. In the middle of the nineteenth century, one of the "solutions," which may help to explain the apparent decline in fertility, arrived in the form of renewed pressure on infants and young children. The material effects of poverty—undernutrition, poor housing, disease—all had their role to play. In addition, where mothers worked there is little doubt that children tended to suffer, as economic necessity drove women back to work as soon as possible after giving birth (Hewitt 1958:126–127). For babies left with care-takers, survival depended on how the infant could be fed in the absence of a nursing mother (p. 133). Cow's milk was usually too expensive and not particularly healthy anyway. Patent baby foods did not even appear in England until the 1860s to provide a formulated substitute for maternal milk. And, even once they did, their effect was equivocal, with some physicians (who were scarcely inclined to give working-class mothers much credit at the best of times) arguing that "the mortality among artificially fed infants is very much greater than among infants fed even partly on breast milk" (Reid 1895:500), usually due to diarrhea (Hewitt 1958:147–148). In general, then, the infant of necessity entrusted to someone outside the immediate family was at considerable risk. As Pinchbeck and Hewitt (1973:405–406) write:

There is no doubt . . . the infant mortality rates were inflated by the deaths of babies ill-fed and often ill-used by those in whose care they were left by their mothers. Some starved to death; others died from being fed totally unsuitable food . . . many more were victims of the reckless use of the narcotics—opium, laudanum, morphia—which were the major ingredients of the Godfrey's Cordial, Atkinson's Royal Infant's Preservative, and Mrs. Wilkinson's Soothing Syrup, administered to calm children and which in many cases "established a calm that was but a prelude to a deeper quiet."

Perhaps one of the most instructive pieces of evidence of the adverse effect of female employment on infant survivorship comes from the period during the U.S. Civil War when a "cotton famine" in Lancashire precipitated the lay-off of hundreds of thousands of workers. Mortality data suggest that the decline in the number of women working actually had an ameliorative effect on the infant death rate (Hewitt 1958:118).

Another factor which must be considered in relation to any decline in working-class fertility is that hard work and poor nutrition contributed to subfecundity, due to delayed menarche and amenorrhea (Frisch 1978a); though lactational afertility, under the circumstances we have just outlined, is not likely to have had much effect.

None of this, of course, excludes the possibility that the conflict between work and reproduction was also being resolved through mortality controls such as abandonment and infanticide. A survey of press reports in the 1860s "reveals the frequent findings of dead infants under bridges, in parks, in culverts and ditches, and even in cesspools" (Langer 1974:361).

Thus, there is good reason to argue that the working-class birthrate per se did not necessarily decline; what clearly occurred was an increase in infant mortality due to the cumulative effect of worsening urban poverty combined with various direct and indirect forms of parental neglect. What it means is that, well into the middle of the nineteenth century, there is little evidence in the reproductive patterns of the working class of a "demographic transition" to a low mortality, low birthrate regime.

Trends elsewhere in the population are another matter, and we must bear in mind that the timing of the reduction in mortality and fertility differed greatly from one class to another. Indeed, it would be fatuous to suppose otherwise, in light of the wide differentials in the costs and benefits conferred by capitalist industrialization. As cottage industry had given way to the factory system and rural employment was displaced by a new urban-industrial mode of production characterized by low wages, oppressive work conditions, poor housing, and an inadequate diet, working-class mortality began to rise, especially among the young, and expected life span diminished (Hewitt 1958:77; E. P. Thompson 1963:314–331; House of Commons 1845:357). E. P. Thompson has concluded that, on evidence, "the living and working conditions of artisans and of some rural laborers were rather healthier

in the second half of the 18th century than that of factory operatives or out-workers in the first half of the 19th" (1963:330). The
other side of the coin of working-class deprivation, however, was
the efflorescence of the middle class, a not entirely unrelated phenomenon (Hobsbawm 1979:233), whose life-style was marked by
improved housing, a comfortable diet, and remunerative and
unexhausting work. As a result, English trends in mortality and
survivorship were by no means uniform, any more than prosperity
was; both, indeed, were class-determined. Thus, in Preston in
1841, the percentage of deaths in the under 5 category was 18
among the gentry, 36 for tradespeople, and 55 among industrial
workers (House of Commons 1845:358). Similarly, longevity as a
whole was affected by one's place in the economic and social order,
as comparative statistics from various major cities showed:

Table 4.7
Average Age at Death by Class

	Liverpool	Manchester	Rochdale
Gentry and professional	43	38	34
Trades	19	20	26
Operatives	15	17	18

Source: House of Commons 1845:356.

As Thompson (1963) and a few others before him have commented, such class differences have frequently been obscured by
emphasis upon national averages where progressive trends have
tended to reflect improvements in living conditions predominantly
confined to the upper class and an expanding middle class. For
these classes, a demographic transition did indeed occur in the
first half of the last century as they absorbed the greater measure
of benefits engendered by the industrial revolution. Middle-class
men, for example, began to defer marriage (Sigsworth and Wyke
1972:85) in favor of economic achievement; within marriage, the
survivorship of their offspring improved and business rather than
children was increasingly targeted for investment of economic resources as the costs of rearing children outstripped their economic
utility (Minge-Klevana 1978). In contrast, the labor value of children among the working class, if we may judge by the history of
factory legislation (Hutchins and Harrison 1966; Pinchbeck and

Hewitt 1973), remained significant well into the second half of the nineteenth century and, in some quarters, even later.*

The result of class and intra-class disparities in mortality and the value of children was manifested in an increasing difference in fertility between different economic and social groups in the latter half of the nineteenth century. In 1919, the Fertility Commission surveyed the childbearing history of married women, classified according to their husband's occupations and the period in the 1800s during which they had married. Fertility rates (based on total children born) were given as a percentage of the corresponding rates for occupied persons of all classes married during similar dates. It found divergent trends (table 4.8).

Thus, the "demographic transition" was relatively late in reaching a large proportion of the English population, despite widespread assumptions that it had. The evidence is not new; but, these assumptions have rested upon a pervasive and tenacious

Table 4.8
Total Children Born (Crude) (Number of Children Born, Standardized)

Social-Occupational Class	1851–	1861–	1871–	1881–86
Professional and higher administration in finance	86(89)	85(88)	78(81)	72(76)
Employers in industry and retail trade	98(99)	95(96)	90(93)	86(89)
Skilled workers	101(101)	102(101)	102(101)	102(100)
Intermediate workers	100(99)	100(100)	101(101)	102(101)
Unskilled workers	105(103)	105(104)	109(107)	112(116)

Source: Hewitt 1958:87.

* The working class itself was not a homogenous population. By the middle of the last century there was an obvious "aristocracy of labor," consisting chiefly of skilled workers, which could be said to have made modest gains from industrialization, even if the world of the middle class remained distant and unobtainable. One measure of their relative advantage, however, was that their trade unions were among the groups which lobbied for restrictions on children's and women's employment at a time when it was vital to the welfare of many other working class families (Pinchbeck and Hewitt 1973:405).

belief in the essentially progressive character of the industrial revolution, a viewpoint which has not yet been subject to much re-
vision in the demographic literature.

Class and Sexual Mores

If fertility patterns varied according to a class's relationship to the
means of production, inevitably so too did the character of social
and sexual relations within classes. One of the chief mediating
factors was the status of female labor. Working-class women, of
course, had always been involved in the productive activities of
their households. But, with the Industrial Revolution, much of
their economic contribution shifted to outside the home where
previously their hardships had been more easily ignored than in
the mine or factory (Hewitt 1958:3). In some sectors of industry,
as we have noted, female labor came to predominate over that of
men (Thompson 1963) and the proportion of working women who
were married was often quite high (Hewitt 1958:14). This was in
contrast to the experience of the middle and upper class where,
during the same period, women were losing many previous economic functions. Many of these were, in fact, being taken over by
domestic servants recruited from the working class—to the extent
that, by 1851, the largest single occupational category in England
was that of individuals in nonfarming domestic service (Mathias
1969:260), and this remained the case even well into the present
century (Butler 1916).

Such class-based differences in the economic value of female
labor had important demographic implications. Some, such as the
effect of industrial employment on infant welfare and mortality,
we have already alluded to. The situation for middle- and upper-
class women was exceedingly different, for they were being increasingly relegated to a redundant condition, caught between
labor-saving devices and domestic servants. This was paralleled
by a declining fertility that was probably effected by varied contraceptive practices, including coitus interruptus and pessaries
(Frisch 1978a:28), supplemented by a diversion of male sexual enterprise outside the domestic sphere.

Relevant to this last point was the way the contrast in situation of middle- and working-class women led to the elaboration of a peculiarly dichotomous ideology of female sexuality. Thus, middle-class women were widely represented as asexual, while working-class women were envisaged as more primitive, vulgar, and sexual (Marcus 1966:32). (In parallel, during much of this period, middle-class writing about impoverished urban districts tended to assimilate to them the image that contemporary explorers were painting of their journeys on dark continents among primitive heathens. This is rendered most explicit in William Booth's *In Darkest England and the Way Out* in 1890.) The former representation can be regarded effectively as a contribution to the middle-class contraceptive armory. The latter, for its part, was fueled from several directions. First, there was the fact that a significant, if vague, number of working-class women turned professionally or occasionally to prostitution, drawing many of their customers from the middle class. Despite the fact that such prostitution was the result of poverty and unemployment—and there is some suggestion that "the standard of living of prostitutes was perceptibly higher than other women" (Walkowitz 1977:76)—it was also widely viewed as evidence of the sexual availability of an entire class. (Is it a coincidence that prostitutes came to be referred to as "working women"?) Second, there was a common assumption in the middle class that factories, where men and women intermingled without normal drawing-room social customs to constrain them, were "hot-beds of immorality" (Hewitt 1958:54). Thus, whenever concern arose in the middle class over the sanctity of the family or the purity of women, it tended to generate a wave of opposition to female employment as well—without very much consideration as to where working-class families would make up the lost income.

If one may judge from Steven Marcus' intriguing analysis of Victorian pornography (1966), as middle-class women were entering a period of economic redundancy and a kind of sexual equivalent, which must have had the effect of minimizing their vulnerability to the risks of pregnancy and childbirth, working women were increasingly perceived by economically advantaged men as fair game sexually. It is as if the industrial age, having given expression to the view that money could purchase another human being's labor power had necessarily advanced the notion that this included sexual labor as well. It was this generalized sexual sub-ordination of women of the working class which subsidized the Victorian morality that came to apply to sexual relations within the middle class. As such, the poverty which underlay a higher fertility at the bottom of the economic scale not only contributed directly to a higher standard of living at the top, but had an indirect effect on a dampening of middle-class marital fertility to the extent that working-class women provided an outlet for the sexual incli-nations of men of other classes.

To a remarkable extent, in spite of both middle-class philan-thropy and depredations, working-class familial institutions sur-vived. Not only did their birthrate remain fairly high, but it is arguable that the working class remained a repository of far more conservative attitudes toward sexuality (in the sense, for example, of being less tolerant of nonreproductive sex).

While class differences in the costs and benefits of child rearing account for the lingering high fertility and conservative sexuality of the working class, it should not be forgotten that ecclesiastical and civil authority effectively constrained their options far more than those of the middle and upper class. In fact, the time differ-ence in the appearance of a "demographic transition" that we have noted for working-class and middle-class sections of the popula-tion was in no small part dictated by legal pressures intended to curtail working-class efforts to control their fertility—despite Mal-thusian alarms about uncontrolled population. (We address this contradiction more fully below.) Such measures were not new. In 1624, as we noted earlier, Parliament had passed legislation to prevent infanticide. But, this was finally conceded to be unwork-able in 1803, when the government took aim at abortion instead, feeling that abortionists, if not women having abortions, could be readily identified and prosecuted. In 1828 and 1837, the law was strengthened (McLaren 1984:114, 131–136). At the same time, there was evidence of a growing campaign against those who sought to democratize access to information about means of regulating fer-tility. By the 1870s, when concern was mounting about a decline in the reproduction of the labor supply, this began to take on a special force, culminating in the supreme irony of the imprison-ment of Charles Bradlaugh and Annie Besant (themselves working-class Malthusians) in 1877 for disseminating birth control literature in the conviction that poverty was attributable largely to overpopulation (Ledbetter 1972:1–2)—a view with which the ruling class nonetheless hardly concurred.

Ireland, Malthus, and the Myth of Imprudent Reproduction

The relationship between England and Ireland during the eighteenth and nineteenth centuries provides one of the most instructive examples of the effects of colonialism on demographic processes.

One hundred and fifty years ago, the Irish were largely perceived by the English much as the English upper and middle class viewed the working class in England; their poverty was regarded as chiefly their own fault and, as Malthus was to suggest, due to a lack of restraint in the matter of childbearing. The economic crises that were to beset Ireland, especially what became known as the Great Potato Famine in the 1840s—were, as such, to become the paradigmatic example henceforward of the plight of all developing countries where blame could be conveniently placed upon uncontrolled, irrational procreativity.

The hegemony of England over Ireland may be traced back to the Anglo-Norman invasions which began as early as the twelfth century. Thus, long before the Industrial Revolution, Ireland, according to the English historian James Froude, "was regarded as a colony to be administered, not for her own benefit, but for the convenience of the mother country" (quoted in MacNeil 1886:15). Military incursions, land confiscations, and paralegal interventions all conspired to create a situation by the early eighteenth century in which Ireland had no independent legal existence to speak of: all laws passed by its parliament had, since 1495, to be approved by the English Privy Council, and most native Irish Catholics were politically and economically disenfranchised.

Yet, according to the Malthusian scenario as it developed in the first half of the nineteenth century, it was not English colonialism that was the cause of Ireland's economic difficulties, but the introduction of the potato from the Americas. The Irish were regarded as fundamentally lazy and this cultigen was deemed to play a role similar to that of poor relief in England, subsidizing large families among the poverty-stricken. In recent times this viewpoint has been encapsulated in the geographer Thomas Freeman's terse summation of the demographic trends in Ireland during the sixty years preceding the Famine: "Apparently content with little, the Irish increased and multiplied" (1950:106). Similarly, according to historian Michael Drake, population rose because "Irish men and women were prepared to live almost exclusively on potatoes" (1969:66). Or, as it was phrased at the time: "The fatal luxuriance with which this vegetable flourished in the soil of Ireland, caused population to run fearfully ahead of the requirements and capabilities of the country. Millions have been hurried into existence, for whom no place was ready, no occupation provided; numbers multiplied, not in proportion to the development of the national resources and increase of general productiveness, but in the ratio of the prolific potato" (*Thoughts on Ireland*, 1847:37). Thus, when famine struck, it was seen by adherents of this view—especially in England among those who had some responsibility for colonial policy in Ireland—as a "natural" disaster which would serve to readjust population to available food supply.

The fact remains, however, that the rise in Irish population which seems to have first evidenced itself around 1750 took place long after the potato had first been introduced into Ireland. Thus, as Cullen (1968:79) has argued, there is probably more reason to see the increasing dependence of the peasantry on the potato (which became particularly great in the second half of the eighteenth century), not as a cause of population growth, but rather as a response to it and to the factors which lay behind it—in particular, the raising of rents by landlords in order to force Irish tenant farmers onto smaller plots. Since the potato was a particularly "acre-economizing crop," Cullen, in contrast to the standard Malthusian position, has concluded that "Far from being some kind of stigma on the character of the Irish peasantry or a manifestation of some inherent laziness or fecklessness, the adoption of the potato was a perfectly rational and justifiable response to economic circumstances" (1968:81).

Nor is there evidence that, as the Malthusians argued, the Irish population was pressing "fearfully ahead of the requirements and capabilities of the country." Quite the contrary, the potato was actually the major source of Irish prosperity during the second half of the eighteenth century when Ireland, as the great Georgian edifices of Dublin testify, was among the richest countries of Europe. (Indeed, it was this fact that especially tempted the English, from whom Ireland had obtained a degree of legislative independence in 1783, to establish a Union of the two countries as a means toward exploiting Ireland's treasure at a time when the war against France was imposing a huge financial burden upon England. This Union was effected in 1801.) Its prosperity, however, was not equitably apportioned, but depended, in fact, on the growing impoverishment of the Irish peasantry.

The Colonizing Effects of the English Market

Up until the middle of the eighteenth century, the colonial economy of Ireland had been largely oriented toward grazing cattle and the development of a provisions trade which had played a critical role in the supply of meat to England's Caribbean colonies, a role which evolved simultaneously with the suppression of any other industries which represented competition with English trade. During most of this period, there was relatively little demand on rural labor—the extensive use of land for cattle obviating the need for a large work force—and Ireland seems to have been generally characterized by a relatively stable population, a condition which was certainly reinforced by periodic food scarcity in the subsistence sector (Connell 1965).

Major changes took place, however, with industrial development in England and the associated English drive for new markets. Both factors pressed severely upon England's domestic resources—chiefly food supplies for the fast-growing urban proletariat and for an army actively engaged abroad in campaigns to preserve or expand England's share in the emergent world capitalist system. Cheap foodstuffs became an essential element in guaranteeing the leading position of English industry, and it was to the Celtic fringe, both Scotland and Ireland, that England first looked for the imports that could moderate domestic prices, restrain trade union activism and demands for higher wages, and hold down the costs of production upon which the competitive advantage of English industry was based (Ainsworth-Davis 1924:81; Orwin and Whetham 1971:25; Trow-Smith 1959; Ross 1983a, 1983b). One indication of the critical role which England's Irish colony was compelled to assume is the shift that took place in the direction and quantity of Irish meat exports. In the 1760s Ireland exported a total of 213,000 barrels of beef, 50 percent of which went to the plantations, 48 percent to the continent; and only 1 percent to Britain. By 1800 the total export of beef had fallen to 147,382 barrels, of which 79 percent went to Britain. Unlike beef, Ireland's export of pork increased between 1764 and 1800 from 30,328 barrels to 107,530 but the same shift toward the British market ensued; from virtually zero in 1764 to 87 percent in 1800 (O'Donovan 1940:114–116).

What these figures also indicate is the important structural shift in land use that came about under pressure from the English market. It was not simply that the latter was becoming the monopoly consumer of Irish livestock, but that cattle grazing was declining in significance as far as overall utilization of Irish land was concerned, as it gave way to more intensive agricultural purposes, represented by increasing production of grain for the urban population in England. Thus, Irish grain exports rose from 31,423 barrels in 1771–1773 to over 863,000 barrels by 1791 (Newenham 1805:48–50), while beef exports fell by one-third. This more intensive use of the land, however, was contingent on an increased work force which landlords sought to achieve by encouraging their tenants to grow more potatoes as a means of getting married earlier and of raising children on smaller holdings. Thus, the potato was one of the few major food crops that was not tithed (Gill 1925:35–36; Coote 1801:191–193).

The drive to expand acreage in cereals squeezed the area available for subsistence, creating increased competition among land-hungry rural inhabitants, a situation which permitted landlords to push up rents, which in some districts rose as much as 85 percent between 1746 and 1783 (J. Johnson 1970:229). The result is that, through cereal production for England and higher rents, landlords were able to turn their aggressive pronatalist policies into considerable economic prosperity for themselves. There is, thus, little evidence for the Malthusian proposition that the population increase in Ireland during the second half of the eighteenth century had a damaging effect on the whole Irish economy; quite the contrary, it seems to have been the primary factor behind an unprecedented increase in the prosperity of the ruling class. As Thomas Newenham observed in 1805, "We know that within these last five-and-twenty years the rent of land has doubled in most places and trebled in many. We know that a vast number of superb country mansions, besides splendid townhouses, have been built within these last twenty years: a circumstance which clearly evinces a very great increase of wealth among the landlords of Ireland" (p. 143).

Irish peasant families, however, lived on a steadily contracting subsistence base, in contrast to a century or two earlier when their diet had been more varied. It consisted primarily of the potato and the products of a pig which was itself raised on potatoes (although the pig often had to be foregone and paid as rent). That the peasant economic position was being subjected to ever greater pressure during the second half of the eighteenth century was evidenced by the dramatic rise in exports of Irish pork (see above).

Thus the potato was more the instrument of landlord policy than the addiction of a lazy peasantry. It was scarcely itself responsible for the rise in Irish population which took place after 1750. This seems, moreover, to accord with observations from elsewhere in Western Europe. Thus, Morineau had noted for France, that "in considering the regions where population growth had taken hold after 1745, one cannot help but recognize that while some of them had adopted the potato, others (Languedoc, Ile-de-France) had not. . . . There is no universal correlation between the spread of the potato and demographic growth" (1979:22–23).

The Political Economy of Irish Population Growth

As we have suggested, and as others such as Cullen have also noted, there is much more reason to argue for a positive association between rising population and intensification in agricultural production—for which the potato was certainly a facilitating factor.

But the critical issue, as in other colonial regimes, seems essentially to have been the demand for rural labor which such intensification increased and the resulting shifts in the cost/benefits of rearing children. In part, as we have seen, this demand came about from English pressure for greater quantities of grain—first officially manifested in the passage in 1748 of Foster's Corn Law which lifted prior restrictions on the importation of Irish cereal (Hechter 1975:85). The demand for grain grew even greater during the Napoleonic Wars, when England's continental sources were cut off. By the war's end, the high price and scarcity of grain were implicated in the growing working-class protest against the injustices of the new industrial system. As Samuel Bamford wrote at the time:

A series of disturbances commenced with the introduction of the Corn Bill in 1815 and continued, with short intervals, until the close of the year 1816. In London and Westminster riots ensued and were continued for several days, while the Bill was discussed; at Bridport there were riots on account of the high price of bread; at Bideford there were similar disturbances to prevent the export of grain; at Bury by the unemployed to destroy machinery; at Ely, not suppressed without bloodshed; at Newcastle-on-Tyne by colliers and others; at Glasgow, where blood was shed, on account of soup kitchens; at Preston, by unemployed weavers; at Nottingham by Luddites who destroyed 30 frames; at Merthyr Tydvil, on a reduction of wages; at Birmingham by the unemployed; at Walsall by the distressed; and December 7th, 1816, at Dundee, where, owing to the high price of meal, upwards of 100 shops were plundered. (quoted in Morton 1979:364)

Under such conditions, it is not surprising, given its proximity and the political and economic authority which England commanded over Ireland, that Irish food should have been seen as essential to the stability and continued development of English commerce. Thus between 1805 and 1825, Irish exports of oats and oatmeal increased eightfold (Greene 1956). Nor is it surprising that the export of Irish food should have affected the demand for labor, the cost/benefits of rearing children and hence the reproductive behavior of Irish peasants.

But, there was another factor as well, of equal or even of greater importance, which has long been overlooked, which led rural families in Ireland, under increasing economic stress, to increase fertility in order to attempt to improve their precarious subsistence: the production of flax and, from it, linen yarn. Flax cultivation and the hand-spinning of its fiber into yarn were old cottage industries in rural Ireland. Indeed, Irish linen had been among the earliest fixtures in the colonial system which harnessed Irish resources to English commercial needs.

It was English policy, as much in Ireland as in India and other colonies, to discourage competing industries, particularly in the important field of textiles. But it was in England's interest actually to stimulate Irish flax and linen production. Nonetheless, the market for such linen yarn remained modest until the rise of cotton textile manufacturing in England in the middle of the eighteenth century. As we have seen, cotton manufacturing represented not simply a displacement of woolen manufacturing as the preeminent industry in England but a quantum leap in the scale of production. (Cotton could be supplied by colonial regions in almost unlimited quantity compared to its predecessor which had been obtained largely from British sheep herds.) Cotton, however, had one significant technical limitation: it could not be machine-produced with a warp strong enough to manufacture an all-cotton cloth. The result was that the rise of machine-woven cotton came to depend upon the import of large quantities of Irish hand-spun linen yarn to produce a material known as "fustian." In addition, considerable quantities of linen cloth were also exported to England (Newenham 1805:201).

As a result, therefore, of the domestic and colonial expansion of the English economy in the mid-eighteenth century, flax cultivation and the spinning of linen yarn became strategically important rural cottage industries in Ireland. This was especially true in the poor western province of Connacht, where both activities were attractive to land-hungry peasants whose subsistence base, due precisely to that same expansion of the English economy, was shrinking and whose dependence on the potato was increasing commensurately. Flax, moreover, combined readily with potato production on small peasant holdings and, indeed, seemed to grow especially well on land previously used to raise potatoes (Gill 1925:36*n*), something which may have further encouraged potato cultivation during this period. But, the advantages to growing flax were, from the peasant's standpoint, even more varied. As Conrad Gill has noted in *The Rise of the Irish Linen Industry*:

A flax crop yielded on the whole a larger return from a given area than any other crop which a peasant could grow, and, secondly . . . the careful hand-labour needed in its harvesting made it particularly valuable for very small holdings. Further, the preparation of yarn, although it was ill-paid labour, brought at any rate some increase to the trifling income of the cottier's household. In certain parts of the country flax crops were the more attractive because they were exempted by custom from tithe. Moreover, it was found that flax could be grown satisfactorily after potatoes—which were also exempted from tithe—and thus a small farmer . . . could use a flax crop in establishing a simple rotation. (1925:35–36)

The expanding English market for linen yarn tended to increase the Irish peasants' fertility rate by markedly enhancing the labor value of children in harvesting and spinning. Spinning, moreover, gave a special economic value to young women (R. Thompson 1802:174) which seems to have been implicated in an increase during this period in the rate of marriage, as well as in the tendency for it to take place at a younger age. Thus, it seems quite unlikely to be coincidental that the rate of Irish population growth reached its zenith during the same period when the country's linen export trade more than trebled (Gill 1925:163), or that the center of flax production was Connacht, the province where, according to Connell (1965:429), "women married earliest," and "parcellation of the land was most acute."

How the Irish Were Made Redundant

The crux of the Malthusian position has been that population rose steadily, pressing on Irish food supplies (primarily on the potato) until such time as Nature infected that tuber with a fatal blight which, through starvation and disease, checked the demographic pressure. But the proposition that, in the post-Napoleonic War period, Irish population was "excessive," and that "the population had increased up to the limit of subsistence" (Griffith 1926:61–62), was not a scientific assessment but, rather, a political judgment. As Robert Owen had noted from his own calculations of Irish resources in 1823, it was "evident that this hitherto ill-fated island is competent to maintain, not only all its own inhabitants, but more than double the whole population of Great Britain and Ireland, in comfort heretofore unattained by any nation or people, at any period of the world" (1823:22).

The evidence, if nothing else, was that Ireland was, in fact, not only managing to sustain not only its own population but contributing vast quantities of food to the English larder as well! The impression conveyed to the English public through a burgeoning Malthusian literature, however, was that the Irish had been so reduced to lassitude by the easy availability of the potato that they were disinclined to cultivate any further economic ambition.

Thus, in the very midst of the Famine, in 1846, a letter-writer in the London *Times* remarked of the Irish: "they inhabit a country a great part of which is at least equal in fertility to our own, with more that is capable of being made so. There is no reason, except their own willful mismanagement, why they should not grow as fine crops of wheat as are raised in the Lothians, and, after feeding themselves, export the surplus to our shores" (1880:14). But the truth was that, year after year, while the Irish peasant had been forced to depend on the potato, Ireland had been feeding England, not a "surplus," but what the Irish themselves could have been eating if the structure of a colonial system imposed upon them and refined over several centuries had not obligated them to forgo such nourishment in order to pay their rents.

This system had so evolved that the question of the subsistence of the peasantry was entirely secondary (much as in India during the same years; see below) to the maintenance of those food exports which were so essential to the perpetuation of English industrial life and to the expansion overseas of English commercial interests. In most years, this meant that the peasants were reduced to destitution, with many men forced to seek seasonal work in England on farms or helping to construct canals and railways (Kerr 1943:380; J. Johnson 1970:236–238; O'Connor 1974:24–25), and with some even going as far away as Cuba to build railroads for sugar companies (Moreno 1976:135).

In 1845–1848, with conditions so desperate that an estimated one million died and an equal number emigrated, Ireland still continued to export prodigious stores of grain and livestock, including, in 1846 alone, almost half a million pigs (O'Donovan 1940:192). As the London *Times* (1880:45) was forced to concede, "while England was avowedly feeding Ireland . . . whole fleets of provisions were continually arriving from the land of starvation to the ports of wealth and the cities of abundance."

The Irish population became "excessive" in the post-Napoleonic period only in the sense that, in a given economic climate, the peasants whose tenancies had previously been encouraged in order to produce grain and flax now stood in the way of the market for beef and pork. In part, this market was created by English urban growth, though, as we have seen, the majority of the English working class was poorly nourished and saw relatively little meat in their diet. A disproportionate share went to the upper and middle class, while another regular recipient of Irish meat seems to have been the British army (Ross 1983b). This came into its own in the nineteenth century, when it was engaged in hostilities in defence of colonial markets somewhere in the world every year of Victoria's lengthy reign (Farwell 1972:1).

To supply this market, the previous trend toward land subdivision was replaced by one of consolidation, as landowners aggressively transformed cultivable land back into pasture, forcing thousands of tenant families to attempt to eke out a living by the roadsides and the edges of small towns (Foster 1846:341), where visitors saw in their wretched appearance and crowding together all the apparent symptoms of what Malthus had foretold. Few writers were as discerning as the Halls who, on the eve of the Great Famine, noted the economic reality that lay behind what was so readily seen as imprudent procreation.

The county of Meath is the great grazing ground of Ireland, and consists almost entirely of pasture-land, vying in its external aspect with the richest of the English counties, and, perhaps, surpassing any of them in fertility. . . . Much of the apparently prosperous character is, however, hollow and insubstantial; the large farmers are indeed wealthy, but of small farmers there are few or none: the policy of the "graziers" has been, for a long time, to devote the produce of their soil to the raising of cattle; and the "clearing of estates" in Meath has, therefore, been proceeding at a very disastrous rate. . . . The small plots of ground are "wanted for cattle"; and as the cabins cannot exist without them, they are in rapid course of removal . . . The towns, into which the poor have been driven, are thronged with squalid countenances; starvation stalks at noonday through their streets. (Hall and Hall 1841–43:373)

By 1841, over two-thirds of the arable land in County Meath was in pasture, a reflection of what was happening throughout Ireland at the time (Wakefield 1812:381; T. Freeman 1957:168). The result, in one writer's phrase, was to create "vast districts of fertile pasture almost unpeopled, and congregated clusters of unsightly hovels swarming with want and misery" (*Thoughts* 1847:44). But, so long as the economic imperative to clear the land existed, the landlords found it in their interest to promote the vision of an island in Malthusian turmoil; thus, they "began to utter bitter complaints of surplus population: they began to ventilate their grievances through the English and Irish press, saying that their land was overrun by cottiers and squatters—the main cause of all this being kept in the background" (O'Rourke 1902:46).

One important aspect of the aftermath of the famine years, 1845–1848, deserves special mention here, germane as it is to the illumination of the relationship between the myth of irrational procreation and the harsh realities of the colonial economy. Promoting the view that the Famine was a "natural" event, Charles Trevelyan, who was in charge of English famine relief in his role as Assistant Secretary of the Treasury, counseled that little should be done to intervene on the part of human agencies,* maintaining that, as Malthus had predicted, the Famine was "a direct stroke of an all-wise and all-merciful Providence" (Trevelyan 1848:201) because it had checked the tendency of the Irish poor to reproduce beyond the subsistence capacity of the island and would restore a more harmonious relation between population and food resources.

Yet, nothing of the sort happened. Indeed, taking advantage of the Famine, the English Parliament enacted legislation which actually worsened the situation among the Irish peasantry by expediting the process of land concentration and eviction (Kennedy 1973:28–29). Thus, between 1845 and 1851, the number of plots of less than one acre fell from 135,000 to 38,000, while those between 1 and 15 acres declined from 493,000 to 280,000 (Steele 1974:3).

* Trevelyan had been educated at the East India Company's college at Haileybury at the time when Thomas Malthus was a member of the faculty there (Steven and Lee 1921–22: 12:886–887, 19:1135).

At the same time, live cattle exports rose from almost 202,000 in 1846–1849 to about 558,00 by 1870–1874 (O'Donovan 1940); and by 1880 it could be written that "agriculture of most other kinds has been steadily dwindling down; 519,307 acres out of a total tillage area of 5,500,000 had gone out of cultivation in ten years. The wheat culture was ruined. . . . The breadth of land even under oats had declined by 320,000 acres . . . 50.2 percent of the entire surface area of the country and two-thirds of its wealth were devoted to the raising of cattle" (Dublin Mansion House Relief Committee 1881:2).

It is hardly surprising then, that, while England's population continued to rise, that of Ireland declined, in part through a falling birth rate, but largely because of emigration which far exceeded the rate of population increase. As the role of Ireland as England's cattlefarm was reaffirmed and consolidated in the wake of the Great Famine, the countryside was the stage for a persistent and massive exodus: almost two million people left between 1848 and 1855 and another 3.5 million up to the eve of World War I (Lee 1973:6).

The Pressure of Poverty on Fertility

A part of the general theory of the demographic transition is that as economic prosperity reduced infant and childhood mortality, it eventually brought about a structurally related decline in the perceived necessity of large families. The obverse logic of this is that high infant mortality (and the poverty so often responsible for it) has been a principal reason for high birth rates. We have seen how Malthusian ideology stood this view on its head, blaming excess fertility for poverty. But, to suggest that there is some universal principle, correlating poverty with high fertility, whichever way the causal arrow points, represents a dangerous oversimplification.

For a social system to merit more children, it must have some elasticity. In most cases, this pertains to the potential for child labor to be utilized. But where the economic advantage of children is declining and the general employment situation is poor, people are inclined to curtail their fertility. This point has been made by modern researchers such as Mencher (1980) in her recent work in southern India. And it seems to be exemplified by demographic trends among the Irish peasantry in the decades prior to the Great Famine, as the general condition of rural life worsened. We have already seen how, in the decades between the end of the Napo- leonic Wars and the Famine, many pressures were placed upon the Irish peasantry in the ultimate interest of the English economy. In the face of such circumstances, a succession of writers none- theless pointed to a burgeoning population as the origin of Ire- land's problems—an argument which rested upon a general consensus that Irish reproductive habits were inherently irrational and thus ignored the material consequences of family size. But, there was little disagreement over the deterioration in the condi- tion of the rural economy.

It is only recently that new evidence on Irish population during this critical period has made it clear that, in fact, peasant repro- ductive strategies were not insensitive to increasing economic mis- ery. While population continued to rise, the new evidence shows that the rate of growth slowed down in the decades before the Famine, as marriage was delayed and couples had fewer children (Morgan 1976; Vaughn and Fitzpatrick 1978). There are a number of reasons for this. As already noted, much cultivable land was being converted to pasture, entailing a shrinkage in the average size of peasant holdings and an epidemic of evictions. There was also, over the same period, a critical change in the market for Irish yarn as a result of technological advances in the factory production of cotton textiles, a development which added to the incentive for landlords to expand pasturage where formerly cottiers had har- vested flax. With the decline of flax production which had given work to young children came a major disincentive to maintain previous levels of fertility.

The Social Determination of Excess Population

The slowing down of population growth in the decades before the Famine was associated, in its aftermath, with a pattern of delayed marriage and celibacy in Ireland which was virtually unique for Europe (Lee 1973). Yet, despite this and in contrast to Malthusian prognostications about the remedial effect of the Famine, the threat of famine did not abate. The western province of Connacht, where population declined 28.8 percent between 1841 and 1851, and continued to fall through the next three decades (p. 2) was the scene of terrible famine again in 1879–1880 (Dublin Mansion House Committee 1881:77). Such events put the issue of Irish "population pressure," as the Malthusians represented it, into perspective: under a colonial regime which placed rigorous priority on export production, the Irish peasantry could never be self-sufficient or enjoy a healthy indigenous economic life, *at any level of fertility.* Excess population was a condition determined at any point in time by the production strategies imposed on Ireland by its absentee rulers. While Irish reproductive behavior might reasonably respond to the material effects of such strategies, it could never do so in a way that could anticipate all the exigencies of colonial rule.

The Irish Pattern Repeated in India

The lesson of Ireland is a generic one. In such countries anywhere in the world the appearance of a "surplus" population derived largely from the impact of colonial capitalism, from the loss of indigenous control over strategic resources—above all, land—and the ensuing subservience of local labor to the process of capital accumulation in the colonizing country. Development in such colonies was set backward as the European powers methodically transformed them into producers of raw materials and markets for European manufactures. Local industries were discouraged and even destroyed; rents and taxes were imposed or elevated to levels far in excess of those imposed previously by native rulers, thus placing new pressures on local subsistence. As Gunnar Myrdal has written of South Asia: "The development of plantations was initiated and controlled by foreigners. Managerial functions and ultimate control were in the hands of aliens. Dividends and a large part of the salaries were remitted abroad or used to purchase foreign goods rather than to stimulate demand on the local market. . . . The plantations [thus] spurred the industrialization of the Western countries but not of South Asia. The plantations were, in effect, extensions of the metropolitan countries" (1968:449).

It is only by acknowledging this central condition, the loss of political and economic autonomy, that one can begin to understand the subsequent demographic experience of the colonialized world. Certainly, it is prerequisite to the recognition, as we have seen in the case of Ireland, that "overpopulation," as an explanation of underdevelopment, grossly misrepresents the historical relationship between people and the resources upon which their health and livelihood depend and the way in which that relationship has been shaped and distorted by colonial imperatives.

Such "Malthusian" crises as famine, so frequently employed as a "natural" measure of population pressure, must be regarded in the same socio-cultural and historical framework. In the case of Ireland (if one surveys the period from 1740 to 1880), the fact that famines occurred regardless of whether peasant fertility was high or low lends considerable weight to this argument. The same is true of India, where, during the centuries of English rule, though rates of population growth were low, famines increased in intensity and frequency (Bhatia 1967:8). (Indeed, such famines obviously inhibited population increase.)

As elsewhere, the underdevelopment of India and its demographic consequences must be traced to the priority which European rule accorded to its own domestic markets. As we have seen, England in the seventeenth and eighteenth centuries sought to protect its textile industry against the threat of cheap and better-made Indian cloth. Under the rule of the East India Company only a limited effort was made to curb Indian textile production because the Company, as opposed to English woolen merchants, profited from the export of Indian calicoes and muslins to England. As noted earlier, parliamentary action was eventually taken to protect the native English market. But, the long-term threat presented by Indian cloth was not finally eliminated until the English state assumed direct control—a process that began with the official abolition of the company's monopoly in 1813 (Morton 1979:462).

With this direct administrative link, Indian textile production was exposed to a flood of English cotton manufactures while, at the same time, Indian imports into England were checked by prohibitively high duties (Mukerjee 1974:404). Trends in trade statistics convey the import of these developments: in the two decades from 1814 to 1835, English exports of cotton piece-goods to the Indian subcontinent soared from 818,208 yards to 51,777,277 (Bhatia 1967:17).

Behind these numbers, and the flooding of India with the products of the Lancashire mills, lay a profound transformation in the condition of rural India. Most important was an acceleration of the rate of capitalist penetration of the countryside, with its impact on land tenure and subsistence. Rents, for example, increased considerably under English rule, forcing many peasants off the land and increasing the proportion in the hands of moneylenders and landlords—which meant that revenue was siphoned out of the countryside at an unprecedented rate. Though deprived of capital, the rural sector was nonetheless compelled to absorb ever greater numbers of people who had previously earned their living in the craft industries which English colonial policy was rapidly destroying (Dutt 1940:184–187).

At the same time, however, the potential of Indian agriculture was being eroded, chiefly through an administrative neglect never witnessed in pre-British days. As Sir Arthur Cotton, a pioneer in modern irrigation works in India, wrote in 1854: "Public works have been almost entirely neglected throughout India . . . The motto hitherto has been 'Do nothing, have nothing done, let nobody do anything. Bear any loss, let the people die of famine, let hundreds of lakhs be lost in revenue for want of water, or roads, rather than do anything" (quoted in Dutt 1940:194).

The result was that much arable land became waste, formerly reclaimed districts reverted to swampland where malaria and other diseases took hold and soil productivity in many regions declined (Mukerjee 1974:342; Dutt 1940:204). As this ecological degeneration occurred, increased hardship and further indebtedness forced many holdings to be sold while more and more people were seeking to subsist off the land. The consequence was that the average size of peasant holdings shrivelled and the economic basis of rural subsistence grew accordingly more precarious. As more people came to depend on agriculture, they did so less as peasant cultivators than as landless laborers.

But ultimately, what placed the greatest stress upon the rural economy was that it was made to bear the burden of colonial

taxation, to pay for the enormous costs of English imperial administration and the so-called Indian public debt which was one of its
principal manifestations. This, in turn, inevitably forced Indian
agriculture to shift steadily from subsistence crops to commercially
favored products, in order to raise the cash to meet rising rents
and taxes (Bhatia 1967:24–34). Thus, at the expense of Indian diet,
as in Ireland, agricultural production was geared to the necessities
of English industry. As Knowles has observed: "The importance
of India to England in the first half of the nineteenth century lay
in the fact that India supplied some of the essential raw materials—
hides, oil, dyes, jute and cotton—required for the industrial revolution in England" (1928:305). Simultaneously, traditional foodgrains, while they now constituted a diminishing percentage of
rural production, were equally under pressure to be exported to
bring in needed cash, rather than to be consumed in India—regardless of whether food was locally in short supply.

One of the most dramatic consequences of this diversion of resources was an increasing frequency and severity of famines, a
pattern which began under the rule of the East India Company
and accelerated under the subsequent administration of the English Raj. Such events could scarcely be adjudged "natural" oc-
currences when colonial policy was so visibly implicated. Warren
Hastings, governor of Calcutta, had made this altogether clear
when he wrote to the Board of Directors of the East India Company
in 1772: "Notwithstanding the loss of at least one-third of the inhabitants of the province [of Bengal], and the consequent decrease
of cultivation, the nett [sic] collections of the year 1771 exceeded
even those of 1768. It was naturally to be expected that the diminution of the revenues should have kept pace with other consequences of so great a calamity. That it did not was owing to its
being violently kept up to its former standards" (quoted in Mukerjee 1974:353).

Nor was it any less obvious by the middle of the nineteenth
century what the connection was between the colonial export
economy and rural crises. As Bhatia notes: "It is significant that
almost all official narratives of famines during the period 1860–79
excepting that of 1860–61 make a prominent mention of the depletion of stocks by exportation in the preceding year, as a con-

tributing cause of the existing distress among the people" (1967:31).

Linked as such famines were to the scale of exports, it was virtually inevitable that the transition to Crown rule, with its policy of making India subsidize its own exploitation and of developing Indian exports as the basis of English trade with China (Wolf 1982:288), would have made such catastrophes more frequent (Bhatia 1967:8). But perhaps nothing increased the level of Indian exports as much as the completion of the Suez Canal in 1869 which halved travel time between England and Asia (B. Brown 1974:133). The result was that "famines and scarcities [were] four times as numerous during the last thirty years of the nineteenth century as they were one hundred years earlier, and four times more widespread" (Digby, quoted in Dutt 1940:132).

Yet, English policy moved, much as in the case of Ireland, in the direction of strict laissez-faire, a position reinforced as much as anything by a clear recognition that compassion and colonial profit were at loggerheads. Thus, in contrast to the days of the Moghuls, when "state regulation of supplies and control of prices of foodgrains during famines was an accepted principle of State policy" (Bhatia 1967:104), and even in contrast to East India Company policy, English administration in India through the last century grew increasingly evasive and noninterventionist in the matter of famines (p. 105). Rather, effective encouragement was given to commercial interests to profit from famine prices, while nothing was done to curtail the exodus of crucial resources. As Bhatia observes, "to stop exports of food was, in a way, to curtail imports of foreign cloth and default on payment of "home charges" which the British Parliament and its subordinate Government in India could never permit" (p. 110).

That such exports were important to English industry and had significant consequences for English demographic trends we have already observed, but periodic famines and associated epidemics took an enormous toll (McAlpin 1983). Through most of the nineteenth century, Indian population probably grew slowly at about 4 percent per decade (Clark 1967:108; McAlpin 1983). Between 1870 and 1910, while the population of England and Wales increased by 58 percent (the European average was 45.4 percent), that of

India rose by only 18.9 (Dutt 1940:64). If the argument must be made that Indian famine was in some sense the result of "population pressure," it was the pressure of English population upon India.

Java: The Dutch "Culture System" and Population Increase

As in the instance of Ireland, Java under Dutch jurisdiction presents a classic illustration of increasing social misery seemingly attributable to "irrational" and "uncontrolled" population growth. In fact, however, it represents one of the clearest examples of a dependent colonial people forced to an increase in numbers which, rather than impelling a deterioration of living standards, forestalled an even greater degree of deprivation.

In Java, early Portuguese colonial influence had been preceded by Islam, spreading eastward with the sea trade. Under Islamic influence, a vigorous class of Indonesian traders and merchants held their own in competition with the Portuguese, whose effects on the region were to be slight in comparison with their successors, the Dutch. Newly emancipated from Spanish rule themselves, the Dutch were one of the most formidable mercantile powers in seventeenth century Western Europe, with Amsterdam one of the great financial centers of that period. In 1602, they formed the United East India Company (the V.O.C., Vereenigde Oostindische Compagnie) which readily removed what was left of Portuguese trade in the archipelago and commenced a policy of armed conquest through the islands to establish a monopoly over regional commerce. Maneuvering among rival Javanese kingdoms, the V.O.C. inaugurated a period during which the polities of Indo-Javanese civilization were steadily eroded while its own dominion over Java and the Outer Islands (Sumatra, Borneo, and the Celebes) was consolidated. By the mid-eighteenth century, the Dutch had become the paramount political authority on the island of Java, which was the focus of their commercial interests in Indonesia.

Profits were made in a variety of ways: by forced planting of export crops (indigo, coffee, sugar) over which the Company exercised monopoly privileges; by simple tribute taxation in kind (rice, timber, cotton, beans); by money taxes; and by exports from sugar and coffee plantations worked by forced labor. This phase of Dutch colonial rule, which incurred considerable wrath among the people of Java, lasted until 1798 when the Dutch government dismembered the V.O.C. (much as the English Crown was beginning to do during the same period to the East India Company) (Fisher 1964). The end of company rule was partly political, partly financial (it had teetered toward bankruptcy by paying astronomical dividends to its backers). But, it meant, for several decades, an end to Dutch control in the area as the Napoleonic Wars curtailed the overseas enterprises of mainland Europe. In the interim, the English, who had previously been excluded from the East Indies by Dutch sea power (Morton 1979:208), filled the colonial vacuum.

When the Dutch were able to reassert their dominion over the region in 1816, they set about transforming the island into a vast agribusiness. As yet, despite its traditional position as the center of Indonesian culture, a comparatively small proportion of Java's land was under cultivation. The Dutch intensified agricultural production, chiefly for export, at a furious rate, under a colonial policy known as the *cultuur stelsel* or "culture system" (Furnivall 1948:20). They were met, however, by mounting resistance among the Javanese peasantry which developed into a bloody war for independence in 1825, a war in which some 200,000 Javanese lost their lives but which failed to dislodge the Dutch. Indeed, by the end of the war in 1830, the political and economic position of the Dutch was more secure than ever (Fisher 1964:255–256).

In the aftermath of the war, the Culture System turned much of Java into a European-run plantation. Its central principle was that villagers were obligated to pay colonial taxes, not in money but in those crops which the Dutch mandated, chiefly sugar and coffee (Furnivall 1948:21). Java's nonirrigated lands were planted with coffee to such an extent that by 1850 there were 300 million trees on the island (Geertz 1963:66) (enough to make the phrase "a cup of Java" synonymous with "a cup of coffee" in many parts of the world). At the same time, in order to encourage villagers to plant sugarcane in their paddy fields, Dutch authorities undertook an expansion of irrigation facilities, again through the deployment of forced labor.

But, most important is the fact that the Dutch, unlike many other colonial powers, sought to preserve and build their profits upon the Javanese village economy. Hence, the government had prohibited the sale of village paddy lands. On the other hand, while official policy called for the peasants themselves to rotate the planting of sugar and rice in their own fields, one-fifth (later, one third) of village lands were required to be devoted to sugar (Wolf 1982:334). From the Dutch point of view, this system had obvious merits. It preserved an illusion of indigenous ownership and so reduced the political hazards of creating an agro-industrial class of landless laborers, much as occurred in the Caribbean (cf. Mintz 1974). And it guaranteed a ready reserve force of labor for seasonal work in the cane fields. This was assured, not only by the fact that the traditional village was the key unit of sugar production, but because (as we will explore more fully below) the general pattern of agricultural intensification under the Dutch was especially conducive to population growth at the village level. Taking advantage of the extra water made available from the expansion of sugar production and working ever more intensively in their paddies to compensate for the diversion of land into cash crops, the Javanese actually managed to produce enough rice to raise their population by 700 percent during the nineteenth century (from 4 to 30 million). In contrast, in the less colonialized outer territories of Indonesia, population rose only from about 4.7 to 7.7 million (Fisher 1964:289).

Dutch rule in Java in the last century represents a classic episode in colonial development. The network of roads that were constructed to develop and control regional trade was, to take just one example, "far more elaborate than that of any other tropical region" (Fisher 1964:259). Through such infrastructural innovations as roads and new irrigation works, intensive agriculture spread throughout much of the Javanese lowlands. Yet the net result of all this "development" was decidedly uneven, as most of the wealth which export crops produced was ultimately banked in the Netherlands. In Amsterdam, the products of the Indies sub-

sidized a period of great prosperity in the second half of the nineteenth century, evidenced by the construction of the important
North Sea Canal, 1865–1876, and a rapid expansion of population
(Werkman 1983:712). But in Java, the average peasant diet by the
end of the last century was barely adequate (Fisher 1964:291). And,
when independence finally came in 1949, rural Java was demonstrably worse off than it had been at the beginning of Dutch rule
350 years earlier. No significant beginnings had been made toward
industrialization; population had swollen to 60 million and caloric
intake had never risen above 2,000 calories a day; and the entire
island, with its millions of tiny holdings, had been converted into
"one vast rural slum" (Geertz 1963; Harris 1980).

Inevitably, this state of affairs has been widely attributed to overpopulation. In turn, Javanese population growth has been variously attributed to the material benefits said to have been
conferred by European rule—including, in one writer's euphemis-
tic phrase, "the creation of new means of livelihood" (Fisher
1964:288–289)—or to peasant improvidence and ignorance. As we
have already suggested, living standards were actually in decline
(Alexander in press) and, in fact, so great were rice exports in the
early nineteenth century that many parts of Java were threatened
with famine (Fisher 1964:258). Nor can one justifiably argue that
the Javanese suddenly became more ignorant or improvident upon
the arrival of European imperialists, except in some way in which
the Dutch would unavoidably be implicated.

The impetus behind the rise in Javanese population seems,
rather, to have been the heightened demand for rural labor that
was implicit in the operation of the Culture System (Dobby
1967:239), which required communities to try to maintain subsistence production of rice at the same time that they were obliged
to increase their output of such export crops as sugarcane (and
divert a certain percentage of their rice for export as well). As
Alexander describes the impact of colonial demand on the pattern
of labor investment in the rural sector:

A village forced to cultivate sugar on one-third of its land had to increase
agricultural labor inputs fifty percent by virtue of that fact alone, a task

made much more difficult because of the simultaneous labor peaks in the cropping cycles of the two cultigens. In addition, if the village was to maintain rice production at former levels, it had to increase labor inputs on the remaining two-thirds of its land. And this was only the beginning: villagers also had to transport the cane, provide labor for the mills, muster men for construction of roads and extension of the irrigation system, and meet corvee obligations to both Dutch and indigenous rulers. (in press)

Contrary to Geertz's (1963) notion that rice production was maintained at a constant rate per capita despite rising population, new evidence indicates that rice productivity actually deteriorated and that the extra labor demands could not be met without a decline in living standards (B. White 1983:13–14). Thus, the demands of the colonial regime compelled the rural Javanese to try to sustain their own subsistence or, rather, to slow the pace of its decline by finding new labor resources, which they did by increasing fertility and the use of child labor (B. White 1973).

Alexander has suggested that the increase in fertility may also be traced to the growing involvement of women in the cultivation of sugarcane and as part of the labor force in sugar mills (in press). This, he argues, would probably have led to a decline in breast-feeding, which in turn would have reduced the traditional period of postpartum sexual abstinence, since the latter was enforced in Java by the view that semen was harmful to a mother's milk (Alexander in press). We would not expect this factor to lead to a sustained increase in child rearing, however, given the large array of alternative means of fertility/mortality control, if it were not the case that the labor value of children was on the rise, both in the field and in the home.

From several points of view, then, Java seems to represent a quintessential demonstration of a situation where "increase in population was a demographic response to demand for labor within the family, created by the need to intensify subsistence production in the face of colonial demands on land, labor, and produce" (B. White 1973:217). It is worth commenting, then, that, for all the distance that separates them, the circumstances underlying the rise in Javanese population and those behind demographic growth in England at about the same time were basically similar. The explanation lies in the fact that colonial underdevelopment was not confined just to remote colonies, but included as well the inner city districts which grew up within the metropolitan centers of world capitalism as the industrial revolution unfolded (Harrison 1983).

The Shadow of Malthus

As we have seen, during the development of the political economies dominated by the quest for profits, peasant and working class parents recurrently found themselves squeezed between the proverbial "rock and a hard place": higher reproductivity was frequently their best short-term defense against miseration, even though, in the long run, the aggregate result was catastrophic. But, even this was not solely or even primarily because population outstripped production, but because food and other resources were being expropriated by the ruling class. What such scenarios of "overpopulation" establish, then, is *not* "improvidence," but the fact that population regulating systems could be overwhelmed, distorted, or defeated by exploitative kinds of political economies. Under such circumstances, the Malthusian charge of improvident overbreeding reveals itself as a variation on the familiar theme of "blaming the victim."

As a special and more elaborate version of this theme the ideas of Malthus became the conventional wisdom of industrial capitalism and the age of colonialism. But, one thing that is clear is that there was comparatively little in Malthus that was new. Robert Wallace, also a cleric, had published a book called *Various Prospects* in 1761 which spelled out the disproportionate relationship between population and means of subsistence (Beer 1984:70–71). What was of critical importance about Malthus' views, first published in a short pamphlet in 1798, was its timing. This work first appeared at a pivotal time in European, and particularly English, history, when capitalists were freeing themselves from many of the lingering political and institutional confines of preindustrial capitalism and were in search of a credible ideology to rationalize their desire for untrammeled economic opportunity. Between its first publication and the last statement of his views in 1830, his thesis was revised and modified to reflect and attend to the needs of the ruling class that sponsored him (endowing him with a professorship at the East India College).

Most important to these sponsors was the fact that the great social and economic transformation which was enriching them was also giving birth, as we have seen, to new problems in regard to labor. New means were required to check its new needs and expectations which grew out of a deepening deprivation. But, it was also felt necessary to sweep away some of what were regarded as cumbersome and costly vestiges of previous generations, chief among which was the old Elizabethan Poor Law. The Poor Law had never been a charitable measure; indeed, it had been essentially a way of policing the movements of the poor by restricting public assistance to their home parishes. Nonetheless, in the early nineteenth century, in the midst of the growing misery of the English working class, it had come to represent in many minds the natural entitlement of the poor to some form of social support (Beer 1984:85). Such a view, however, was hardly consonant with new laissez-faire attitudes or the ideals of the new capitalists who sought to maximize the cheapness and mobility of labor and to guarantee that workers would be abundantly available in times of economic boom but, in times of crisis and unemployment, would look after themselves until it was time to reappear at the factory gates. Much depended then upon the abolition of the Tudor Poor Law and, with the help of Thomas Malthus, this was finally accomplished in 1834 with new legislation that "set the seal on unfettered free trade in the labour market" (Dobb 1963:275).

Malthus' ideas on population were never ideas in the abstract, but always interconnected with the social and economic arguments of the day, taking the part of free-market capitalists. Of this, the writer William Hazlitt was in no doubt at all when he wrote in 1807 that Malthus' *Essay on Population* was used by its author "to shut up the workhouse, to snub the poor, to stint them in their wages, to deny them any relief from the parish, and preach lectures to them on the new-invented crime of matrimony" (pp. 21–22). But one of the reasons for the rapid eminence which Malthus attained was that, although he provided specific arguments on many individual issues, he offered a general rationale for the needs of laissez-faire capitalism which had the exquisite advantage of appearing in the guise of universal scientific truth.

In the first place, he advanced the view that poverty (and, indeed, a whole spectrum of economic and social ills) was not a social product but a natural one, arising from an inevitable pressure of population upon resources, and that people were poor because they represented a surplus which necessarily drove down wages according to the natural process of supply and demand. It followed that institutions such as the Poor Law, in Malthus' view, were agencies of a false optimism which sought to help people but actually exacerbated their difficulties by tending to encourage marriage and breeding precisely among those who already suffered from what he regarded as redundant numbers. On the other hand, we know from an admission that he made in a letter in 1807, "that the Poor Laws do not encourage early marriage *so much* as might naturally be expected" (quoted in Digby 1983:99), that Malthus was aware that the poor might not be quite so imprudent after all; but, the disparity between such knowledge and what he published serves to underscore the essentially ideological thrust of his intellectual enterprise.

This ideological aspect is nowhere more clear than in one of Malthus' last essays, where he actually concedes that the disparity between agricultural production and population is not entirely natural but a function of economic organization. So overlooked is this that we feel it is worth quoting:

Yet it is unquestionably true, that the laws of private property, which are the grand stimulants to production, do themselves so limit it, as always to make the actual produce of the earth fall very considerably short of the power of production. (Malthus 1830:36)

The reason was essentially that, because capitalists must earn a profit, they would exclude from use land that might be cultivable, but at too great a cost. Interestingly, he went on to observe that, under an alternative system of common property, it might be possible to exploit such land without regard for profits and so allow a far greater population to subsist. But, "it is quite obvious that such a state of things would inevitably lead to the greatest degree of distress and degradation" (p. 37). Thus, it was because Malthus regarded capitalism as the only morally acceptable form of social order and private property as the result of the laws of nature (pp. 71–72), that he could see no resolution to the problem of population except what he termed "the laws of nature," or the operation of positive checks—disease, famine, and general misery—which led to increased mortality. That is to say, recurrent epidemics and endemic starvation were obviously preferable to any threat to the capitalists who guaranteed his sinecure.*

The one practical form of human intervention he envisaged was in the form of preventive checks that helped reduce births. These included various means he regarded as "vice" but included as well what he called "moral restraint," by which he meant primarily the postponement of marriage. The latter he hoped would be coupled with the prudence to avoid sex before marriage and to delay marriage itself until such time as a husband and wife could support all the children they might produce. There is no doubt that he was aware that exclusive reliance on moral restraint, as he envisaged it, to delay sex, marriage, and pregnancy was an impractical way of regulating population growth; but, to those who objected that the degree of self-control necessary was unrealistic, Malthus replied that "The Christian cannot consider the difficulty of moral restraint as any argument against its being his duty" (1960:491).

In the absence of moral restraints, however, there was obviously an array of preventive checks to fertility which included noncoital sex, prostitution, abortion, infanticide, and contraception, all of which Malthus regarded as instances of "vice and misery." Thus, while rationalizing starvation wages and exploitation by postulating a "natural tendency of the labouring classes of society to increase beyond the demand for their labour, or the means of their adequate support" (Malthus 1830:74), Malthus either discounted evidence that such a tendency was not as clear as he asserted or else firmly opposed the most immediate practical efforts that the working class could make to adjust the numbers of their children

In this respect, as in his general theory of population and subsistence, Malthus echoed Robert Wallace, who had argued that a communist republic could abolish poverty and elevate the general welfare, but that it would inevitably collapse from overpopulation. In contrast, all the miseries that such a republic would banish would, in a capitalist economy, serve to curtail population (Beer 1984:71).

to their economic circumstances and to attempt to minimize the intensity of their deprivation. Condemning all such options indiscriminately, he left nothing else to bring population into line with the food supply except the "positive checks" of disease, famine, and war.

There is, of course, an explanation for Malthus' scorn for methods of fertility control, and it lies in the realization that it was in large measure his task to reconcile the particular contradictions between production and reproduction which, as we earlier noted, industrial capitalism had intensified. As Heinsohn and Steiger (1983) point out, Malthus was eminently aware that "the natural desire for children" could be defeated by "human reason and ingenuity," the agents of which he regarded as "vice." Much as he talked about the threat posed by rampant procreation, his failure to advocate any controls other than moral restraint reflected the interests of the class whose principal ideologue he had become, which in that period appeared to have little to gain by seeing the working class enabled to control its own fertility (and to acquire the potential, at least, to reduce the size of the labor reserve and push up wages). After all, most capitalists regarded industrial expansion as predicated on population increase—to such a degree that the English working class, far from being excessive, actually had to be supplemented by imports of Irish labor—and Malthus himself subscribed to the general view that population pressure was a stimulus to production. Thus, his "apprehension that [people] would not have sufficient children was at least as great as his well-known fear of misery caused by an increasing population" (Heinsohn and Steiger 1983:231). (Indeed, greater, for there is not much evidence that other people's misery was a source of much concern to him at all.)

In Malthus' own words, "it is clearly the duty of each individual not to marry till he has a prospect of supporting his children; but it is at the same time to be wished that he should retain undiminished his desire of marriage in order that he may exert himself to realize this prospect, and be stimulated to make provisions for the support of greater numbers" (1960:485). In other words, Malthus was not *anti-natalist*. His argument against the Poor Laws, after all, was only that they hastened people into marriage. By the same token, moral restraint was meant to apply only before marriage. Once married, men and women were not meant to indulge in fertility-dampening vices but to be free to breed to their natural capacity. Malthus wanted to see them have a "large family" (p. 488); in fact, he expected each couple to have five or six children (p. 585).

The resolution of the paradox of combining premarital abstinence and a fear of overpopulation with an exhortation to unrestrained marital fertility is that Malthus was most interested not only in making certain that parents had large numbers of children, but that they shouldered the costs of rearing them, freeing employers and the state from the need to subsidize the reproduction of the labor force. If unemployment and low wages created difficulties, he was willing to make occasional concessions such as public assistance to working-class families with more than six children, on the charitable assumption that they could not have foreseen that they would be so prolific before they got married (p. 585). But, otherwise, it was up to the laws of the market place; which meant that, while an endless supply of workers conferred innumerable benefits upon industry, the miseries it entailed for those workers were entirely their own.

Despite the mendacity of Malthus' political morality, and the shadow it casts over our own time, his contribution to an understanding of some of the factors involved in demographic processes must inevitably be acknowledged. He was among the first, for example, to see the relationship between birth control and death control. Indeed, it is to Malthus that we owe the idea that human population growth is subject to systematic controls—however much he sought to replace them with the least effective or humane measure—and that, in the absence of one kind of control, others are certain to be employed. This idea, and some of its implications, is a central theme of the next chapter.

5. Population Regulation and the Development Process

A reluctance to face up to the existence of systemic death control as an optimizing strategy in preindustrial modes of reproduction not only distorts our perception of the classic demographic transition, but it continues to hamper our understanding of modes of reproduction in contemporary less-developed nations. This lack of understanding in turn provides the basis for population policies espoused by governments, churches, and other organizations which claim to be life-protecting but which are in fact life-destroying.

The primary mechanism of morbidity-mortality control currently employed by contemporary societies in which the transition to modern modes of population regulation remains incipient is probably the unequal rationing of foods within households. Two focii of nutritional risk can be identified: (a) rationing of mother's milk; and (b) rationing of other proteinaceous and calorific foods. The differentials involved may be either sex and age specific or sex and age neutral. A second prominent mechanism of mortality control is the rationing of medical care and of nonnutritional psycho-biological nurturance, again with and without age or sex specific targets.

Sex-Specific Mortality Control

As noted in chapter 3, the evidence for direct or indirect preferential female infanticide and pedicide in Europe is equivocal prior to recent times. However, by the nineteenth century every European country for which reliable data are available shows evidence of culturally mediated mortality control (Johansson 1984:472) either in the form of distorted sex ratios or actual mortality rates. This "excess female mortality" (EFM) was at its greatest in the early phase of industrialization and gradually disappeared with developed urbanization and industrialization and their associated demographic transitions. In England and Wales in 1833–1844, mild EFM was recorded for ages 10–14, 15–24, and 25–34. But since industrialization had begun eighty years before, one can assume that it had been more intense and involved more age cohorts earlier in the century. The best data are from Sweden. Males aged 10–14 have higher mortality rates from about 1751 to 1871; from about 1871 to 1921 females aged 10–14 have the higher rate; thereafter males lose their advantage. A similar sequence occurred for the age group 5–9 except that the deterioration in the relative death rate of females was postponed until about 1880.

Johansson interprets these shifts in EFM as responses to the relative value of female labor: under the traditional agricultural mode of production, Swedish girls and boys were equally valuable as farm workers; with urbanization and industrialization, agricultural production was commercialized, and males were preferred as wage laborers, causing families to devalue daughters relative to sons. Parents, however, were not permitted to remove unwanted daughters in infancy but "were pressured to keep them alive while stinting them of food, clothing, and other material resources" resulting in a form of "deferred infanticide" in late childhood (5 to 9 years) and early adolescence (10–14 years). Industrialization and urbanization however, "eventually minimized the differential value of sons and daughters to the family economy, first by providing more employment opportunities for young girls and second, in their later stages, by removing child labor altogether. Ultimately as standards of living rose well above subsistence, favoritism toward sons, if it continued at all, ceased to have mortality consequences" (p. 485).

While agreeing with the general thrust of this analysis, we are not convinced that the eighteenth- and early nineteenth-century mortality rate data accurately reflect the true extent of EFM, since there is clearly a strong possibility that death rates in the 0–1 age group were distorted by the failure even to record as births un-wanted female babies who were the victims of more direct forms of infanticide. As Johansson (p. 477) herself recognizes, the fact that female infants 0–1 years gained a steady mortality advantage during the nineteenth century, going against the trends for chil-dren and juveniles, suggests that this was the case. If so, the ap-pearance of EFM in the late nineteenth century may simply reflect the suppression of direct and indirect infanticide and a consequent shifting of the burden of death control to early childhood and adolescence, without any increase in the overall rate of EFM.

A cost/benefit interpretation of EFM is also strongly supported by data from colonial North America. Death rates for females aged 1–9 were sometimes more than twice as high as those for males. This corresponds to a sex-specific demand for indentured child labor on farms and the fact that "For every one white female im-ported, eight to ten males were indentured and transported" from England to the colonies (Johansson, p. 472). Although women's labor value was high under frontier homesteading conditions, they remained at a disadvantage with respect to heavy field labor and could not earn their keep as hired field hands. EFM disappeared in the United States during the nineteenth century as young women were increasingly drawn into the urban wage labor force as a prelude to marriage and as children of both sexes were in-creasingly confined to school.

EFM in South Asia

It should come as no surprise that high levels of EFM characterize many contemporary less developed countries. In South and East Asia, as we have seen, direct preferential female infanticide was widely practiced in India, China, and Japan. While direct forms of female infanticide have largely been suppressed, markedly skewed sex ratios, mortality rates and life expectancies provide evidence of continuing EFM in much of South Asia. Recent studies on dis-aggregated census data have shown that EFM cannot possibly be dismissed as an artifact of enumeration procedures and informant bias, as had long been argued.

Miller's (1981) study of district-level sex ratios in India marks a turning point in this regard. Miller found that more than one third of India's rural districts had sex ratios (for all ages combined) higher than the expected 105:100, ranging up to 118 in Rajasthan's Jaisalmer district. The important point, however, is that these EFM districts are not distributed randomly but occur in a solid block across India's north central and northwest states. In rural Uttar Pradesh in the north in 1970–1975, for example, female children aged 0–4 had mortality rates that were 30 percent above those for males (Jeffery et al. 1984a:1210). Longitudinal studies in the neighboring Punjab show female child mortality rates that are almost double the male rates. Female children who have elder sisters and no brothers seem to be especially at risk, since families generally want two sons and most would be satisfied if they had no daughters. To the east and south a totally different pattern prevails in which juvenile sex ratios are below 105, ranging down to a low of 90 in Koraput district, Orissa. And, in fact, the contrast may be greater because of underaging of unmarried, postmenarche girls in the north and northwest (by parents who wish to improve their marital prospects), which would lead to overcounting of premenarche girls and thus to underestimations of EFM in that group. Thus, as Miller observes, "nationwide sex ratio data, sample survey data on childhood mortality, longitudinal population records in several locations and ethnographic evidence all point to inequalities in mortality as the prime cause of unbalanced sex ratios" (1983:113).

As Bardhan has commented, however, it has not been unusual to attribute these regional contrasts in sex ratios to the lower status that females in the north and northwest have as a result of long Muslim rule (1982:1448). But, barring the possibility that there are significant religious differences in reporting the deaths of female infants, census data suggest that the male bias in sex ratios is due far more to regional than to religious factors. Thus, for all ages, the sex ratio in Uttar Pradesh in 1971 was 114 for Muslims, 112 for Hindus; in Kerala, it was 981 for Muslims and 972 for Hindus (p. 1448). The significance of a religious factor is further reduced by the differences reported for the two Muslim states of Pakistan and Bangladesh. A high EFM appears to be characteristic of Pakistan, just west of Punjab, while Bangladesh, contiguous with eastern India, has sex ratios that are intermediate between those of southern and northern India.

The explanation proposed by both Miller and Bardhan of such sex specific mortality differences accords with our cost/benefit approach in emphasizing the techno-economic aspects of production and their implications for the relative value of male and female labor—and, by extension, for the relative survivorship of children of one sex or the other. As Bardhan notes:

In all the states of East and South India (except Karnataka) the predominant crop is paddy which—unlike wheat and dry-region crops—tends to be relatively intensive in female labor. Transplantation of paddy is an exclusively female job in many paddy areas; besides, female labor plays a very important role in weeding, harvesting, threshing and various kinds of processing of paddy. By contrast, in dry cultivation and even in wheat cultivation under irrigation, the work involves more muscle power. (1982:1448)

Thus, a low EFM in southern India reflects the higher value of female labor in connection with the predominance of rice as the staple subsistence crop. In northern India and Pakistan, on the other hand, wheat is the staple and as plowing takes the place of transplanting as the critical operation, women's labor value is diminished. As a result, according to the 1961 census, in the southern state of Kerala about one woman in five was a worker (and 47 percent of female workers are cultivators or agricultural laborers), while in Uttar Pradesh one in twenty was a worker (with only 8 percent in the agricultural sector) (Segal 1965:140–141). The situation of Bangladesh is somewhat more complicated with its intermediate level of EFM. Rice is the staple, although it is being replaced in some areas by wheat. There is also a much higher degree of landlessness than in southern India, which forces males and females to compete for employment in agriculture where premium wages are awarded to males. As a result, unlike in southern India, men, not women, do most of the transplanting and harvesting of rice. Women's work, however, is not so devalued as in northern India and Pakistan because their involvement in wage work is greater. Hence, the intermediate level of EFM.

The higher benefits to be derived from rearing boys in northern India and Pakistan is also reflected in the prevailing custom of "husband purchases" (dowry), which contrasts with the forms of marital exchange that characterize southern India where the transfer of wealth between families is either symmetrical or favors the wife's family. The penalty of dowry is without any doubt an immediate source of familial anti-female sentiment which contributes to the general risk to female survivorship (Mukhopadhyay 1984:16–18). In India as a whole, for example, a long-term decline in female employment (which has sharply increased since 1960) may well underlie an apparent escalation in dowry levels which, in turn, has led to an intensification of tensions between intermarrying families and "dowry deaths," which "result from the conscious and deliberate murder of a girl by her in-laws as a result of the conflicts arising from dowry payments" (p. 18). In conformity with the principle of infrastructural determinism, we would like to emphasize that differences in marital exchanges, such as those between northern and southern India, should be seen in the long term as the *effects*, rather than the causes of modes of production and reproduction (Dyson and Moore 1983). (For a general explanation of the infrastructural causes of varieties of locality, descent, marriage, and family organization, see Harris 1985:250–288.)

Miller and Bardhan's interpretation receives additional support from an unexpected source: studies of the factors responsible for the age, sex, and species ratios of India's bovine population (Vaidyanathan et al. 1983). In the age group 3+ years, male cattle outnumber female cattle by as much as two to one and female mortality greatly exceeds male mortality rates in the same states where human male juveniles heavily outnumber human females. The correlation arises from the preference for male cattle as plow animals. A reversed situation occurs in the east and south where buffalo are used to puddle the paddy fields and where fewer plow animals are needed due to the small size of holdings. In the south, cattle are therefore raised primarily for their milk rather than their muscle power. Interestingly enough, the unwanted calves—males in the south, females in the north—are generally slowly starved to death by limiting their access to the cow's udder—a practice which prevents the cow from going dry in the absence of its calf while culling the unwanted sex. This withholding of mother's milk among bovines corresponds to a similar practice against humans (see below) as a mechanism of optimizing reproductive benefits. Hindus regard the deliberate killing of cattle as only slightly less of a crime than the deliberate killing of humans. Few farmers therefore openly admit that they are deliberately shortening the life of either calves or babies. This fact is relevant to the notion that population-regulating systems must necessarily involve conscious decision making. In the Indian case as in so many others, mortality control is not only achieved largely through unconscious decisions, but its very existence is vigorously denied. A similar denial is encountered among mothers in rural Bangladesh who appear not to be aware of the fact that they provide their female children with fewer calories and proteins than their male children (Chen, Huq, and Souza 1981:67).

Means of Achieving EFM: Nutritional Controls

In Ecuador, nine out of ten highland provinces show EFM among children 1–5 years of age. Among 1,000 children one year old, an average of 3.97 more girls than boys died; at two years the difference was 5.32 per thousand. McKee (1984) has found a statistically significant correlation between these indices of EFM and the average age of weaning: girls are weaned on the average at 10.93 months; boys on the average 20.27 months. The ideological justification for this difference is that mothers are said to transmit qualities of sexuality and aggression to infants via nursing; girls who are nursed as long as boys are thought to become hypersexual, aggressive, and rebellious—traits that are to be encouraged among males but suppressed among females.

Males are also favored with more mother's milk in Peru, Taiwan, Ireland, Bangladesh, India, Guatemala, Jordan, Liberia, and Nepal. Ideological justifications vary. In rural Taiwan, for example, earlier weaning for girls is used to lead to earlier menopause, which brings welcome relief from the burden of childbearing. In Ireland, boys are said to need to be nursed longer in order to fill them with the "milk of human kindness" so that they will take care of their aged parents. Despite such varied rationales, however, there is a common theme: earlier weaning is good for girls;

late weaning is good for boys (McKee 1984). A link with childhood EFM has not been demonstrated in all of these cases—not surprisingly, since nutritional deficiency is rarely registered as a basic or associated cause of death in most developing countries (Victoria and Vaughan 1985:257). Nonetheless, it can reasonably be assumed that such a bias would tend to favor male infant survivorship, in light of the many recognized merits of breast feeding. As Berg notes:

Breast milk is healthful; it meets most of the matabolic needs of the baby; it contributes to good growth; it is clean, thus lowering the risk of intestinal illness and general infection. Furthermore, it provides a host of protective factors. Breast-fed babies are more resistant to malaria and to infection caused by bacteria or viruses (including the polio virus). And they are less likely to suffer from rickets and iron-deficiency anemia (1973:97).

Favored treatment of boys during nursing is only one part of a continuing widespread disparity in the quality and quantity of male and female diets. In many less developed countries these disparities begin in infancy and persist through adolescence and adulthood, and are implicated in the elevated mortality rates frequently found among women of childbearing age.

Maher's research among Berber-speakers of the Middle Atlas region of North Africa illustrates how dietary inequalities are incorporated into everyday life. Although women perform much of the agricultural work and many also spin wool, weave carpets, and otherwise contribute to the household economy financially in addition to routine domestic activities, the products of their labor are essentially controlled by their husbands. Reflecting this prevailing male privilege outside the home, men similarly command priority in regard to food consumption, especially in circumstances where subsistence is problematical (Maher 1981:76–80). Maher reports:

Men eat before women and consider prized food items such as meat to be their prerogative. Women and children learn to refuse meat, and on formal occasions, to eat what the men leave. . . . The standard meal in the hamlets is composed of bread which is dropped in a vegetable relish, sometimes garnished with a small chunk of meat which is shared among all present. People bless themselves before and after eating, and refrain from talking and laughing. . . . Women carry this modesty to extremes. If they are guests, they will often swear that they have eaten already. And if they are not that they are not hungry. One woman used to assure her fellow diners that she preferred bones to meat. Men, on the other hand, are supposed to be exempt from facing scarcity which is shared out among women and children. (pp. 80–81)

In much of India as well, because women tend to work for less than men or are unwaged and thus control little income, their lower status within the home frequently translates into a subordinate claim to quality foods. Thus, within low-income rural households, one finds a continuum of dietary privilege, with females (in particular the wife) at the bottom. According to Katona-Apte:

At meals, the wife feeds her husband first, then the children, boys before girls; only then does she eat. Often she eats separately with her daughters. If available, the major portions of such nourishing foods as meat, fish, egg, or milk, and sweets, are served to the males, because it is believed that they need it for strength or growth, and often not much is left over for the females. It is not unusual to find households where the women are vegetarians, but the males are not (1975:45).

Similar biased patterns of eating are found in a considerable variety of culturally distinctive settings. They probably gave males a nutritional advantage in nineteenth century Sweden (Johansson 1984:483). The same is true for working-class families in nineteenth-century England. As Rowntree and Kendall observed of one Berkshire family, consisting of a wife, husband, and nine children (one of whom, a boy, was old enough to work): "The wife manages to get a piece of meat for the two breadwinners every day, or nearly every day. Like many another, she apportions out the meat at the beginning of the week, and keeps back so much 'to look at.' It is said in this neighborhood of the women and children, 'they eat the potatoes and look at the meat'" (1913:315).

A similar bias occurs in much of rural Latin America, where women serve and males eat first. The extent to which such patterns, themselves widely reported, actually result in significant differences in health or mortality has seldom been documented, however.

A link between sex-biased nutritional intake and EFM has been demonstrated for rural Bangladesh, however, by the Matlab Food and Nutrition Study (Chen, Huq, and Souza 1981). In the study population, EFM was recorded for ages 1–11 months, 1–4 years, 5–14 years, and 15–44 years, with the highest discrepancy during ages 1–4 years when the female death rate was 45 percent higher than the male death rate (per 1,000 population). Male intake of calories for all ages was 20 percent higher than female intake; and protein intake was 21 percent higher. When these figures are adjusted for weight as well as for activity levels, however, even though the extra demands of pregnancy and lactation are included, the discrepancy is greatly reduced except for ages 0–4 years. The basic reason for this is that, as they grow older, women weigh less and less relative to men—averaging 5 kg less during adulthood (p. 61). On the other hand, since an unknown portion of this weight difference is itself a result of greater undernutrition for women, it is difficult to decide the extent to which weight differences should in fact be used to adjust downward the difference in nutritional intake between males and females (p. 63).

A further complication is that the elevated female mortality during childhood selects for individuals who are able to survive on marginally adequate diets and who may be genetically predisposed to resist the deleterious effects of stunted growth. There is growing recognition that chronically malnourished populations may be culturally and biologically selected for their ability to survive on energy rations that are 20 to 30 percent below what is regarded as normal for well nourished communities (Prentice 1984:24). This selection would be extremely powerful "particularly in the case of child-bearing women" (p. 23).

Pregnancy, Perinatal, and Lactation Diets

What is especially noteworthy about the systematic and cross-culturally persistent deprivation of high quality animal foods to which females are subjected is the fact that many belief systems urge similar or even more intense dietary deprivations during pregnancy and lactation (Sharma 1955; Trant 1954; Wellin 1955; Rosenberg 1980; Ferro-Luzzi 1980; Wilson 1980).

Several alternative interpretations of these pregnancy and lactation taboos are possible, since virtually no reliable studies of before-and-after changes in the actual diet of pregnant and lactating women have been carried out. Thus, although maternal nutritional status is being increasingly recognized as an important factor in perinatal outcome, affecting birth-weight and mortality (Durward 1984), no one really knows how much such taboos in fact result in a less adequate diet than is "normal" for women who are not pregnant or breast-feeding; hence, it is practically impossible to say to what extent they may heighten health risks for mother or newborn.

For many preindustrial and developing societies, however, it is not too difficult to understand why the pressures of scarcity might induce curtailments of food intake wherever practicable. Thus, though objectively pregnancy and lactation elevate a woman's metabolic requirements, it is commonly the case that they are perceived as a time of diminished needs, particularly where there is a reduction in economic activity:

We can speculate that a chronic shortage of food forces people to make choices as to who is to get which foods and how much of them. In India, this choice favors those who are expending visible physical energy. Rationalization for not feeding women after delivery is that she is not expending energy and so would not be able to digest the food. The same is true while she is lactating. Since she is not visibly contributing any labor, she may be viewed as an economic burden on the family. (Katona-Apte 1975:47)

In fact, of course, women may continue to be physically active into late pregnancy and during lactation, but some reduction in economic productivity is to be expected during the perinatal period. One possible explanation for the apparent ability of nutritionally deprived women to bear and nurse normal children (see above) is that their activity levels are reduced in ways which have hitherto escaped measurement (Beaton 1984:399).

It should not be forgotten, however, that female physiology is well adapted for nurturing a fetus or breast-feeding a child at its own expense (Wishik and Stern 1975). Thus, restrictions on a woman's diet might not necessarily jeopardize the health of her new offspring while, at the same time, they might also coexist with her continued productivity, though often at her physical expense. This represents a dilemma that women have frequently faced in preindustrial (and, indeed, in industrial) societies for precisely the reason that they represent the fulcrum upon which the reproductive and productive demands of their families are precariously balanced. Confronted by the problem of weighing their own additional needs against the ongoing needs of their family, pregnant and lactating women must often make arduous choices, including acquiescence to dietary beliefs that curtail their personal consumption. Whether they make those decisions, or they are imposed upon them, the result may be, as Maher (1981:81) notes in her study of Berber-speaking women in North Africa, that "Lactating mothers in the hamlets are usually skeletal and clearly supply the needs of the nursing child from their own strength and not from an increased intake of food or rest."

It is clear that in such deprived economies, extra rations during pregnancy or lactation may be regarded as a "luxury" which women cannot hope to enjoy without adversely affecting the diets of their economically active spouses and older children. That women are often both economically productive as well as pregnant (Shorter 1982:52–53) may seem to be disregarded; but, it precisely expresses the nature of preindustrial male-dominated sexual hierarchies.

It must obviously be considered that a major effect of these taboos may be to prevent impoverished pregnant and lactating women and their families from assuming the costs of the extra-nutritional demands of childbearing—costs which are often taken for granted in more affluent populations, but can be quite onerous for families on a tenuous or marginal income. Even in England today, recent evidence suggests that "the cost of an adequate diet for an expectant mother may be beyond the means of families dependent on benefits or on low wages" (Durwood 1984:14). The cumulative economic saving that results from dietary restrictions may be very considerable in societies which lack efficient contraception. This, in fact, may have become increasingly so in recent years in many countries where, as we discuss below, development has actually deepened poverty in many sectors, the prices of staple foods have risen (often dramatically), real wages have fallen considerably, and the incidence of undernourishment or malnutrition has frequently increased (Navarro 1982:186; Rupesinghe 1985:253, 255–256).

The impact that such deprivation may have on women compels us to emphasize that, in estimating the reproductive potential of contemporary human populations, we must not only consider the extent to which production can be intensified, but the degree to which the human body—in this case, the female—can be exploited in the process. This is far from being an exclusively economic consideration, for it also involves, as we have suggested, questions of human physiology and the limits of its adaptibility. We must keep in mind that childbearing and childrearing are often promoted at the expense of women themselves, by processes of physical exploitation predicated on the specifically female role in the reproduction of labor (De Ste. Croix 1981:45, 99–100).

Another important point to consider in this regard is that, if Barbara Harrell (1981) is correct in her view that lactation or pregnancy tends to be the "norm" for postmenarche, premenopausal women in preindustrial societies, then the "normal" diet is, in fact, the more restricted one defined by various taboos and practices (or, at best, one that is not augmented at a time of elevated need), punctuated by occasional, brief periods of less curtailed diets which would tend to have little overall effect on women's nutritional status. To take a cynical view, the implication is that adult women could look forward to nutritional parity with men only in the unlikely event that they manage not to become pregnant.

We should bear in mind, however, that women are not passive victims of culturally mediated deprivation. As we discussed in an earlier chapter, it should not be presumed that they never regard the benefits of a new child as outweighed by the costs which are imposed on them. This may be reflected in the quality of nurturance and patterns of neglect, and in turn affect the incidence of infant and child mortality, as we shall see in the following section.

Medical Selective Neglect

Contemporary preindustrial mortality regulating practices include other forms of neglect or abuse which interact with nutritional rationing and which may or may not be directed at one sex more than the other. Such measures include the rationing of medical care, and material and psychological support. For example, a large part of EFM in Sweden was associated with different susceptibility to and differences in the treatment of tuberculosis. Boys were not only better able to resist infection because of their superior nutritional status but they were favored during the extended course of treatment which included withdrawal from work, rest, high protein diets, and warm, clean clothing (Johansson 1984). In northern India, midwives are paid more for delivering boys than girls, especially if the boy is the firstborn son of a wealthy family. Midwives who deliver girls are often scolded and criticized (Jeffery, Jeffery and Lyon 1984a:1209; Jeffery, Jeffery and Lyon 1984b:238). Presumably the quality of their care reflects the differences in fees.

The Matlab Food and Nutrition Study demonstrated a link not only between sex-biased nutritional intake and EFM, but between investment in medical care for children and EFM. Parents in the study population were urged to bring children suffering from diarrhea (a leading cause of childhood mortality) to the free clinic maintained for this purpose. Independent field data showed that the male rate of diarrhea attacks was 10 percent higher than the female rate, but males were brought to the clinic 66 percent more often than females. As we have seen, the female childhood mortality rate was 45 percent above the male rate. Not only was the Matlab clinic free, but free transportation for guardian and child was also furnished. Yet this did not eliminate costs associated with the guardian's and child's foregone labor (Chen, Huq, and Souza 1981:64–65).

A similar sex-based bias in the use of health care seems to occur in India where delay in seeking medical treatment may be a major reason that the mortality rate from the twenty leading killer diseases is consistently higher for female children in the age group 0–4 than for males (Mukhopadhyay 1984:27). Studies by the National Institute of Nutrition also suggest that, "Whilst the incidence of diseases due to malnutrition is higher among females, hospital admission and treatment for these diseases is much higher for males" (p. 27).

Sex-Neutral Mortality Control and "Ethno-Eugenics"

Scrimshaw reports that Ecuadorean mothers who are burdened with more children than they can cope with ignore the instructions of health workers to boil the water in infant formulas and reappear at the same clinic with infants suffering from acute diarrhea, after each of their subsequent pregnancies (1978).

Scheper-Hughes (1984) attributes much of infant and child mortality patterns among the poor in northeast Brazil to sex-neutral practices, which she identifies as "ethno-eugenics." Her sample of 72 women in a hillside shantytown of rural migrants reported a total of 686 pregnancies, an average of 9.5 per woman. Of these, 85 were terminated by induced or spontaneous abortions, and there were 16 stillbirths. Out of 588 live births, 251 died between ages 0–5, an average of 3.5 per woman. These deaths were concentrated at the beginning and end of the women's reproductive histories, a pattern which Scheper-Hughes attributes to the inexperience of mothers with their firstborn and to their economic, physical and psychological inability to cope with the needs of the last born. (A more likely explanation for the higher mortality of the firstborn is that they were conceived while their mothers were still in their teens and were still growing, increasing the likelihood that their babies would be underweight—Frisancho, Matos and Flegel 1983). Some women indicated the deceased last-born had been unwanted and that "it was a blessing that God decided to take them in their infancy" (Scheper-Hughes 1984:539).

More important than birth order in determining a mother's tendency to invest in or distance herself from a particular infant was the mother's perception of the child's innate constitution and temperament as it relates to "readiness or fitness for life." Mothers expressed a preference for "quick, sharp, active, verbal, and developmentally precocious children." Children with the opposite traits were subject to "medical selective neglect" and "ethno-eugenics." Mothers speak of children who "'wanted to die,' whose will and drive toward life was not sufficiently strong or developed." The weak child succumbs to one of the crises of childhood; infections of the umbilical cord; infant diarrhea, or teething.

Some pediatric diseases are regarded as incurable; but their diagnostic symptoms are so broad that almost any childhood disorder can be interpreted as a harbinger of death: fits and convulsions; lethargy and passivity; retarded verbal or motor function; a ghost-like or animal-like appearance. Writes Scheper-Hughes: "At this stage of the research I do not know what exactly prompts a folk diagnosis of this kind, but I suspect that its flexibility allows mothers a great deal of latitude in deciding which of their children are not favored for survival as 'normal' children" (1984:541).

When a child marked with one of these fatal diseases dies, mothers do not display grief. They say there was no remedy, that even if you treat the disease, the child "will never be right," that such children "wouldn't be able to defend themselves in life," that it is "best to leave them to die," and that no one wants to take care of such offspring. It should be noted that lack of grief over the death of infants in rural and poverty class Latin America is excused if not encouraged by the widespread Catholic folk belief that such infants are not affected by original sin and rise immediately to heaven to become "little angels" (Toor 1947:161; Hutchinson 1957:145; Scheper-Hughes 1984:540).

Recognition that parents are often obliged by circumstances to invest in only those infants and children who are most likely to be able to endure life's hardships may help to clarify certain practices which appear to be superficially incompatible with optimizing behavior. In India, for example, women consider dietary restrictions during gestation not only as a means of ensuring a small baby and hence an easier delivery, but, contrary to established medical knowledge, they also insist that high birth-weight babies are weaker than low birth-weight babies (Nichter and Nichter 1983). There is some evidence that under conditions of extreme poverty the Indian mother's preference for small babies may be eugenically correct. If low birth-weight infants survive the increased risk of mortality which their reduced size imposes, smaller body size may enhance their long-term survival within an endemically undernourished population (Frisancho et al. 1973). Part of their success may be attributable to the fact that small children eat less and hence cost less; they are therefore fed better relative to their larger siblings. One can speculate further that the smaller body type found in India and in other less developed nations results from generations of cultural selection for the genotypes of economical children as well as from the ongoing necessity of getting along on impoverished diets (Prentice 1984).

Some words of caution about the significance of medical selective neglect and ethno-eugenics would seem appropriate. We would like to stress once again that optimizing is not the same as optimal. As Scheper-Hughes points out, the folk symptomology of fatal pediatric disease in Brazil corresponds to the symptoms of "malnutrition and parasitic infections interacting with physical and psychological neglect." To the extent that mothers practice medical selective neglect and ethno-eugenics, they are reacting to life-threatening conditions which are not of their own making: shortage of food, contaminated water supplies, unchecked infectious diseases, lack of day care for children of working mothers, absence of affordable medical care, and the other stigmas and penalties of extreme poverty. While recognizing the fact that Brazilian mothers are systematically "culling" (our word) their unwanted children and that part of the appallingly high rate of mortality is a result of the rationing of infant and child care, we must not fall into the trap of blaming the victims. These population-regulating practices are, in Scheper-Hughes' words, "indignities and inhumanities forced upon poor . . . women who must at times make choices and decisions that no woman and mother should have to make" (1984:541).

Development and Changing Costs of Children

It is clear that the people of less-developed countries possess means adequate for lowering their rate of population increase through adjustments in fertility-mortality rates which need not depend on modern contraceptive technology. The existence of EFM and of ethno-eugenic practices demonstrate the extremes to which they are already involved in optimizing their material interests precisely by their refusal to rear children who have certain "undesirable" characteristics. One can only conclude that if they do not rear even fewer children it is because to do so under the conditions imposed by their current mode of production would be against their material interests.

What the conditions in question are has already been suggested in our discussion of the demographic history of England, Ireland, and Java. As we have seen, there is a phase in the commercialization and intensification of agriculture in conjunction with industrial and urban growth during which the value of children as a source of labor and family income is enhanced. As Mamdani (1973) was among the first to demonstrate, more children and larger households in much of the less-developed world means a higher, not a lower standard of living in the short run. In resisting family planning programs, Punjab villagers explained: "Why pay 2,500 rupees for an extra hand? Why not have a son?" (1973:77).

A number of attempts have been made to measure the economic value of children in peasant communities. White (1976) has shown for contemporary rural Java that boys of 12–14 years contribute 33 hours of economically valuable work per week and girls aged 9–11 about 38 hours. Altogether, children contribute about half of all work performed by household members. Much household labor involves handicrafts, petty trade, and processing of various foods for sale. Income from these activities, while extremely low per hour, varies directly with labor input. Similar findings are reported for Nepal (Nag et al. 1978).

Costs are more difficult to measure, but White shows that children themselves do most of the work needed to rear and maintain their siblings, freeing mothers for income-producing tasks. In any event, larger households are more efficient income-producing units in rural Java because a smaller proportion of total labor time is required for maintenance. Given these conditions, White finds that the prevailing strategy of reproduction which involves about five births and four surviving children per woman (achieved through relatively late marriage, and birth spacing of about three years) "seems an entirely appropriate response" (1982:605). It is nonetheless a mode of reproduction that yields an alarming 2 percent per annum increase in Java's population.

Cain has quantified both benefits and costs for male children in the Bangladesh village of Char Gopalpur: "Male children become net producers at the latest by the age of 12. Furthermore, male children work long enough hours at high enough rates of productivity to compensate for consumption during their earlier periods of dependence by the age of 15. Therefore, in general . . . parents . . . realize a net economic return on male children for the period when they are subordinate members of the parental household" (1977:225).

To judge from the European experience, however, the value of child labor is unlikely to remain high as the development process unfolds. With the expansion of urban, industrial, technical, and white-collar employment opportunities, the net return from child rearing can be increased by investment in fewer but better educated offspring. Indeed, there is considerable evidence that the value of child labor has been decreasing in villages which have moved furthest in the development process. Gupta (1978), for example, found that in Rampur village close to New Delhi, fertility declined as wage opportunities increased outside of the village. Tractors, tube wells and pumps reduced the demand for child labor. In addition, parents wanted their children to get more education to prepare for higher quality jobs in New Delhi. In a similar situation in Sri Lanka (Tilakaratne 1978), employers of wage labor now prefer adult males rather than children who may only be able to work part time as a result of attending school. More white collar jobs are available for which children are unsuited because they have not achieved the required levels of literacy and mathematical skills. Even families headed by manual workers desire to have children participate in white-collar high status jobs and to give more schooling to them. Marriage to an educated and well-employed man or woman has become the ideal and this can be done only by postponing marriage which in turn depresses fertility.

Caldwell and his colleagues traced fertility declines in nine Indian villages located near the city of Bangalore to changes in the costs and benefits of rearing children. Three factors accounted for the trend against child labor: land holdings had become fragmented and too small to absorb labor of children in agriculture; new nonfarm employment opportunities requiring arithmetic skills and literacy had opened up; educational facilities had been introduced or improved within the village (Caldwell et al. 1983).

The importance of distinguishing earlier from later phases of the shift from agricultural to industrial, commercial, and urban modes of production is shown by Nag and Kak's (1984) restudy of Mamdani's village of Manupur in the Punjab. Nag and Kak report a sharp increase in the number of couples practicing contraception and a sharp reduction in the number of sons regarded as desirable. In the ten years between Mamdami's research and the restudy, intensification of the region's mode of production has altered the demand for child labor. Shortening or elimination of fallow has led to the disappearance of grazing land within the village, and boys can no longer make themselves useful tending cattle. Disappearance of cattle and increased reliance on chemical fuels and fertilizer has also done away with the childhood task of collecting dung cakes and with the introduction of herbicides, children are no longer needed for weeding. Furthermore, there has been a substantial rise in the proportion of Manupur workers employed in industrial, commercial, and government sectors. Further mechanization of farm operations, expanded use of credit, and the need to keep books has made Manupur parents consciously concerned to expand their children's educational horizons. Secondary school enrollment has increased from 63 percent to 81 percent for boys and from 29 to 63 percent for girls. Parents now want at least one son to have a white-collar job so that the family will not be entirely dependent on agriculture; many parents want both sons and daughters to attend college.

To sum up: the demographic transition from high fertility to low fertility modes of reproduction depends in general on the emergence of new material conditions that create adverse economic balances for large families. The expansion of bureaucratic, commercial, and technical employment opportunities rapidly shifts the emphasis from numbers to quality. One poor farmer's child, freed from household chores and proto-industrial petty commodity production, kept in school, and pushed or pulled into becoming a doctor, bureaucrat, truck owner, businessman, or teacher can provide a greater return flow to parents (and siblings) than five children who stay home and do menial work. Of course, only a small percent of children rise to such exalted heights, but the more schooling they have, the better their chances, the higher their income. As the amount of child labor available to the household decreases, the costs of child rearing fall more heavily on mothers; and these costs in turn increase if pregnancy and childcare prevent women from participating in wage labor employment outside the home and village. Prolonged education for both sexes also means delayed marriage for both sexes and delayed marriage is strongly correlated with reduced fertility (Nag 1983a:64). This impulse toward lower fertility gains added momentum if an optimized number of children can be achieved at lower levels of fetal, infant, and child wastage. With lowered survivorship optimums, resources can be concentrated on providing improved nutrition, health care, and nurturance. (Government provision of schools, roads, clinics, and hospitals is obviously needed if any of this is to occur.)

The Indian situation, from which many of our examples have been drawn, is instructive in a cautionary way, however, for it also shows that new economic opportunities and/or improvements in welfare services do not necessarily constitute a transformation of the prevailing mode of production. The southwestern state of Kerala effectively demonstrates that, while improvements in healthcare and education may substantially modify the material conditions in which children are born and reared and thus help to effect a significant modification in behavioral strategies associated with family size, child care, and treatment of women, they are not always associated with positive *economic* trends. Thus, Kerala, one of the poorest, least industrialized, and worst nourished states in India (Centre for Development Studies 1975), is perhaps the most "progressive" demographically with one of the lowest birthrates and the lowest death rate (Mukhopadhyay 1984:26). The explanation for this contradiction lies in the fact that advances in social services were well within the scope of the resources available to the state government. On the other hand, the kind of development which could radically transform the Kerala economy, traditionally based on extractive industries and backward agriculture, would have required substantial capital investment and therefore have depended on national policy initiatives. That these have not been forthcoming underscores the fact that not all instances of underdevelopment are solely the product of exogenous capitalist interests.

The Conditions of Demographic Change

We cannot fail to note that our analysis of the conditions under-lying the demographic transition finds a curious echo in a portion of the amended official Third World population policy of the United States government, as presented to the United Nations International Conference on Population in Mexico City in 1984. In the words of the head of the U.S. delegation, James Buckley:

So long as the great majority of couples see an economic advantage in having a large number of children, they will tend to have them. This desire is prevalent in the least developed countries where children begin to con-tribute to family income at an early age, and are the main source of sup-port for parents too old to work. Once a society achieves a certain level of real economic development, however, the incentives to childbearing will change—especially where women have achieved higher education and broader economic opportunities, and are able to obtain their rightful place in society. (1984:679)

While these few remarks properly focus on the material basis for the preference for large families, subsequent sections of the U.S. statement reveal a notable failure to acknowledge the historical and structural constraints that make it so difficult for developing countries to achieve the kind of economic development which would change "the incentives to childbearing." This is not sur-prising, however, in the light of U.S. foreign policy interests and the commitment of the government and business community to a particular concept of development which is favorable to U.S. in-vestment.

Many Third World countries recognize the need to take more aggressive measures to alter the costs and benefits of reproduction. In the short run, efforts have been varied. Just as many developed nations that are presently concerned about falling fertility rates (Wattenberg and Zinsmeister 1986) offer bonuses, tax benefits, ma-ternity leaves, and other inducements for people to reproduce, similar rewards or disincentives have been implemented to en-courage them not to have children. In Egypt, for example, "the working woman is deprived by law of her maternity benefits after the third child, and more and more voices have been raised re-cently wanting also to deprive her of other rights, such as promotion, periodic salary increase, etc., if she gives birth to more than two children" (El Saadawi 1980:64). In China in recent years, couples have been rewarded for having fewer than two children (IPPF 1984:16–17).

We must emphasize, however, that while it cannot be expected that governments must or will necessarily stand idly by, allowing population growth to eat up production gains while awaiting the outcome of long-term development (Holden 1984; Finkle and Crane 1985), we do not regard such measures as a substitute for substantive economic change. In the end, the principle of infrastructural determinism predicts that the effect of such incentives ("politics in command") can be sustained only to the extent that development does take place.

It is in this respect that the U.S. position, predicated on its own geopolitical interests, disregards an essential question in the general issue of development. The reproductive imperatives in most Third World countries today are rooted in a colonial inheritance, which has often been perpetuated in their present neocolonial status. To ignore this is to distort one's perspective on the kind of economic change that such countries require.

In a survey of the economic conditions associated with demographic growth, for example, the economist Julian Simon noted that India first experienced sustained population growth after 1600. Yet, "Agricultural methods continued the same despite population pressure. . . . India's agricultural techniques failed to change *despite* the fact that more productive (per unit of land) techniques were known. . . . But the Indian farmers either did not adopt the more intensive techniques or practiced them badly" (1977:208). He observed that "this is quite at variance with the European experience, where techniques changed rapidly during the last four centuries" (p. 208). This critique of the failure of Indian agriculture to advance, even in the face of population growth, a critique which strongly echoes nineteenth-century English criticism of the Irish, studiously avoids any mention of British colonial rule or the constraints it imposed on the rural Indian economy (see chapter 4). As a consequence, we are left with a contrast between Indian laziness and Europe's apparent spirit of enterprise. The implication of such historical assessments is that what Third World countries require to be able to feed their people is to emulate the European model of development.

Most Third World countries, like India, have a colonial inheritance of highly rigid, undiversified export-oriented economies. Caught between fluctuating or declining prices for their exports of cash crops or raw materials—jute, cacao, tin, etc.—and escalating prices for the manufactured goods they import from industrialized nations (Crittenden 1981), the less-developed countries have faced burgeoning trade deficits which have impelled them to seek loans from institutions such as the World Bank and the International Monetary Fund. Dominated by the United States, which is one of their leading sources of capital, the World Bank and the IMF have typically attached stringent terms to such loans, aimed at creating an economic climate that encourages foreign capitalist investment and export industries (Hayter and Watson 1985; Feder 1983). These terms usually include cuts in public sector spending, wage controls, and the curtailment of state subsidies of staple foods—all of which eventually have translated into a loss of purchasing power among the poor and often, as a result, into a rise in infant and child mortality.

That is not to say that there has not been "development." In much of Latin America, for example, the World Bank has stimulated cattle production to create a beef export industry. In this, it has been spectacularly successful; but as a result domestic beef consumption has fallen sharply throughout the region. Thus, in Guatemala, "beef production nearly doubled from 1960 to 1972, yet domestic per capita consumption of beef fell by approximately 20 percent during the same period" (Pelto and Pelto 1983:325). In many countries, moreover, the expansion of pasture has critically reduced the acreage devoted to subsistence crops (p. 325), further jeopardizing local diets.

Brazil and Mexico have been among the most preeminent examples of capitalist development in developing countries. Brazil during the 1960s underwent what was commonly referred to as a "miracle," with economic growth averaging 6 percent annually. Characteristically this was built upon incentives to capital investment coupled with a deteriorating level of wages among the working class which have been causally linked to a rise in urban infant mortality (Wood 1982:215–216). Substantial cuts also were made in state health expenditures and services of precisely the kind we have suggested favor infant survivorship—paralleling the experience in most countries where the World Bank and the IMF have imposed their strictures (Rupesinghe 1985). The overall result of the "Brazilian miracle" can be summarized by saying that, where in 1960 the poorest 10 percent of the population received 1.17 percent of national income, by 1970 this had been reduced to 1.11 percent; while, during the same period, the upper 5 percent's share rose from 27.69 to 34.86 percent (Malloy and Borzutzky 1982:86).

The story was much the same in Mexico. During the 1960s and 1970s, GNP rose an average of 6.2 percent per year and the average per capita income grew at 2.9 percent annually. But, as in Brazil and so many other developing countries, income distribution worsened (p. 86). An anthropometric and nutritional survey conducted in a district of tropical Mexico in 1958, just prior to inauguration of an extensive agricultural development program, and again in 1971, found that, although *average* food intake had risen significantly, the overall increase was biased in favor of the higher income group. In contrast, about 30 percent of the population, the poorest peasants, showed no improvement in dietary intake or incidence of malnutrition. (A decrease in infant and child mortality seemed likely therefore to be largely attributable to health improvements, such as malaria eradication and the establishment of a health center, rather than to agricultural development) (Hernandez et al. 1974).

The accumulated heritage of such schemes is that today, Brazil and Mexico are among the most heavily indebted nations in the world and poverty is more deeply entrenched than ever before. The scale of their debts, and those of dozens of other countries ranging from Peru to Sri Lanka, ensures that interest payments consume the bulk of their export earnings, depleting the capital resources that are ultimately required to enhance the living conditions of the majority of their people (Mass 1976:139–140).

By 1973, the president of the World Bank, Robert McNamara, admitted that "The data suggest that the decade of rapid growth [the 1960s] has been accompanied by greater maldistribution of income in many developing countries. . . . Policies aimed primarily at accelerating economic growth in most developing countries have benefited mainly the upper 40% of the population" (quoted in Feder 1983:652). By 1979, McNamara confessed that no one really knew how to solve the problem of massive poverty and unemployment in the Third World (p. 656). But, he and others at the World Bank, IMF, and in Washington did know that, whatever the solution might be, from their point of view it could not include redistribution of wealth and income on a significant scale.

Nonetheless, current World Bank policy supports "family planning" (Bernstein 1984:E3). In contrast, the U.S. government position on population is essentially what we might describe as "free market demographics." Thus, at Mexico City, "it urged a 'market economy' system on governments, as a means of slowing population growth" (IPPF 1984:6). By this it means the operation of economies unfettered by controls or planning that would inhibit capital investment and free enterprise. In the end, it is argued, this will permit development, which in turn will curb fertility. As we have seen, however, this is precisely a kind of development which time and again has tended to intensify the dilemma faced by most Third World countries.

It is hard, under such circumstances, to give credence to U.S. concern for the emergence of new fertility regimes in the Third World. Indeed, the demonstrated relationship between U.S.-style development and intensification of poverty, decline in income and food purchasing power, and even increases in infant mortality, is probably not unfavorable to corporate and transnational financial interests, since such trends can be highly conducive to maximizing profits. As Navarro notes, with respect to diminished food consumption: "First, it means cheaper 'nontraditional industrial exports' (i.e., the cost of maintenance of labor power is lower); second, the reduction in internal food consumption allows a reallocation of land use patterns, thereby favoring the parallel consolidation of agricultural and agro-industrial export crops. Underconsumption in food and undernourishment constitute the necessary ingredients for the development of a commercial export-oriented agriculture" (1982:186).

The United States, however, has not been content to let the

matter rest with the abandonment of the poor to the exigencies of the "free market." Like Malthus, it has actively campaigned against forms of fertility control, thus giving support to the view that it favors free enterprise as much in the domain of reproduction as in that of production. Among other things, the Reagan administration has categorically rejected support for the use of medical abortions as a means of reducing the number of unwanted children in less-developed countries. Thus, it was proclaimed at Mexico City:

First, where U.S. funds are contributed to nations which support abortion with other funds, the U.S. contribution will be placed into segregated accounts which cannot be used for abortion; second, the U.S. will no longer contribute to separate nongovernmental organizations which perform or actively promote abortion as a method of family planning in other nations and third, before the U.S. will contribute funds to the United Nations Fund for Population Activities, it will first require concrete assurances that the UNFPA is not engaged in, and does not provide funding for, abortion or coercive family planning programs. Should such assurances not be possible, and in order to maintain the level of its overall contribution to the international effort, the United States will redirect the amount of its intended contribution to other, non-UNFPA family planning programs. (Buckley 1984:678)

In fact, since that statement, the United States has withdrawn support not only from UNFPA but from the International Planned Parenthood Federation (IPPF) as well, although the merest fraction of the IPPF budget is concerned with abortion, and then only in terms of "responding to modest requests from some 10 or 12 of its 119 member Family Planning Associations who want help in this respect" (IPPF 1984:7). The obvious implication is that the U.S. government has a broader opposition to fertility control than is indicated by its specific attack on abortion. The latter, however, epitomizes its ideological position and its implications.

That there is any humanitarian content to the threats posed in this statement can scarcely be credited by anyone familiar with the enormous waste of infant, child, and female lives incurred throughout the less-developed world wherever the demographic transition is still only incipient. While no one would deny that contraception is less wasteful than medical abortion, it would seem equally difficult to deny that medical abortion is less wasteful than infanticide or the prolonged abuse and neglect of ethno-eugenic practice. While it is difficult to provide empirical proof that the suppression of feticide translates into augmented levels of direct and indirect infanticide and pedicide, such a consequence is logically entailed in the theory—endorsed by the U.S. delegation—that "economic advantage" regulates fertility.

U.S. policy avoids the force of this logic only by separating the abstraction of "having" children from the reality of *rearing* children. As we have seen, the notion that human life begins at conception, at birth, or in infancy are all equally fallacious from a biosocial point of view. The rearing of a new human being is a continuous process which begins in sexual behavior before conception and which continues long after birth in the nurturant behavior of those upon whom each new individual depends. In pursuit of the "economic advantage" that determines whether a new individual will be reared, failure to interrupt the process at an earlier point means that it will be interrupted at a later point. Thus, under conditions which prevail throughout much of the world today, failure to prevent conception will tend to be followed by indirect or direct feticide; and failure to prevent birth will tend to be followed by direct or indirect pedicide. If economic advantage determines fertility, then to be pro-life to the fetus is to be pro-death for the infant or child (not to mention the plight of the mother whose life is risked by illegal or incompetent techniques).

While we hold that family planning programs which foster the knowledge and practice of modern contraceptive techniques will not be effective in reducing family size and rates of population growth unless they are accompanied by changes in the mode of production (or by governmental subsidies for small families), we see no reason why fertility controls cannot be substituted for mortality controls at every step in the development process. It is clearly of humanitarian interest to all, regardless of the immediate effect on population growth, to substitute to the greatest extent possible, modern contraceptive and other prenatal forms of fertility control for the covert postnatal mortality controls which continue to be heavily relied on by contemporary preindustrial systems of population regulation. In reflecting on population regulation in the long term, there is much circumstantial evidence to indicate that in repressing abortion or direct infanticide, "pro-life" world religions and governments have inadvertently contributed to an increase in indirect infanticide and pedicide. Now that the facts of preindustrial population regulation are better known, their failure to press vigorously for compensating controls prior to birth, including medical abortion, constitutes a hypocrisy equal to that of Malthus when he condemned all forms of fertility control other than "moral restraint," while knowing full well that "moral restraint" alone would condemn most of the working class to perpetual poverty.

References

Abelson, A. E. 1976. "Altitude and Fertility." *Human Biology* 48(1):83–91.

Abernathy, Virginia. 1979. *Population Pressure and Cultural Adjustment.* New York: Human Sciences Press.

Aikin, J. 1968. (orig. 1795). *A Description of the Country from 30 to 40 miles Round Manchester.* Newton Abbot: David and Charles.

Ainsworth-Davis, J. 1924. *Meat, Fish, and Dairy Produce.* The Resources of the Empire Series. London: Ernest Benn.

Alexander, P. In press. "Labor Expropriation and Fertility: Population Growth in Nineteenth Century Java." In W. Handwerker, ed., *Culture and Reproduction: Reconstructing the Demographic Paradigm.* Boulder: Westview Press.

Allen, L. L. et al. 1982. "Demography and Human Origins." *American Anthropologist* 84:888–896.

Anderson, M. 1971. *Family Structure in Nineteenth-Century Lancashire.* London: Cambridge University Press.

Anderson, P. 1974. *Passages from Antiquity to Feudalism.* London: Verso.

Angel, L. 1972. "Ecology and Population in the Eastern Mediterranian." *World Archaeology* 4:88–105.

—— 1975. "Paleocology, Paleodemography, and Health." In S. Polgar, ed., *Population, Ecology, and Social Evolution,* pp. 167–190. The Hague: Mouton.

Appleby, A. 1978. *Famine in Tudor and Stuart England.* Liverpool: Liverpool University Press.

Aries, P. 1965. *Centuries of Childhood.* New York: Random House.

Balickci, Asen. 1967. "Female Infanticide on the Arctic Coast." *Man* 2:615–625.

Baran, P. 1957. *The Political Economy of Growth.* New York: Monthly Review.

Bardhan, P. 1982. "Little Girls and Death in India." *Economic and Political Weekly (India)* September 4:1448–1450.

Barth, F. 1961. *Nomads of South Persia: The Basseri Tribe of the Khamseh Confederacy.* Boston: Little, Brown.

Beaton, George. 1984. "Adaptation to and Accommodation of Long-Term Low Energy Intake: A Comment on the Conference on Energy Intake and Activity." In Ernesto Pollitt and Peggy Amante, eds., *Energy Intake and Activity,* pp. 395–403. New York: Liss.

Beer, M. 1984 (orig. 1919). *A History of British Socialism*. Nottingham: Spokesman.

Berg, A. 1973. *The Nutrition Factor: Its Role in National Development*. Washington, D.C.: The Brookings Institution.

Bernstein, R. 1984. "The Malthusian Time Bomb is Still Ticking." *New York Times* July 29:E3.

Bhatia, B. M. 1967. *Famines in India: A Study of Some Aspects of the Economic History of India (1860–1965)*. London: Asia Publishing House.

Bielenstein, Hans. 1947. "The Census of China During the Period 2–742 A.D." *Bulletin of the Museum of Far Eastern Antiquities* 19:125–165.

Binford, L. and W. J. Chasko. 1976. "Nunamiut Demographic History." In E. Zubrow, ed., *Demographic Anthropology: Quantitative Approaches*, pp. 63–143. New York: Academic Press.

Birdsall, Nancy. 1983. "Fertility and Economic Change in Eighteenth and Nineteenth Century Europe: A Comment." *Population and Development Review* 9:111–123.

Birdsell, J. 1968. "Some Predictions for the Pleistocene Based on Equilibrium Systems Among Recent Hunter-Gatherers." In R. Lee and I. DeVore, eds., *Man the Hunter*, pp. 229–249. Chicago: Aldine.

Bolian, C. 1971. "Manioc Cultivation in Periodically Flooded Areas." Manuscript.

Bongaarts, John. 1980. "Does Malnutrition Affect Fertility? A Summary of the Evidence." *Science* 208:564–569.

—— 1982. "Malnutrition and Fertility." (Reply to Rose Frisch). *Science* 215:1273–1274.

Bongaarts, John, F. Odile, and Ron Lesthaeghe. 1984. "The Proximate Determinants of Fertility in Sub-Saharan Africa." *Population and Development Review* 10:511–537.

Boserup, E. 1981. *Population and Technological Change*. Chicago: University of Chicago Press.

Boswell, J. 1980. *Christianity, Social Tolerance, and Homosexuality: Gay People in Western Europe from the Beginning of the Christian Era to the Fourteenth Century*. Chicago: University of Chicago Press.

Braidwood, R. 1960. "The Agricultural Revolution." *Scientific American* (September), pp. 3–10.

Braudel, Fernand. 1973. *Capitalism and Material Life*. New York: Harper/Colophon.

Briggs, J. 1974. "Eskimo Women: Makers of Men." In C. Matthiasson, ed., *Many Sisters: Women in Cross-Cultural Perspective*, pp. 261–304. New York: Free Press.

Brookfield, H. and P. Brown. 1963. *Struggle for Land: Agriculture and Group Territories among the Chimbu of the New Guinea Highlands*. Melbourne: Oxford University Press.

Brown, Barratt M. 1974. *The Economics of Imperialism*. Harmondsworth: Penguin Books.

Brown, J. 1970. "A Note on the Division of Labor by Sex." *American Anthropologist* 72(5):1073–1078.

Buchbinder, G. and R. Rappaport. 1976. "Fertility and Death among the Maring." In P. Brown and G. Buchbinder, eds., *Man and Woman in the New Guinea Highlands*, pp. 13–35, American Anthropological Association Spec. Pub. No. 8.

Buckley, James. 1984. "Conference on Population." *Vital Speeches of the Day* (September), 1:677–679.

Buikstra, Jane, L. Konigsberg, and J. Bullington. n.d. "Fertility and the Development of Agriculture in the Prehistoric Midwest." Department of Anthropology, Northwestern University. Mimeo.

Bullen, Beverly et al. 1985. "Induction of Menstrual Disorders by Strenuous Exercise in Untrained Women." *New England Journal of Medicine* 312:1349–1353.

Bury, J. 1932. *The Idea of Progress*. New York: Dover.

Butler, C. 1916. *Domestic Service. An Enquiry by the Women's Industrial Council*. London: G. Bell and Sons.

Butzer, K. 1971. *Environment and Archaeology: An Ecological Approach to Prehistory*. Chicago: Aldine.

Butzer, K. and L. G. Freeman, eds. 1976. *Early Hydraulic Civilization in Egypt*. Chicago: University of Chicago Press.

Cain, Mead. 1977. "The Economic Activities of Children in a Village in Bangladesh." *Population and Development Review* 3:201–227.

—— 1983. "Fertility as an Adjustment to Risk." *Population and Development Review* 9:688–702.

Caldwell, John. 1977. "The Economic Rationality of High Fertility: An Investigation Illustrated with Nigerian Survey Data." *Population Studies* 31:5–27.

—— 1982. *Theory of Fertility Decline*. New York: Academic Press.

—— 1983. "Direct Economic Costs and Benefits of Children." In R. Bulatao et al., eds., *Determinants of Fertility in Developing Countries: Supply and Demand for Children*, pp. 458–493. New York: Academic Press.

Caldwell, John, P. H. Reddy, and Pat Caldwell. 1983. "The Causes of Demographic Change in Rural South India: A Micro Approach." *Population and Development Review* 8:689–727.

Carneiro, R. 1960. "Slash-and-Burn Agriculture: A Closer Look at Its Implications for Settlement Patterns." In A. Wallace, ed., *Men and Cultures*, pp. 229–234. Philadelphia: University of Pennsylvania Press.

—— 1961. "Slash-and-Burn Cultivation Among the Kuikuru and Its Implications for Cultural Development in the Amazon Basin." In J. Wilbert, ed., *The Evolution of Horticultural Systems in Native South America, Causes and Consequences: A Symposium*, pp. 46–47. *Antropologica*: Supplement Publication No. 2.

—— 1968. "The Transition from Hunting to Horticulture in the Amazon

Basin." *Proceedings of the Eighth International Congress of Anthropological and Ethnological Sciences*, Tokyo and Kyoto, pp. 244–248.

—— 1970. "A Theory of the Origin of the State." *Science* 169:733–738.

—— 1983. "The Cultivation of Manioc Among the Kuikuku of the Upper Xingu. In R. Hames and W. Vickers, eds., *Adaptive Responses of Native Amazonians*, pp. 65–111. New York: Academic Press.

Cashdan, Elizabeth. 1985. "Natural Fertility, Birth Spacing, and the 'First Demographic Transition.'" *American Anthropologist* 87:650–653.

Cavilli-Sforza, L. 1983. "The Transition to Agriculture and Some of Its Consequences." In Donald Ortner, ed., *How Humans Adapt: A Biocultural Odyssey*, pp. 103–120. Washington, D.C.: Smithsonian Institution Press.

Cavilli-Sforza, L. and W. Bodmer. 1971. *The Genetics of Human Population*. San Francisco: W. H. Freeman.

Centre for Development Studies. 1975. *Poverty, Unemployment, and Development Policy*. New York: United Nations.

Chadwick, D. 1862. *On the Social and Educational Statistics of Manchester and Salford*. Manchester: Cave and Sever.

Chagnon, N. 1968. *Yanomamo: The Fierce People*. New York: Holt, Rinehart, and Winston.

—— 1973. "The Culture-Ecology of Shifting (Pioneering) Cultivation among the Yanomamo Indians." In D. Gross, ed., *Peoples and Cultures of Native South America*, pp. 126–142. Garden City, N.Y.: Doubleday/ Natural History Press.

—— 1974. *Studying the Yanomamo*. New York: Holt, Rinehart and Winston.

—— 1979. "Is Reproductive Success Equal in Egalitarian Society?" In N. Chagnon and W. Irons, eds., *Evolutionary Biology and Human Social Behavior: An Anthropological Perspective*, pp. 373–401. North Scituate, Mass.: Duxbury Press.

Chagnon, N., M. Flinn, and T. Melancon. 1979. "Sex Ratio Variation among Yanomamo Indians." In N. Chagnon and W. Irons, eds., *Evolutionary Biology and Human Social Behavior: An Anthropological Perspective*, pp. 290–320. North Scituate, Mass.: Duxbury.

Chagnon, N. and P. Hames. 1979. "Protein Deficiency and Tribal Warfare in Amazonia: New Data." *Science* 20(3):910–913.

Chang, C. 1982. "Nomads without Cattle: East African Foragers in Historical Perspective." In E. Leacock and R. Lee, eds., *Politics and History in Band Societies*, pp. 269–282. Cambridge: Cambridge University Press.

Chen, L., E. Huq, and S. Souza. 1981. "Sex Bias and the Family: Allocation of Food and Health Care in Rural Bangladesh." *Population and Development Review* 7:55–70.

Clark, C. 1967. *Population Growth and Land Use*. New York: St. Martin's Press.

Clarke, W. 1966. "From Extensive to Intensive Shifting Cultivation: A Succession from New Guinea." *Ethnology* 5:347–359.

Coale, A., ed. 1975. *Economic Factors in Population Growth*. New York: Halsted Press.

Coe, M. and K. Flannery. 1966. "Microenvironments and Mesoamerican Prehistory." In J. Graham, ed., *Ancient Mesoamerica*, pp. 46–50. Palo Alto, Calif.: Peek Publications.

Cohen, Mark. 1977. *The Food Crisis in Prehistory*. New Haven: Yale University Press.

—— 1983. "The Significance of Long-Term Changes in Human Diet and Food Economy." Paper prepared for Wenner-Gren Conference on Food Preferences and Aversions, Cedar Key, Fla.

Cohen, M. and G. Armelagos, eds. 1984. *Paleopathology and the Origins of Agriculture*. New York: Academic Press.

Cohen, Myron. 1976. *House United, House Divided: The Chinese Family in Taiwan*. New York: Columbia University Press.

Cole, D. 1975. *Nomads of the Nomads: The Al Murrah Bedouin of the Empty Quarter*. Chicago: Aldine.

Collier, F. 1964. *The Family Economy of the Working Classes in the Cotton Industry, 1784–1833*. Manchester: Manchester University Press.

Connell, K. 1965. "Land and Population in Ireland, 1780–1845." In D. V. Glass and D. Eversley, eds., *Population in History: Essays in Historical Demography*, pp. 423–433. London: Edward Arnols.

Cook, S. and W. Borah. 1971. *Essays in Population History: Mexico and the Caribbean*. Berkeley: University of California Press.

Coontz, S. 1957. *Population Theories and the Economic Interpretation*. London: Routledge and Kegan Paul.

Coote, C. 1801. *General View of the Agriculture and Manufactures of the King's County*. Dublin: Graisberry and Campbell.

Cowlishaw, G. 1978. "Infanticide in Aboriginal Australia." *Oceania* 48:262–263.

Crittenden, A. 1981. "I.M.F. Puts Pressure on Bangladesh." *New York Times*, November 30:D1, D7.

Cullen, L. 1968. "Irish History without the Potato." *Past and Present* 40:73–83.

Dahlberg, F. 1976. "More on Mechanisms of Population Growth." *Current Anthropology* 17(1):164–166.

Davis, D. 1945. "The Annual Cycle of Plants, Mosquitoes, Birds, and Mammals in Two Brazililan Forests." *Ecological Monographs* 15(3):243–295.

Davis, Kingsley. 1951. *The Population of India and Pakistan*. Princeton: Princeton University Press.

Day, W. 1862. *The Famine in the West*. Dublin: Hodges, Smith.

Deane, P. 1979. *The First Industrial Revolution*. Cambridge: Cambridge University Press.

DeMause, Lloyd. 1974. "The Evolution of Childhood." In L. DeMause, ed., *The History of Childhood*, pp. 1–73. New York: Psychohistory Press.

Denevan, W. 1970. "The Aboriginal Population of Western Amazonia in Relation to Habitat and Subsistence." *Revista Geografica,* vol. 72.

—— 1976. "The Aboriginal Population of Amazonia." In W. Denevan, ed., *The Native Population of America in 1492,* pp. 105–134. Madison: University of Wisconsin Press.

Denevan, W. et al. 1984. "Indigenous Agroforestry in the Peruvian Amazon: Bora Indian Management of Swidden Fallows." *Intersciencia* 000:000.

De Ste. Croix, G. 1981. *The Class Struggle in the Ancient Greek World, from the Archaic Age to the Arab Conquests.* London: Duckworth.

Devereux, G. 1967. "A Typological Study of Abortion in 350 Primitive, Ancient, and Pre-Industrial Societies." In H. Rosen, ed., *Abortion in America,* pp. 95–152. Boston: Beacon Press.

Dickemann, M. 1975. "Demographic Consequences of Infanticide in Man." *Annual Review of Ecology and Systematics* 6:107–137.

—— 1979. "Female Infanticide, Reproductive Strategies, and Social Stratification. A Preliminary Model." In N. Chagnon and W. Irons, eds., *Evolutionary Biology and Human Social Behavior: An Anthropological Perspective,* pp. 321–367. North Scituate, Mass.: Duxbury Press.

—— 1984. "Concepts and Classification in the Study of Human Infanticide." In Glenn Hausfater and Sarah Hrdy, eds., *Infanticide: Comparative and Evolutionary Perspectives,* pp. 427–437. New York: Aldine.

Digby, A. 1983. "Malthus and Reform of the Poor Law." In J. Dupâquier and A. Vauve-Chamoux, eds., *Malthus Past and Present.* London: Academic Press.

Divale, W. and M. Harris. 1976. "Population, Warfare, and the Male Supremacist Complex." *American Anthropologist* 78:520–538.

Dobb, M. 1963 (orig. 1947). *Studies in the Development of Capitalism.* New York: International Publishers.

Dobby, E. 1967 (orig. 1950). *Southeast Asia.* London: University of London Press.

Dover, K. J. 1978. *Greek Homosexuality.* New York: Vintage.

Drake, M. 1969. "Population Growth and the Irish Economy." In L. Cullen, ed., *The Formation of the Irish Economy,* pp. 65–76. Cork: Mercier Press.

Dublin Mansion House Relief Committee. 1881. *The Irish Crisis of 1879–80.* Dublin: Browne and Nolan.

Duby, G. 1972. "Medieval Agriculture 900–1500." In C. Cipolla, ed., *The Fontana Economic History of Europe: The Middle Ages,* pp. 175–220. London: Collins.

—— 1974. *The Early Growth of the European Economy.* Ithaca: Cornell University Press.

Dufour, D. 1983. 'Nutrition in the Northwest Amazon: Household Dietary Intake and Time-Energy Expenditure." In R. Hames and W. Vickers, eds., *Adaptive Responses of Native Amazonians*, pp. 329–355. New York: Academic Press.

Dumond, D. 1975. "The Limitation of Human Population. A Natural History." *Science* 187:713–721.

Dupaquier, J. and A. Vauve-Chamoux, eds. 1983. *Malthus Past and Present.* New York: Academic Press.

Durward, L. 1984. *Poverty in Pregnancy: The Cost of an Adequate Diet for Expectant Mothers.* London: Maternity Alliance.

Dutt, R. P. 1940. *India Today.* London: Gollancz.

Dyson-Hudson, Rada and Neville Dyson-Hudson. 1969. "Subsistence Herding in Uganda." *Scientific American* 220:76–89.

Dyson, Tim and Mick Moore. 1983. "On Kinship Structure, Female Autonomy, and Demographic Behavior in India." *Population and Development Review* 9:35–60.

Eisenberg, J. et al. 1972. "The Relation Between Ecology and Social Structure in Primates." *Science* 176(4037):863–874.

El Saadawi, N. 1980. *The Hidden Face of Eve: Women in the Arab World.* London: Zed Press.

Elliot, K. and J. Whelan, eds., 1976. *Health and Disease in Tribal Societies.* New York: Elsvier.

Ellison, T. 1886. *The Cotton Trade of Great Britain.* London: Effingham Wilson.

Ember, C. 1983. "The Relative Decline in Women's Contribution to Agriculture with Intensification." *American Anthropologist* 85(2):285–304.

Engels, F. 1958. *The Condition of the Working Class in England.* Stanford: Stanford University Press.

Farwell, Byron. 1972. *Queen Victoria's Little Wars.* New York: Harper and Row.

Feder, E. 1983. "Plundering the Poor: The Role of the World Bank in the Third World." *International Journal of Health Services* 13(4):649–660.

Fedrick, J. and P. Adelstein. 1973. "Influence of Pregnancy Spacing on Outcome of Pregnancy." *British Medical Journal* 4(5895):753–756.

Ferro-Luzzi, G. E. 1980. "Food Avoidance at Puberty and Menstruation . . . in Pregnant Women . . . during the Peuperium in Tamiland." In John Robson, ed., *Food, Ecology, and Culture: Readings in the Anthropology of Dietary Practices*, pp. 92–108. New York: Gordon and Breach.

Finch, J. 1842. *Statistics of Vauxhall Ward, Liverpool, Shewing the Actual Condition of More than Five Thousand Families.* Liverpool: Joshua Walmsley.

Finkle, Jason and Barbara Crane. 1985. "Ideology and Politics at Mexico City: The United States at the 1984 International Conference on Population." *Population and Development Review* 11:1–28.

Fisher, C. 1964. *South-East Asia: A Social, Economic and Political Geography.* London: Methuen.

Ford, C. and F. Beach. 1970. *Patterns of Sexual Behavior.* New York: Harper and Row.

Foster, T. 1846. *Letters on the Condition of the People of Ireland.* London: Chapman and Hall.

Frank, A. 1970. "On Dalton's 'Theoretical Issues in Economic Anthropology.'" *Current Anthropology* 11(1):67–71.

Freeman, M. M. R. 1971. "A Social and Ecological Analysis of Systematic Female Infanticide Among the Netsilik Eskimo." *American Anthropologist* 73:1011–1018.

Freeman, T. 1957. *Pre-Famine Ireland: A Study in Historical Geography.* Manchester: Manchester University Press.

Fried, Morton. 1967. *The Evolution of Political Society.* New York: Random House.

Frisancho, A. R. et al. 1973. "Adaptive Significance of Small Body Size Under Poor Socioeconomic Conditions in Southern Peru." *American Journal of Physical Anthropology* 39:255–262.

Frisancho, A. R., J. Matos and P. Flegel. 1983. "Maternal Nutritional Status and Adolescent Pregnancy Outcome." *American Journal of Clinical Nutrition* 38:739–746.

Frisch, R. 1978a. "Population, Food Intake, and Fertility." *Science* 199:22–30.

—— 1978b. "Reply to Trussel." *Science* 100:1509–1513.

—— 1984. "Body Fat, Puberty, and Fertility." *Biology Review* 59:161–188.

Frisch, R. and J. McArthur. 1974. "Menstrual Cycles: Fatness as a Determinant of Minimum Weight for Height Necessary for Their Maintenance or Onset." *Science* 185:949–951.

Furnivall, J. 1948. *Colonial Policy and Practice: A Comparative Study of Burma and Netherlands India.* Cambridge: Cambridge University Press.

Geertz, C. 1963. *Agricultural Involution: The Process of Ecological Change in Indonesia.* Berkeley: University of California Press.

Gill, C. 1925. *The Rise of the Irish Linen Industry.* Oxford: Clarendon Press.

Glamann, K. 1974. "European Trade 1500–1750." In C. Cipolla, ed., *The Fontana Economic History of Europe: The Sixteenth and Seventeenth Centuries,* pp. 427–526. London: Collins.

Glass, D. V. 1940. *Population Policies and Movements in Europe.* Oxford: Clarendon Press.

Golley, F. et al. 1969. "The Structure of Tropical Forests in Panama and Colombia." *Bioscience* 19:693–696.

Goody, J. 1976. *Production and Reproduction.* Cambridge: Cambridge University Press.

—— 1983. *The Development of the Family and Marriage in Europe.* New York: Cambridge University Press.

Graham, S. 1985. "Running and Menstrual Dysfunction: Recent Medical Discoveries Provide New Insights into the Human Division of Labor by Sex." *American Anthropologist* 87:878–882.

Greene, R. 1956. "Agriculture." In E. Edwards and T. Williams, eds., *The*

Great Famine: Studies in Irish History, 1845–52, pp. 89–128. Dublin: Irish Committee of Historical Sciences.

Griffith, G. 1926. *Population Problems of the Age of Malthus*. Cambridge: Cambridge University Press.

Gross, D. 1975. "Protein Capture and Cultural Development in the Amazon Basin." *American Anthropologist* 66:526–549.

—— 1982. "Proteinas y cultura en la Amazonia." *Amazonia Peruana* 3:127–134.

—— 1984. "Time Allocation: A Tool for the Study of Cultural Behavior." *Annual Review of Anthropology* 13:519–558.

Gulliver, P. 1955. *The Family Herds*. London: Routledge and Kegan Paul.

Gupta, Monica Das. 1978. "Production Relations and Population: Rampur." *Journal of Development Studies* 14(4):177–185.

Gwatkin, D. and S. Brandel. 1982. "Life Expectancy and Population Growth in the Third World." *Scientific American* 246(5):57–65.

Haas, Jonathan. 1982. *The Evolution of the Prehistoric State*. New York: Columbia University Press.

Hajnal, J. 1965. "European Marriage Patterns in Perspective." In D. V. Glass and D. Eversley, eds., *Population in History*, pp. 101–143. Chicago: Aldine.

Hall, Mr. and Mrs. S. C. 1841–43. *Ireland: Its Scenery, Character, Etc*. London: Jeremiah How.

Hames, R. 1983. "The Settlement Pattern of a Yanomamo Population Bloc: A Behaviorial Ecological Interpretation." In R. Hames and W. Vickers, eds., *Adaptive Responses of Native Amazonians*, pp. 393–427. New York: Academic Press.

Hames, R. and W. Vickers, eds. 1983. *Adaptive Responses of Native Amazonians*. New York: Academic Press.

Hamilton, Margaret. 1982. "Sexual Dimorphism in Skeletal Samples." In R. Hall, ed., *Sexual Dimorphism in Homo Sapiens*, pp. 107–163. New York: Praeger.

Hamilton, Sahni, B. Popkin, and D. Spicer. 1984. *Women and Nutrition in Third World Countries*. South Hadley, Mass.: Bergin and Garvey.

Handwerker, W. 1983. "The First Demographic Transition: An Analysis of Subsistence Choices and Reproductive Consequences." *American Anthropologist* 85(1):5–27.

—— 1985. "Scope of Perspective in Fertility Models." *American Anthropologist* 87(3):653–656.

—— In press. "Introduction." In W. Handwerker, ed., *Culture and Reproduction: Reconstructing the Demographic Paradigm*. Boulder: Westview Press.

Hanley, Susan. 1977. "The Influences of Economic and Social Variables on Marriage and Fertility in Eighteenth and Nineteenth Century Japanese Villages." In Ronald Lee et al., eds., *Population Patterns in the Past*, pp. 165–200. New York: Academic Press.

Harpending, H. 1976. "Regional Variation in Kung Populations." In R. Lee and I. DeVore, eds., *Kalahari Hunter-Gatherers*, pp. 152–165. Cambridge: Harvard University Press.

Harrell, Barbara. 1981. "Lactation and Menstruation in Cultural Perspective." *American Anthropologist* 83:796–823.

Harris, David. 1978. "Adaptation to a Tropical Rain-Forest Environment: Aboriginal Subsistence in Northeastern Queensland." In N. Blurton Jones and V. Reynolds, eds., *Human Behavior and Adaptation*, pp. 113–134. London: Tayler and Francis.

—— 1981. "The Prehistory of Human Subsistence: A Speculative Outline." In D. N. Walcher and N. Kretchmer, eds., *Food, Nutrition, and Evolution*, pp. 15–35. New York: Masson.

Harris, M. 1967. "Reply to John Bennet." *Current Anthropology* 9:252–253.

—— 1975. *Culture, People, Nature: An Introduction to General Anthropology.* New York: Harper and Row, 2d ed.

—— 1977. *Cannibals and Kings: The Origins of Cultures.* New York: Random House.

—— 1979. *Cultural Materialism.* New York: Random House.

—— 1981. *America Now: The Anthropology of a Changing Culture.* New York: Simon and Schuster.

—— 1984. "Animal Capture and Yanomamo Warfare: Retrospect and New Evidence." *Journal of Anthropological Research* 40:183–201.

—— 1985. *Culture, People, Nature: An Introduction to General Anthropology.* 4th ed. New York: Harper and Row.

—— 1986. *Good to Eat: Riddle of Food and Culture.* New York: Simon and Schuster.

Harrison, P. 1983. *Inside the Inner City.* Harmondsworth: Penguin.

Hassan, F. 1975. "Determination of the Size, Density, and Growth Rate of Hunting-Gathering Populations." In S. Polgar, ed., *Population, Ecology, and Social Evolution*, pp. 27–52. The Hague: Mouton.

—— 1978. "Demographic Archaeology." In M. Schiffer, ed., *Advances in Archaeological Method and Theory*, pp. 49–103. New York: Academic Press.

—— 1981. *Demographic Archaeology.* New York: Academic Press.

Hatcher, John. 1977. *Plague, Population, and the English, 1348–1530.* London: Macmillan.

Haviland, W. 1967. "Stature at Tikal: Implications for Ancient Maya Demography and Social Organization." *American Antiquity* 32:326–325.

Hawkes, K. and J. O'Connell. n.d. "Pleistocene Foraging and Population Growth Rate." Manuscript.

—— 1981. "Affluent Hunters? Some Comments in Light of the Alyawara Case." *American Anthropologist* 83:622–626.

Hawkes, K. et al. 1982. "Why Hunters Gather: Optimal Foraging and the Ache of Eastern Paraguay." *American Ethnologist* 9(2):379–398.

Hayden, B. In press. "Resources, Rivalry, and Reproduction: The Influence of Basic Resource Characteristics on Reproductive Behavior." In W. Handwerker, ed., *Culture and Reproduction*. Boulder: Westview Press.

Hayter, T. and C. Watson. 1985. *Aid: Rhetoric and Reality*. London: Pluto Press.

Hazlitt, W. 1807. *A Reply to the "Essay on Population" by the Reverend T. R. Malthus*. London: Longman, Hurst, Rees and Orme.

Hechter, M. 1975. *Internal Colonialism: The Celtic Fringe in British National Development, 1536–1966*. Berkeley: University of California Press.

Heinsohn, G. and O. Steiger. 1983. "The Rationale Underlying Malthus's Theory of Population." In J. Dupaquier and A. Vauve-Chamoux, eds., *Malthus Past and Present*, pp. 223–232. New York: Academic Press.

Helm, June. 1980. "Female Infanticide, European Diseases, and Population Levels Among the Mackenzie Dene." *American Ethnologist* 7:259–284.

Hepburn, A. 1980. *The Conflict of Nationality in Modern Ireland*. London: Edward Arnold.

Henry, L. 1961. "Some Data on Natural Fertility." *Eugenics Quarterly* 8:81–91.

Herlihy, David. 1977. "Deaths, Marriages, Births, and the Tuscan Economy (ca. 1300–1500)." In Ronald Lee et al., eds., *Population Patterns in the Past*, pp. 235–264. New York: Academic Press.

Hernandez, M. et al. 1974. "Effect of Economic Growth on Nutrition in a Tropical Community." *Ecology of Food and Nutrition* 3:283–291.

Hewitt, M. 1958. *Wives and Mothers in Victorian Industry*. London: Rockliff.

Hickerson, H. 1962. "The Southwestern Chippewa: An Ethnohistorical Study." *American Anthropological Association Memoirs* no. 92.

Hobsbawm, E. 1979. *The Age of Capital, 1848–1875*. New York: New American Library.

Holden, Constance. 1984. "World Bank, U.S., At Odds on Population." *Science* 225:396.

Hopkins, K. 1978. *Conquerors and Slaves. Sociological Studies in Roman History*, vol. 1. Cambridge: Cambridge University Press.

—— 1983. *Death and Renewal: Sociological Studies in Roman History*, vol. 2. Cambridge: Cambridge University Press.

House of Commons. 1836. "Second Report of the Select Committee on the State of Agriculture," *Reports from Committees*, 8(1):225–516.

—— 1845. *Reports from Commissioners*, vol. 8: *State of Large Towns and Populous Districts*.

Howe, M. 1972. *Man, Environment, and Disease in Britain*. New York: Barnes and Noble.

Howell, N. 1979. *Demography of the Dobe !Kung*. New York: Academic Press.

Hrdy, S. 1977. "Infanticide as a Primate Reproductive Strategy." *American Scientist* 65:40–49.

—— 1981. *The Woman That Never Evolved.* Cambridge: Harvard University Press.

Huffman, S. et al. 1978. "Postpartum Amenorrhea: How Is It Affected by Maternal Nutritional Status?" *Science* 200:1155–1157.

Hughes, D. O. 1978. "From Brideprice to Dowry in Mediterranean Europe." *Journal of Family History* 3:262–296.

Hutchins, B. and A. Harrison. 1966 (orig. 1903). *A History of Factory Legislation.* London: Frank Cass.

Hutchinson, H. W. 1957. *Village and Plantation Life in Northeastern Brazil.* Seattle: University of Washington Press.

International Planned Parenthood Federation. 1984. "China: 'Our Arduous Task.'" *People* 11(4):16–17.

—— 1984. "How US Policy Started a Storm." *People* 11(4):6–7.

Isacsson, Sven-Erik. 1984. "Observations on Choco Slash-Mulch Culture." *Occasional Papers in Anthropology* 15:64–89. Archaeology Series, Museum of Anthropology, University of North Colorado.

Jeffery, Roger, P. Jeffery, and Andrew Lyon. 1984a. "Female Infanticide and Amniocentesis." *Social Science Medicine* 19:1207–1212.

—— 1984b. "Only Cord-Cutters? Midwifery and Childbirth in Northern India." *Social Action* 34:229–250.

Jelliffe, D. B. and E. F. Jelliffe. 1978. "The Volume and Composition of Human Milk in Poorly Nourished Communities: A Review." *American Journal of Clinical Nutrition* 31:492–515.

Jelliffe, D. et al. 1962. "The Children of Hadza Hunters." *Journal of Pediatrics* 60:907–913.

Jochim, M. 1981. *Strategies for Survival: Cultural Behavior in an Ecological Context.* New York: Academic Press.

Johansson, Sheila. 1984. "Delayed Infanticide." In Glenn Hausfater and Sarah Hrdy, eds., *Infanticide: Comparative and Evolutionary Perspectives,* pp. 463–485. New York: Aldine.

Johnson, A. 1983. "Machiguenga Gardens." In R. Hames and W. Vickers, eds., *Adaptive Responses of Native Amazonians,* pp. 29–63. New York: Academic Press.

Johnson, J. 1970. "The Two 'Irelands' at the Beginning of the Nineteenth Century." In N. Stephens and R. Glasscock, eds., *Irish Geographical Studies,* pp. 224–243. Belfast: Queen's University.

Katona-Apte, J. 1975. "The Relevance of Nourishment to the Reproductive Cycle of the Female in India." In D. Raphael, ed., *Being Female: Reproduction, Power, and Change,* pp. 43–53. The Hague: Mouton.

Kellum, B. 1974. "Infanticide in England in the Later Middle Ages." *History of Childhood Quarterly* 1(3):367–388.

Kelly, R. C. 1976. *Etoro Social Structure: A Study in Structural Contradiction.* Ann Arbor: University of Michigan Press.

Kennedy, R. 1973. *The Irish: Emigration, Marriage and Fertility.* Berkeley: University of California Press.

Kerr, B. 1943. "Irish Seasonal Migration to Great Britain, 1800–38." *Irish Historical Studies* 4:365–380.

Keys, A. et al. 1950. *The Biology of Human Starvation.* Minneapolis: University of Minnesota Press.

Khazanov, A. M. 1984. *Nomads and the Outside World.* Cambridge: University of Cambridge Press.

Knodel, J. 1977. "Family Limitation and the Fertility Transition: Evidence from the Age Patterns of Fertility in Europe and Asia." *Population Studies* 32:481–510.

Knodel, J. and E. Van de Walle. 1979. "Lessons from the Past: Policy Implications of Historical Fertility Studies." *Population and Development Review* 5:227.

Knowles, L. 1928. *Economic Development of the British Overseas Empire.* London: Boni.

Lancaster, J. 1976. "Sex Roles in Primate Societies." In M. Teitelbaum, ed., *Sex Differences: Social and Biological Perspectives,* pp. 22–61. Garden City, N.Y.: Anchor Press.

Langer, W. 1972. "Checks on Population Growth, 1750–1850." *Scientific American,* pp. 92–99.

—— 1974. "Infanticide: A Historical Survey." *History of Childhood Quarterly* 1(3):353–365.

Laslett, P. 1977. *Family Life and Illicit Love in Earlier Generations. Essays in Historical Sociology.* Cambridge: Cambridge University Press.

—— 1980. "Introduction: Comparing Illegitimacy over Time and Between Cultures." In P. Laslett et al., eds., *Bastardy and Its Comparative History,* pp. 1–68. London: Edward Arnold.

Lea, H. 1957. *Materials Toward a History of Witchcraft.* New York: Thomas Yoseloff.

Leacock, E. 1978. "Women's Status in Egalitarian Society: Implications for Social Evolution." *Current Anthropology* 19:247–275.

—— 1981. *Myths of Male Dominance: Collected Articles on Women Cross-Culturally.* New York: Monthly Review.

Ledbetter, R. 1972. *The Organization That Delayed Birth Control: A History of the Malthusian League, 1877–1927.* Ann Arbor: University Microfilms.

Lee, J. 1973. *The Modernisation of Irish Society, 1848–1918.* Dublin: Gill and Macmillan.

Lee, R. B. 1972. "Population Growth and the Beginnings of Sedentary Life Among the !Kung Bushmen." In B. Spooner, ed., *Population Growth,* pp. 329–342. Cambridge: MIT Press.

—— 1979. *The !Kung San: Men, Women, and Work in a Foraging Society.* New York: Cambridge University Press.

—— 1982. "Politics, Sexual and Non-Sexual, in an Egalitarian Society."

In E. Leacock and R. B. Lee, eds., *Politics and History in Band Societies,* pp. 37–59. Cambridge: Cambridge University Press.

Lee, R. D. and R. Schofield. 1981. "British Population in the Eighteenth Century." In R. Floud and D. McCloskey, eds., *The Economic History of Britain Since 1700,* vol. 1. Cambridge: Cambridge University Press.

LeRoy Ladurie, E. 1978. *Montaillou: Cathars and Catholics in a French Village, 1294–1324.* Harmondsworth: Penguin.

Levine, D. 1977. *Family Formation in an Age of Nascent Capitalism.* New York: Academic Press.

Levine, S. and K. Wrightson. 1980. "The Social Context of Illegitimacy in Early Modern England." In P. Laslett et al., eds., *Bastardy and Its Comparative History,* pp. 158–175. London: Edward Arnold.

Lindenbaum, S. 1979. *Kuru Sorcery: Disease and Danger in the New Guinea Highlands.* Palo Alto, Calif.: Mayfield.

Little, M. and G. Morren, eds. 1976. *Ecology, Energetics, and Human Variability.* Dubuque, Iowa: Wm. C. Brown.

Livingstone, Frank. 1968. "The Effects of War on the Biology of the Human Species." In M. Fried, R. Murphy, and M. Harris, eds., *War, the Anthropology of Armed Conflict and Aggression,* pp. 3–15. Garden City, N.Y.: Natural History Press.

Lizot, J. 1977. "Population, Resources, and Warfare Among the Yanomami." *Man* 23:496–517.

—— 1979. "On Food Taboos and Amazon Cultural Ecology." *Current Anthropology* 20:150–151.

Lovett-Doust, J. and L. Lovett-Doust. 1983. "Sex in Plants: Male Versus Female." *New Scientist* 99(1365):34–36.

McAlpin, M. 1983. "Famines, Epidemics, and Population Growth: The Case of India." In R. Rothberg and T. Rabb, eds., *Hunger and History: The Impact of Changing Food Production and Consumption Patterns on Society,* pp. 153–168. Cambridge: Cambridge University Press.

MacCormack, Carol P. 1982. "Adaptation in Human Fertility and Birth." In Carol P. MacCormack, ed., *Ethnography of Fertility and Birth,* pp. 1–23. New York: Academic Press.

McKee, L. 1984. "Sex Differentials in Survivorship and Customary Treatment of Infants and Children." *Medical Anthropology* 8(2):91–108.

McKeown, T. 1979. *The Role of Medicine: Dream, Mirage, or Nemesis?* Princeton: Princeton University Press.

McLaren, A. 1984. *Reproductive Rituals.* London: Methuen.

MacNeil, J. 1886. *English Interference with Irish Industries.* Place: Publisher.

MacNeish, R. 1972. "The Evolution of Community Patterns in the Tehuacan Valley of Mexico, and Speculation about the Cultural Processes." In P. Ucko et al., eds., *Man, Settlement and Urbanism,* pp. 67–93. Cambridge, Mass.: Schenkman.

Maher, V. 1981. "Work, Consumption, and Authority Within the Household." In K. Young et al., eds., *Of Marriage and the Market: Women's Subordination in International Perspective,* pp. 69–87. London: CSE Books.

Mair, L. 1969. *Witchcraft.* New York: McGraw-Hill.

Malloy, J. and S. Borzutzky. 1982. "Politics, Social Welfare Policy, and the Population Problem in Latin America." *International Journal of Health Services* 12(1):77–98.

Malthus, Thomas. 1830. *A Summary View of the Principle of Population.* London: John Murray.

—— 1960 (orig. 1803). *On Population.* 2d ed. New York: Modern Library.

Mamdani, M. 1973. *The Myth of Population Control: Family, Caste, and Class in an Indian Village.* New York: Monthly Review Press.

Marcus, S. 1966. *The Other Victorians: A Study of Sexuality and Pornography in Mid-Nineteenth-Century England.* New York: Basic Books.

Marriner, S. 1953. "History of Liverpool, 1700–1900." In W. Smith, ed., *A Scientific Survey of Merseyside,* pp. 107–119. Liverpool: University Press of Liverpool.

Marshall, G. 1980. *Presbyteries and Profits: Calvinism and the Development of Capitalism in Scotland, 1560–1707.* Oxford: Clarendon Press.

Marshall, Lorna. 1976. *The Kung of the Nyae Nyae.* Cambridge: Harvard University Press.

Martin, M. and B. Voorhies. 1975. *Female of the Species.* New York: Columbia University Press.

Martin, P. 1978. Comments. *Current Anthropology* 19(1):23.

—— 1985. "Prehistoric Overkill: The Global Model." In P. Martin and R. Klein, eds., *Quarternary Extinctions: A Prehistoric Revolution,* pp. 354–403. Tucson: University of Arizona Press.

Mass, B. 1976. *Population Target: The Political Economy of Population Control in Latin America.* Ontario: Latin American Working Group.

Mathias, Peter. 1969. *The First Industrial Nation: An Economic History of Britain, 1700–1914.* London: Methuen.

May, B. 1981. *The Third World Calamity.* London: Routledge and Kegan Paul.

Meggers, B. 1954. "Environmental Limitation on the Development of Culture." *American Anthropologist* 56:801–824.

—— 1971. *Amazonia: Man and Culture in a Counterfeit Paradise.* Chicago: Aldine.

Meggitt, M. 1977. *Blood Is Their Argument: Warfare Among the Mae Enga Tribesmen of New Guinea Highlands.* Palo Alto, Calif.: Mayfield.

Mellaart, J. 1967. *Catal Huyuk: A Neolithic Town in Anatolia.* New York: McGraw-Hill.

Miller, Barbara. 1981. *The Endangered Sex.* Ithaca: Cornell University Press.

—— 1983. "Daughter Neglect, Women's Work, and Kingship: Pakistan and Bangladesh Compared." *Medical Anthropology* 8(2):109–126.

Minchinton, W. 1974. "Patterns and Structure of Demand 1500–1750." In

C. Cipolla, ed., *The Fontana Economic History of Europe: The Sixteenth and Seventeenth Centuries*, pp. 83–176. London: Collins.

Minge-Klevana, W. 1980. "Does Labor Time Decrease with Industrialization? A Survey of Time Allocation Studies." *Current Anthropology* 21:279–287.

Minturn, Leigh and J. Stashak. 1982. "Infanticide As a Terminal Abortion Procedure." *Behavior Science Research* 17:70–90.

Mintz, S. 1974. *Caribbean Transformation*. Chicago: Aldine.

Mitchell, W. 1980. "Local Ecology and the State: Implications of Contemporary Quechua Land Use for the Inca Sequence of Agricultural Work." In E. Ross, ed., *Beyond the Myths of Culture: Essays in Cultural Materialism*, pp. 139–154. New York: Academic Press.

Mols, R. 1974. "Population in Europe 1500–1700." In C. Cipolla, ed., *The Fontana Economic History of Europe: The Sixteenth and Seventeenth Centuries*, pp. 15–82. London: Collins.

Montgomery, G. and M. Sunquist. 1975. "Impact of Sloths on Neotropical Forest Energy Flow and Nutrient Cycling." In F. Golley and E. Medina, eds., *Tropical Ecological Systems*, pp. 69–98. New York: Springer.

Moran, E. 1979. *Human Adaptability: An Introduction to Ecological Anthropology*. Belmont, Calif.: Duxbury Press.

Moreno, M. 1976. *The Sugarmill: The Socioeconomic Complex of Sugar in Cuba*. New York: Monthly Review Press.

Morgan, V. 1976. "A Case Study of Population Change over Two Centuries: Blaris, Lisburn 1661–1848." *Irish Economic and Social History* 3:5–16.

Morineau, M. 1979. "The Potato in the Eighteenth Century." In R. Forster and O. Ranum, eds., *Food and Drink in History*. Baltimore: Johns Hopkins University Press.

Morren, George. 1977. "From Hunting to Herding: Pigs and the Control of Energy in Montane New Guinea." In R. Feacham and T. Bayliss-Smith, eds., *Subsistence and Survival: Rural Ecology in the Pacific*, pp. 274–313. London: Academic Press.

Morton, A. 1979 (orig. 1938). *A People's History of England*. London: Lawrence and Wishart.

Mosley, M. 1983. "Central Andean Civilization." In J. Jennings, ed., *Ancient South America*, pp. 179–239. San Francisco: Freeman.

Mukerjee, R. 1974 (orig. 1957). *The Rise and Fall of the East India Company*. New York: Monthly Review Press.

Mukhopadhyay, M. 1984. *Silver Shackles: Women and Development in India*. Oxford: Oxfam.

Myrdal, G. 1968. *Asian Drama: An Inquiry into the Poverty of Nations*, vol. 1. New York: Pantheon.

Nadel, S. 1952. "Witchcraft in Four African Societies." *American Anthropologist* 54(1):18–29.

Nag, Moni. 1962. *Factors Affecting Fertility in Nonindustrial Societies: A Cross-Cultural Study.* Yale University Publications in Anthropology No. 66. New Haven, Conn.: Department of Anthropology.

—— 1983a. "Modernization Affects Fertility." *Populi* 10:56–77.

—— 1983b. "The Impact of Sociocultural Factors on Breastfeeding and Sexual Behavior." In R. Bulatao and R. Lee, eds. *Determinants of Fertility in Developing Countries: A Summary of Knowledge,* 1:163–198. New York: Academic Press.

Nag, Moni and N. Kak. 1984. "Demographic Transition in the Punjab Village." *Population and Development Review* 10:661–678.

Nag, Moni, Benjamin White, and Robert Peet. 1978. "An Anthropological Approach to the Study of the Economic Value of Children in Java and Nepal." *Current Anthropology,* pp. 293–306.

Nardi, Bonnie. 1983. "Reply to Harbison's Comments on Nardi's 'Modes of Explanation in Anthropological Population Theory.'" *American Anthropologist* 85:662–664.

Navarro, V. 1982. "The Crisis of the International Capitalist Order and Its Implications for the Welfare State." *International Journal of Health Services* 12(2):169–190.

Needham, J. 1969. *The Grand Titration: Science and Society in East and West.* London: George Allen and Unwin.

Neel, J. V. 1968. "Some Aspects of Differential Fertility in Two American Indian Tribes." *Proceedings: 8th International Congress of Anthropological and Ethnological Sciences,* 1:356–361. Tokyo 1968.

—— 1977. "Health and Disease in Unacculturated Amerindian Populations." In K. Elliot and J. Whelan, eds., *Health and Disease in Tribal Societies.* New York: Elsevier.

Netting, R. 1981. *Balancing on an Alp: Ecological Change and Continuity in a Swiss Mountain Community.* Cambridge: Cambridge University Press.

Newenham, T. 1805. *A Statistical and Historical Inquiry into the Progress and Magnitude of the Population of Ireland.* London: C. and R. Baldwin.

Nichter, Mark and Mimi Nichter. 1983. "The Ethnophysiology and Folk Dietetics of Pregnancy: A Case Study from South India." *Human Organization* 42:235–246.

Noonan, J. T. 1966. *Contraception: A History of Its Treatment by the Catholic Theologians and Canonists.* Cambridge: Harvard University Press.

O'Conner, K. 1974. *The Irish in Britain.* Dublin: Torc Books.

O'Donovan, J. 1940. *The Economic History of Livestock in Ireland.* Dublin: Cork University Press.

O'Rourke, J. 1902. *The History of the Great Famine in 1847, with Notices of Earlier Famines.* Dublin: James Duffy.

Orwin, C. and E. Whetham. 1964. *History of British Agriculture, 1846–1914.* Newton Abbot: David and Charles.

Owen, R. 1823. *Statements Showing the Power that Ireland Possesses to Create*

Wealth Beyond the Most Ample Supply of the Wants of its Inhabitants. London: A. Applegath.

Page, H. and R. Lesthaeghe, eds., 1981. *Child-Spacing in Tropical Africa.* New York: Academic Press.

Pagels, E. 1979. *The Gnostic Gospels.* Harmondsworth: Penguin.

Parker, E. and J. Sanderson. 1871. *Report on the Sanitary Condition of Liverpool.* Borough of Liverpool: Town Council.

Parsons, J. 1976. "The Role of Chinampa Agriculture in the Food Supply of Aztec Tenochititlan." In C. Cleland, ed., *Cultural Change and Continuity: Essays in Honor of James Bennett Griffin,* pp. 233–257. New York: Academic Press.

Pelto, G. and P. Pelto. 1983. "Diet and Delocalization: Dietary Changes since 1750." In R. Rotberg and T. Rabb, eds., *Hunger and History: The Impact of Changing Food Production and Consumption Patterns on Society,* pp. 309–330. Cambridge: Cambridge University Press.

Pinchbeck, I. and B. Hewitt. 1973. *Children in English Society,* (2 vols.); Vol. 2: *From the Eighteenth Century to the Children Act 1848.* London: Routledge and Kegan Paul.

Polgar, S. 1972. "Population History and Population Policies from an Anthropological Perspective." *Current Anthropology* 13(2):203–211.

Pounds, N. 1973. *An Historical Geography of Europe, 450 B.C.–A.D. 1130.* Cambridge: Cambridge University Press.

Power, E. 1932. "Peasant Life and Rural Conditions (c. 1100 to c. 1500.)" In J. Tanner et al., eds., *The Cambridge Medieval History,* vol. 7: *Decline of Empire and Papacy,* pp. 716–750. Cambridge: Cambridge University Press.

Prentice, Andrew. 1984. "Adaptations to Long-Term Low Energy Intake." In Ernesto Pollitt and Peggy Amante, eds., *Energy Intake and Activity,* pp. 3–31. New York: Alan Liss.

Preston, Samuel. 1976. *Mortality Patterns in National Populations: With Special Reference to Recorded Causes of Death.* New York: Academic Press.

Price, T. 1983. "The European Mesolithic." *American Antiquity* 48:761–778.

Raphael, D. 1984. "Weaning Is Always: The Anthropology of Breastfeeding Behavior." *Ecology of Food and Nutrition* 15:203–213.

Rappaport, R. 1983. *Pigs for the Ancestors: Ritual in the Ecology of a New Guinea People.* New Haven: Yale University Press. 2d ed.

Reid, G. 1895. "Infant Mortality and Female Labour in Relation to Factory Legislation." *Journal of The Sanitary Institute* 15(4):497–503.

Renfrew, C. 1973. *Before Civilization: The Radiocarbon Revolution and Prehistoric Europe.* New York: Knopf.

Riches, D. 1974. "The Netsilik Eskimo: A Special Case of Selective Female Infanticide." *Ethnology* 13:351–361.

Roberts, R. 1971. *Salford: The Classic Slum.* Harmondsworth: Penguin.

Roosevelt, A. 1977. "History of Aboriginal Subsistence in a Floodplain Region of Northern Amazonia." Manuscript.

—— 1980. *Parmana: Prehistoric Maize and Manioc Subsistence Along the Amazon and Orinoco*. New York: Academic Press.

Rosenberg, E. M. 1980. "Demographic Effects of Sex-Differential Nutrition." In J. Kandel and G. Pelto, eds., *Nutritional Anthropology: Contemporary Approaches to Diet and Culture*, pp. 181–203. Pleasantville, N.Y.: Redgrave.

Ross, E. 1976. *The Achuara Jívaro: Cultural Adaptation in the Upper Amazon*. Ann Arbor: University Microfilms.

—— 1978a. "Food Taboos, Diet, and Hunting Strategy: The Adaptation to Animals in Amazon Cultural Ecology." *Current Anthropology* 19(1):36.

—— 1978b. "The Evolution of the Amazon Peasantry." *Journal of Latin American Studies* 10(2):193–218.

—— 1983a. "The Riddle of the Scottish Pig." *Bioscience* 33(2):99–106.

—— 1983b. "An Overview of Trends in Human Dietary Variation from Hunter-Gatherers to Modern Capitalism." Paper prepared for Wenner-Gren Conference on Food Preferences and Aversions, Cedar Key, Florida.

—— In press. "Potatoes, Population, and the Irish Famine: The Political Economy of Demographic Change." In W. Handwerker, ed., *Culture and Reproduction: Reconstructing the Demographic Paradigm*. Boulder: Westview Press.

Ross, Eric, ed. 1980. *Beyond the Myths of Culture: Essays in Cultural Materialism*. New York: Academic Press.

Ross, Jane. 1980. "Ecology and the Problem of Tribe: A Critique of the Hobbesian Model of Preindustrial Warfare." In E. Ross, ed., *Beyond the Myths of Culture: Essays in Cultural Materialism*, pp. 33–60. New York: Academic Press.

Roth, Eric. 1985. "A Note on the Demographic Concomitants of Sedentism." *American Anthropologist* 87:380–382.

Rowntree, B. and M. Kendall. 1913. *How the Labourer Lives: A Study of the Rural Labour Problem*. London: Thomas Nelson and Sons.

Rudd, J. 1982. "Introduction." In K. Dayus, *Her People*. London: Virago Press.

Rupesinghe, K. 1985. "The Effects of Export-Oriented Industrialisation in Sri Lanka." *The Ecologist* 15(5/6):246–256.

Russell, J. B. 1972. *Witchcraft in the Middle Ages*. Ithaca: Cornell University Press.

Russell, J. C. 1972. "Population in Europe 500–1500." In C. Cipolla, ed., *The Fontana Economic History of Europe: The Middle Ages*, pp. 25–70. London: Collins.

Sahlins, Marshall. 1972. *Stone Age Economics*. Chicago: Aldine.

Salaman, R. 1949. *The History and Social Influence of the Potato*. Cambridge: Cambridge University Press.

Salzman, P., ed. 1971. "Comparative Studies of Nomadism and Pastoralism. *Anthropological Quarterly* 44(3):104–210.

Sanders, William and Barbara Price. 1968. *Meso-America: The Evolution of a Civilization*. New York: Random House.

Sanders, W., R. Santley and J. Parsons. 1979. *The Basin of Mexico: Ecological Processes in the Evolution of a Civilization*. New York: Academic Press.

Sato, S. 1977. "The Camel Ecology of the Rendille." Paper presented at Seminar on "Pastoral Societies of Kenya," Ethnographic Museum of Japan. Mimeo.

Saucier, J. 1972. "Correlates of the Long Post-partum Taboo: A Cross-Cultural Study." *Current Anthropology* 13(2):238–249.

Scheper-Hughes, N. 1984. "Infant Mortality and Infant Care: Cultural and Economic Constraints on Nurturing in Northeast Brazil." *Social Science and Medicine* 19:535–546.

Schneider, H. 1957. "The Subsistence Role of Cattle Among the Pakot in East Africa." *American Anthropologist* 59:278–301.

Schneider, J. and P. Schneider. n.d. "Unraveling Malthus: The Demographic Transition in a Sicilian Agrotown." Manuscript.

Schrire, Carmel. 1980. "An Inquiry into the Evolutionary Status and Apparent Identity of San Hunter Gatherers." *Human Ecology* 8:9–32.

Schrire, Carmel and W. L. Steiger. 1974. "A Matter of Life and Death: An Investigation into the Practice of Female Infanticide in the Arctic." *Man* 9:161–184.

Schurman, F. and O. Schell, eds. 1967. *The China Reader*. New York: Random House.

Scrimshaw, Susan. 1978. "Infant Mortality and Behavior in the Regulation of Family Size." *Population and Development Review* 4:383–403.

—— 1983. "Infanticide as Deliberate Fertility Control." In R. Bulatao and R. Lee, eds., *Determinants of Fertility in Developing Countries: Fertility Regulation and Institutional Influences*, 2:245–266. New York: Academic Press.

—— 1984. "Infanticide in Human Populations: Societal and Individual Concerns." In Glenn Hausfater and Sarah Hrdy, eds., *Infanticide: Comparative and Evolutionary Perspectives*, pp. 439–462. New York: Aldine.

Segal, R. 1965. *The Crisis of India*. London: Jonathan Cape.

Sella, D. 1974. "European Industries 1500–1700." In C. Cipolla, ed., *The Fontana Economic History of Europe: The Sixteenth and Seventeenth Centuries*, pp. 354–426. London: Collins.

Sharma, D. 1955. "Mother, Child, and Nutrition." *Journal of Tropical Pediatrics* 1:47–53.

Shimmin, H. 1864. *The Courts and Alleys of Liverpool. Described from Personal Inspection*. Liverpool: Lee and Nightingale.

Short, R. V. 1984. "Breast Feeding." *Scientific American* 250(4):35–41.

Shorter, E. 1982. *A History of Women's Bodies*. Harmondsworth: Penguin.

Shostak, M. 1981. *Nisa: The Life and Words of a !Kung Woman*. Cambridge: Harvard University Press.

Sigsworth, E. and T. Wyke. 1972. "A Study of Victorian Prostitution and

Venereal Disease." In M. Vicinus, ed., *Suffer and Be Still: Women in the Victorian Age.* Bloomington: Indiana University Press.

Simon, J. 1977. *The Economics of Population Growth.* Princeton: Princeton University Press.

Skinner, B. F. 1984. "Selection by Consequences." *Behavioral and Brain Sciences* 7:477–510.

Skinner, G. W. "Gender and Power in Japanese Families: Consequences for Reproductive Behavior and Longevity." Paper read at the 84th Annual Meeting of the American Anthropological Association. Washington, D.C. December 4–8.

Slicher Van Bath, B. A. 1963. *The Agrarian History of Western Europe: 500–1850.* London: Edward Arnold.

Smith, A. 1984. *The Emergence of a Nation State: The Commonwealth of England, 1529–1660.* London: Longman.

Smith, E. A. 1983. "Anthropological Applications of Optimal Foraging Theory: A Critical Review." *Current Anthropology* 24:625–651.

Smith, Richard. 1981. "Fertility, Economy, and Household Formation in England over Three Centuries." *Population and Development Review* 7:595–622.

—— 1983. "On Putting the Child Before Marriage. Reply to Birdsall." *Population and Development Review* 9:124–135.

Sorenson, Richard. 1972. "Socio-Ecological Change Among the Fore of New Guinea." *Current Anthropology* 13:349–383.

Spengler, J. 1972. "Demographic Factors and Early Modern Economic Development." In D. Glass and R. Revelle, eds., *Population and Social Change,* pp. 86–98. London: Edward Arnold.

—— 1974. *Population Change, Modernization, and Welfare.* Englewood Cliffs, N.J.: Prentice-Hall.

Steele, E. 1974. *Irish Land and British Politics: Tenant-right and Nationality, 1865–1870.* London: Cambridge University Press.

Steven, L. and S. Lee, eds. 1921–22. *The Dictionary of National Biography.* London: Oxford University Press.

Stocks, A. 1983. "Cocamilla Fishing: Patch Modification and Environmental Buffering in the Amazon *Varzea.*" In R. Hames and W. Vickers, eds., *Adaptive Responses of Native Amazonians,* pp. 239–267. New York: Academic Press.

Stone, L. 1977. *The Family, Sex, and Marriage in England, 1500–1800.* London: Weidenfeld and Nicolson.

Storey, R. 1985. "Estimate of Mortality in a Pre-Columbian Urban Population." *American Anthropologist* 87:519–535.

Strangeland, C. 1966 (orig. 1904). *Pre-Malthusian Doctrine of Population: A Study in the History of Economic Theory.* New York: Augustus M. Kelley.

Stuard, S. 1984. "The Sociobiological Model and the Medieval Evidence." *American Anthropologist* 86(2):410–413.

Sussman, R. 1972. "Child Transport, Family Size, and Increase in Human Population During the Neolithic." *Current Anthropology* 13(2):258–259.

Tanner, W. and A. Zihlman. 1976. "Women in Evolution. Part 1: Innovations and Selection in Human Origins." *Signs* 1(3–1):585–608.

Taylor, I. 1974. "The Insanitary Housing Question and Tenement Dwellings in Nineteenth-century Liverpool." In A. Sutcliffe, ed., *Multi-Storey Living*, pp. 41–87. London: Croom Helm.

Textor, R. 1967. *A Cross-cultural Summary.* New Haven, Conn.: HRAF Press.

Thompson, E. P. 1963. *The Making of the English Working Class.* New York: Vintage.

Thompson, R. 1802. *Statistical Survey of the County of Meath, with Observations on the Means of Improvement.* Dublin: Graisberry and Campbell.

Thoughts on Ireland (Anonymous). 1847. London: James Ridgway.

Tilakaratne, M. W. 1978. "Economic Change, Social Differentiation, and Fertility: Aluthgana." In G. Hawthorn, ed., *Population and Development: High and Low Fertility in Poorer Countries*, pp. 186–197. London: Frank Cass.

Tilly, C., ed. 1978. "Introduction." *Historical Studies in Changing Fertility.* Princeton: Princeton University Press.

The Times of London. 1880. *The Great Irish Famine of 1845–46.* London: The Times.

Toor, Francis. 1947. *A Treasury of Mexican Folkways.* New York: Crown.

Trant, H. 1954. "Food Taboos in East Africa." *Lancet* 2:703–705.

Tranter, N. 1981. "The Labour Supply, 1780–1860." In R. Floud and D. McCloskey, eds., *The Economic History of Britain Since 1700*, 1:204–226. Cambridge: Cambridge University Press.

Treble, J. 1971. "Liverpool Working-class Housing, 1801–1851." In S. Chapman, ed., *The History of Working Class Housing*, pp. 167–220. Newton Abbot: David and Charles.

Trevelyan, C. 1848. *The Irish Crisis.* London: Longman, Brown, Green and Longmans.

Trexler, R. 1973a. "Infanticide in Florence: New Sources and First Results." *History of Childhood Quarterly* (1):98–116.

———. 1973b. "The Foundlings of Florence, 1395–1455." *History of Childhood Quarterly* 1(2):259–284.

Trow-Smith, R. 1959. *A History of British Livestock Husbandry, 1700–1900.* London: Routledge and Kegan Paul.

Trussel, James and Anne Pebley. 1984. "The Potential Impact of Changes in Fertility on Infant, Child, and Maternal Mortality." *Studies in Family Planning* 15:267–280.

Tuke, J. 1880. *Irish Distress and Its Remedies; the Land Question; A Visit to Donegal and Connaught in the Spring of 1880.* London: W. Ridgway.

Tupling, G. 1927. *The Economic History of Rossendale.* Manchester: Manchester University Press.

Ulman, G. 1979. *The Science of Society*. The Hague: Mouton.

United Nations. 197x. *The Determinants and Consequences of Population Trends*, vol. 1. New York: United Nations.

—— 1975. *Demographic Yearbook, 1974*. New York: United Nations.

Vaidyanathan, A., N. Nair, and M. Harris. 1982. "Bovine Sex and Age Ratios in India." *Current Anthropology* 23:365–383.

Van der Walt, L., E. Wilmsen, and T. Jenkins. 1978. "Unusual Sex Hormone Patterns among Desert-Dwelling Hunter-Gatherers. *Journal of Clinical Endocrinology and Metabolism* 46:658–663.

Vaughn, W. and A. Fitzpatrick. 1978. *Irish Historical Statistics: Population, 1821–1971*. Dublin: Royal Irish Academy.

Vickers, W. 1983. "The Territorial Dimensions of Siona-Secoya and Encabellado Adaptation." In R. Hames and W. Vickers, eds., *Adaptive Responses of Native Amazonians*, pp. 451–478. New York: Academic Press.

Victoria, C. and J. P. Vaughan. 1985. "Land Tenure Patterns and Child Health in Southern Brazil: The Relationship Between Agricultural Production, Malnutrition, and Child Mortality." *International Journal of Health Services* 15(2):253–274.

Vining, Daniel. 1985. "Social Versus Reproductive Success: The Central Theoretical Problem of Sociology." *Behavioral and Brain Sciences*.

Vogt, Evon and F. Cancian. 1970. "Social Integration and the Classic Maya: Some Problems in Haviland's Argument." *American Antiquity* 35:101–102.

Wakefield, E. 1812. *An Account of Ireland, Statistical and Political*. London: Longman, Hurst, Rees, Orme, and Brown.

Walkowitz, J. 1977. "The Making of an Outcast Group: Prostitutes and Working Women in Nineteenth-Century Plymouth and Southampton." In M. Vicinus, ed., *A Widening Sphere: Changing Roles of Victorian Women*. Bloomington: Indiana University Press.

Watkins, S. and E. Van de Walle. 1983. "Nutrition, Mortality, and Population Size: Malthus's Court of Last Resort." In R. Rotberg and T. Rabb, eds., *Hunger and History: The Impact of Changing Food Production and Consumption Patterns on Society*, pp. 7–28. Cambridge: Cambridge University Press.

Watson, J. 1965. "From Hunting to Horticulture in the New Guinea Highlands." *Ethnology* 4:195–309.

Wattenberg, B. and K. Zinsmeister. 1986. "The Birth Dearth: The Geopolitical Consequences." *Public Opinion* (December/January), pp. 7–13.

Wellin, E. 1955. "Maternal and Infant Feeding Practices in a Peruvian Village." *Journal of the American Dietetic Association* 31:889–894.

Werkman, E. 1983. "Amsterdam." In *The New Encyclopaedia Britannica (Macropoedia)*, 1:711–715. Chicago: Encyclopaedia Britannica.

Werner, D. 1979. "A Cross-Cultural Perspective on Theory and Research on Male Homosexuality." *Journal of Homosexuality* 4:345–362.

White, Benjamin. 1973. "Demand for Labor and Population Growth in Colonial Java." *Human Ecology* 1:217–236.

—— 1976. "Production and Reproduction in a Javanese Village." Ph.D. dissertation, Columbia University.

—— 1982. "Child Labor and Population Growth in Rural Asia." *Development and Change* 13:587–610.

—— 1983. "Agricultural Involution and Its Critics: Twenty Years after Clifford Geertz." The Hague: Institute of Social Studies, Working Papers Series No. 6.

White, Lynn. 1964. *Medieval Technology and Social Change.* New York: Oxford University Press.

Whiting, J. 1964. "Effects of Climate on Certain Cultural Practices." In W. Goodenough, ed., *Explorations in Cultural Anthropology,* pp. 511–544. New York: McGraw-Hill.

Wilkinson, L. P. 1979. *Classical Attitudes to Modern Issues.* London: William Kimber.

Wilkinson, R. 1973. *Poverty and Progress: An Ecological Model of Economic Development.* London: Methuen.

Wilmsen, E. 1978. "Seasonal Effects of Dietary Intake on Kalahari San." *Proceedings of the Federation of American Societies for Experimental Biology* 37(1):25–32.

—— 1982. "Biological Variables in Forager Fertility Performance: A Critique of Bongaarts Model." Boston University: African Studies Center, Working Papers No. 60.

Wilson, Charles and B. Lenman. 1977. "The British Isles." In C. Wilson and G. Parker, eds. *An Introduction to the Sources of European Economic History, 1500–1800.* Vol. 1: *Western Europe,* pp. 115–154. London: Weidenfeld and Nicolson.

Wilson, Charles and G. Parker, eds. 1977. *An Introduction to the Sources of European Economic History, 1500–1800.* Vol. 1: *Western Europe.* London: Weidenfeld and Nicolson.

Wilson, Christine. 1980. "Food Taboos of Childbirth: The Malay Example." In John Robson, ed., *Food, Ecology and Culture: Readings in the Anthropology of Dietary Practices,* pp. 67–74. New York: Gordon Breach.

Winterhalder, B. and E. Alden Smith, eds. 1981. *Hunter-Gatherer Foraging Strategies: Ethnographic and Archaeological Analyses.* Chicago: University of Chicago Press.

Wishik, S. and R. Stern. 1975. "Impact of Birth Spacing on Maternal and Child Nutrition." *Proceedings of the 9th International Congress of Nutrition,* 2:32–36.

Wittfogel, K. 1957. *Oriental Despotism: A Comparative Study of Total Power.* New Haven: Yale University Press.

Wolf, E. 1969. *Peasant Wars of the Twentieth Century.* New York: Harper.

—— 1982. *Europe and the People Without History.* Berkeley: University of California Press.

Wood, C. 1982. "The Political Economy of Infant Mortality in Sao Paulo, Brazil." *International Journal of Health Services* 12(2):215–229.

Worthington, B. 1979. "Nutrition in Pregnancy." *Birth and the Family Journal* 6:184.

Wrigley, E. A. 1969. *Population and History.* London: Cambridge University Press.

Wrigley, E. A. and R. S. Schofield. 1981. *The Population History of England, 1541–1871: A Reconstruction.* Cambridge: Harvard University Press.

Yesner, D. 1983. "Life in the 'Garden of Eden': Causes and Consequences of the Adoption of Marine Diets by Human Societies." Paper prepared for Wenner-Gren Conference on Food Preferences and Aversions, Cedar Key, Florida.

Zihlman, A. 1983. "Dietary Divergence of Apes and Early Hominids." Paper prepared for Wenner-Gren Conference on Food Preferences and Aversions, Cedar Key, Florida.

Name Index

Abernathy, Virginia, 83
Adams, Brooks, 107–8
Adelstein, P., 8
Aikin, J., 109, 114
Ainsworth-Davis, J., 128
Alexander, P., 146
Allen, L. L., 22
Anderson, M., 112, 116
Anderson, P., 84, 87
Angel, L., 42, 74
Aquinas, St. Thomas, 86, 87, 94
Aristotle, 79
Armelagos, G., 42–43
Asoka, emperor of India, 77
Augustine, St., 84, 85
Augustus Caesar, 78–79, 81

Balicki, Asen, 31, 32
Bamford, Samuel, 130
Bardhan, P., 158, 159, 160
Barth, F., 45, 46
Beach, F., 66
Beaton, George, 165
Beer, M., 148, 149, 184n
Berg, A., 162
Bernstein, R., 180
Besant, Annie, 124–25
Bhatia, B. M., 139, 140, 141–42
Bielenstein, Hans, 77
Binford, L., 27, 38–39
Birdsall, Nancy, 100
Birdsell, J., 31, 32
Bolian, C., 52
Bongaarts, John, 8, 9, 10, 24
Booth, William, 123
Borah, W., 106
Borzutzky, S., 179
Boserup, E., 100, 101
Boswell, J., 67, 82, 83, 84

Bradlaugh, Charles, 124–25
Braidwood, R., 41
Brandel, S., 93
Braudel, Fernand, 93
Brookfield, H., 63
Briggs, J., 22–23
Brown, B., 109, 142
Brown, J., 27
Brown, P., 63
Buchbinder, G., 66
Buckley, James, 176, 181
Buikstra, Jane, 42
Bullen, Beverly, 24
Butler, C., 122
Butzer, K., 37, 77

Caesar, Gaius Julius, 78
Cain, Mead, 172–73
Caldwell, John, 1, 11, 173
Cancian, F., 77
Carneiro, R., 49, 51, 58, 62
Cashdan, Elizabeth, 16, 17
Cavilli-Sforza, L., 17, 32
Chadwick, D., 112
Chagnon, N., 32, 54, 57–58, 59, 60, 61
Chasko, W. J., 27, 38–39
Chen, L. E., 42, 161, 164, 168
Cicero, 78
Clark, C., 77
Clarke, W., 63, 64
Coale, A., 88
Coe, M., 40
Cohen, M., 42–43
Cohen, Mark, 38, 40, 42–43
Cohen, Myron, 78
Cole, D., 45
Collier, F., 111
Connell, K., 127
Constantine, emperor, 83, 84–85

Cook, S., 106
Coontz, S., 100
Coote, C., 128
Cotton, Sir Arthur, 140
Cowlishaw, G., 32
Crane, Barbara, 177
Crittenden, A., 178
Cullen, L., 126, 129

Dahlberg, F., 27
Davis, D., 55
Deane, P., 108
Defoe, Daniel, 113–14
De Mause, Lloyd, 80, 83, 90, 91
Denevan, W., 47n, 49, 51
De Ste. Croix, G., 167
Devereux, G., 5, 28
Dickemann, M., 6, 28, 29, 32, 90, 92, 97, 98, 99
Digby, A., 142, 150
Divale, W., 32, 56–57
Dobb, M., 87, 94, 95, 149
Dobby, E., 146
Dover, K. J., 81
Drake, Michael, 126
Duby, G., 86, 87
Dufour, D., 39
Dumond, D., 22, 34
Durward, L., 165
Dutt, R. P., 107, 140, 142, 143
Dyson, Tim, 160
Dyson-Hudson, Neville, 45
Dyson-Hudson, Rada, 45

Eisenberg, J., 55
El Saadawi, N., 177
Ember, C., 43–44, 49, 50, 70
Engels, F., 115

Farwell, Byron, 134
Feder, E., 178, 180
Fedrick, J., 8
Ferro-Luzzi, G. E., 164
Finkle, Jason, 177
Fisher, C., 144, 146
Fitzpatrick, A., 137
Flannery, K., 40
Flegel, P., 169
Flinn, M., 32
Ford, C., 66

Foster, T., 134
Frank, Andre Gunder, 105
Freeman, M. M. R., 32
Freeman, Thomas, 126, 135
Fried, Morton, 4
Frisancho, A. R., 169
Frisch, R., 7, 8, 23, 24, 26, 119, 122
Froude, James, 125
Furnivall, J., 144

Geertz, C., 144, 146–47, 147
Gill, C., 128, 131, 132
Glamann, K., 93, 108
Glass, D. V., 88
Golley, F., 54
Goody, J., 85, 86
Graham, S., 24
Greene, R., 130
Griffith, G., 132
Gross, D., 12, 54
Gulliver, P., 45
Gupta, Monica Das, 173
Gwatkin, D., 93

Hajnal, J., 88
Hall, Mrs. S. C., 134–35
Hall, S. C., 134–35
Hames, P., 59, 60, 61
Hames, R., 54, 58, 62
Hamilton, Margaret, 56
Hamilton, Sahni, 7–8, 9, 23
Handwerker, W., 16, 18, 23, 33, 38
Hanley, Susan, 98, 102
Harpending, H., 34
Harrell, Barbara, 167
Harris, David, 2, 37, 48, 49, 70
Harris, M., 1, 4, 10, 16, 19, 22, 32, 54, 55, 56–57, 67, 103, 160
Harrison, A., 120
Harrison, P., 71, 148
Hassan, F., 41, 75
Hastings, Warren, 141
Hatcher, John, 93
Haviland, W., 76
Hawkes, K., 38
Hayden, B., 34, 38
Hayter, T., 178
Hazlitt, William, 149
Hechter, M., 130
Heinsohn, G., 152

Helm, June, 32
Henry, L., 15
Herlihy, David, 88
Hewill, M., 118, 119, 122, 123
Hewitt, B., 92, 118, 121
Hickerson, H., 61
Hobsbawm, E., 120
Holden, Constance, 177
Homer, 81
Hopkins, K., 81, 82, 83
Howe, M., 76n
Howell, N., 23, 24, 27, 29, 34
Hrdy, S., 25–26, 29–30, 66
Huffman, S., 24, 25, 42
Hutchins, B., 120
Hutchinson, H. W., 170

Isacsson, Sven-Erik, 40

Jeffery, Roger, 158, 168
Jeffery, P., 158, 168
Jelliffe, D. B., 8, 70
Jelliffe, E. F., 8
Jenkins, T., 24
Jochim, M., 31
Johansson, Sheila, 156, 157, 163, 168
Johnson, A., 48
Johnson, J., 128, 133

Kak, N., 174
Katona-Apte, J., 163, 165
Kellum, B., 90
Kelly, R. C., 67
Kendall, M., 163
Kennedy, R., 135
Kerr, B., 133
Keys, A., 8
Khazanov, A. M., 45
Knodel, J., 13, 15, 17, 105
Knowles, L., 141

Langer, W., 83, 90, 91, 119
Laslett, P., 89
Lea, H., 97
Leacock, E., 44, 70
Ledbetter, R., 125
Lee, J., 136, 137
Lee, R. B., 22, 34, 70
Lee, R. D., 102
Lee, S., 135n

Lenman, B., 113
LeRoy Ladurie, E., 88, 89
Lesthaeghe, R., 17
Levine, D., 113
Levine, S., 89
Lindenbaum, S., 42, 64, 68, 70
Little, M., 47, 63
Livingstone, Frank, 55
Lizot, J., 58, 59
Lovett-Doust, J., 25

McAlpin, M., 142
McArthur, J., 24
MacCormack, Carol P., 5
McKee, L., 161, 162
McKeown, T., 100
McLaren, A., 91, 97, 124
McNamara, Robert, 179–80
MacNeil, J., 125
MacNeish, R., 40
Maher, V., 162–63, 166
Mair, L., 69
Malloy, J., 179
Malthus, Thomas, 112–13, 124, 125, 134, 135, 148–53, 181, 183
Mamdani, M., 172
Marcus, Steven, 123
Marriner, S., 114
Marshall, G., 103
Marshall, Lorna, 31
Martin, M., 68
Martin, P., 37
Mass, B., 179
Mathias, Peter, 106, 107, 109, 111, 122
Matos, J., 169
Meggers, G., 46–47, 51, 53
Meggitt, M., 64
Melancon, T., 32
Mencher, 137
Metellus Macedonius, 78
Miller, Barbara, 157–58, 159, 160
Minchinton, W., 95–96
Minge-Klevana, W., 120
Minturn, Leigh, 7, 29, 30
Mintz, W., 145
Mitchell, W., 74
Mols, R., 93, 95
Montgomery, G., 55
Moore, Mick, 160
Moran, E., 45–46, 47

More, Thomas, 95
Moreno, M., 173
Morgan, V., 137
Morineau, M., 129
Morren, George, 47, 63, 64
Morton, A., 95, 107, 108, 111, 130, 139, 144
Mosley, M., 75
Mukerjee, R., 139, 140, 141
Mukhopadhyay, M., 160, 168, 175
Myrdal, Gunnar, 138

Nadel, S., 69
Nag, Moni, 9, 33, 172, 174, 175
Nardi, Bonnie, 1
Navarro, V., 167, 180
Needham, J., 77
Neel, James V., 6, 60
Newenham, T., 128, 131
Newenham, Thomas, 129
Nichter, Mark, 170
Nichter, Mimi, 170
Noonan, J. T., 84, 86, 87, 89

O'Connell, J., 38
O'Connor, K., 133
O'Donovan, J., 128, 134, 136
O'Rourke, J., 135
Orwin, C., 128
Owen, Robert, 132–33

Page, H., 17
Pagels, E., 85
Parker, E., 115
Parker, G., 100
Parsons, J., 75
Pebley, Anne, 8
Pelto, G., 178
Pelto, P., 178
Pericles, 79
Petty, William, 113
Phillip of Macedon, 79
Pinchbeck, I., 92, 118, 120–21
Plato, 79, 80
Pliny the Elder, 78
Polgar, S., 6, 55, 76
Popkin, B., 7–8, 9, 23
Pounds, N., 87, 92
Power, E., 87
Prentice, Andrew, 164, 171

Preston, Samuel, 15, 120
Price, Barbara, 4
Price, T., 38

Raphael, D., 9
Rappaport, R., 66
Reid, G., 118
Riches, D., 31
Roberts, R., 71
Roosevelt, A., 52, 53
Rosenberg, E. M., 69, 70, 164
Ross, E., 2, 38, 39, 40, 42, 51, 54, 55, 58, 59, 128, 134
Ross, J., 61
Roth, Eric, 41
Rowntree, B., 163
Rudd, J., 101
Rupesinghe, K., 167, 179
Russell, J. B., 94, 96, 97
Russell, J. C., 92, 93, 94

Sahlins, Marshall, 13
Salzman, P., 45
Sanders, William, 4, 75
Sanderson, J., 115
Santley, R., 75
Sato, S., 45
Scheper-Hughes, N., 169, 170, 171
Schneider, H., 45
Schneider, J., 99
Schneider, P., 99
Schofield, R. S., 88, 95, 96, 102, 105, 110, 116
Schrire, Carmel, 32–33, 34
Scrimshaw, Susan, 6, 169
Segal, R., 159
Sella, D., 95
Sharma, D., 164
Shimmin, H., 114
Short, R. V., 8
Shorter, E., 28, 166
Shostak, M., 29
Sigsworth, E., 120
Simon, Julian, 177
Skinner, B. F., 14
Skinner, G. W., 99
Slicher Van Bath, B. A., 87
Smith, A., 96
Smith, E. A., 38
Smith, E. Alden, 38

Smith, R., 88, 116
Sorenson, Richard, 63
Spicer, D., 9, 23
Stashak, J., 7, 29, 30
Steele, E., 135
Steiger, O., 152
Steiger, W. L., 32–33
Stern, R., 24, 165
Steven, L., 135n
Stocks, A., 52
Stone, L., 104
Storey, R., 76
Strangeland, C., 78, 79
Sunquist, M., 55
Sussman, R., 22

Tanner, W., 23
Taylor, I., 114
Textor, R., 49
Thompson, E. P., 119–20, 122
Thompson, R., 132
Tilakaratne, M. W., 173
Tilly, C., 104
Toor, Francis, 170
Trant, H., 164
Tranter, N., 100, 102
Treble, J., 113, 114
Trevelyan, Charles, 135
Trexler, R., 91
Trow-Smith, R., 128
Trussell, James, 8

Vaidyanathan, A., 160
Van de Walle, E., 7, 13, 15, 105
Van der Walt, L., 24
Vaughan, J. P., 162
Vaughan, W., 137
Vickers, W., 54, 58

Victoria, C., 162
Victoria, queen of England, 134
Vining, Daniel, 99
Vogt, Evon, 77
Voorhies, B., 68

Wakefield, E., 135
Walkowitz, J., 123
Wallace, Robert, 148, 151n
Watkins, S., 7
Watson, C., 178
Watson, J., 63
Wattenberg, B., 176
Weber, Max, 103, 104
Wellin, E., 164
Werkman, E., 146
Werner, D., 67
Whetham, E., 128
White, Benjamin, 147, 172
White, Lynn, 86
Whiting, J., 41, 49
Wilkinson, L. P., 78, 79, 80, 82
Wilmsen, E., 10, 24, 26
Wilson, Charles, 100, 113
Wilson, Christine, 164
Winterhalder, B., 38
Wishik, S., 24, 165
Wolf, E., 54, 105, 142, 145
Wood, C., 179
Worthington, B., 29
Wrigley, E. A., 76, 88, 104, 105, 109–10, 116
Wrightson, K., 89
Wyke, T., 120

Yesner, D., 38

Zihlman, A., 22, 23
Zinsmeister, K., 176

Subject Index

Abandonment (infant), 91, 119

Abortifacients, 28, 80

Abortion (feticide), 5, 8, 15, 16, 18, 25, 32, 89, 90, 151, 182; in ancient Greece and Rome, 80, 83; Christianity and, 85; induced, 27–29; and infanticide, 6; out-of-wedlock, 9; repression of, 124, 183; sex-specific, 19; spontaneous, 25–27, 34, 41; U.S. policy opposing, 181–82

Adolescent sterility, 7

Africa, 107

Age at marriage, 9, 78, 88–89, 110

Agrarian rebellions, 77–78

Agrarian systems, 103

Agribusiness, 144

Agricultural economies: child labor in, 39–40; crops in, 47–50

Agricultural intensification, 49–50, 51, 54, 61, 68; distribution of costs of, 69–71; in Dutch-controlled Java, 144–47; in Middle Ages, 87; and population growth: Ireland, 129–32, 136; and population growth: New Guinea, 63, 64, 65, 66; and rise of state, 73, 75; and value of child labor, 172, 174

Agriculture, 40–41, 177; commercialization of, 95, 156, 172; hunting-dependent, 53–55; in India, 140, 141; in Middle Ages, 86–87; and population regulation, 37–71; slash-and-burn, 46–47, 63; slave-based, 82, 84; Third World, 180; work-time comparisons, 50T

Alliances, 11–12

Amazon Basin, 51–53, 55

Amazonia, 4, 58, 69

Amenorrhea, 7, 41, 119; lactational, 8, 9, 10, 24–25, 33, 34, 68; nutrition and, 24–25; postpartum, 38, 49

Amerindians, 32, 55

Amino acids, 48, 49, 58

Amsterdam, 143, 145–46

Andes (the), 48, 49

Animal biomass, 54–55

Animal domesticants, 62–66

Anthropological archaeology, 2

Anthropology, 2

Antinatalist policy, 67

Army, Roman, 82

Asia, 45, 48, 107; infant mortality control, 97–99

Australian hunter-gatherers, 32

Baby food, 118

Bands, 3–4, 51; warfare in, 55–56, 73

Bangladesh, 41–42, 158–59, 161, 164, 172–73

Basseri (people), 46

Bastardy, 88–89, 91

Behavior: intention and, 16–17

Belief systems, in sex-biased nutritional depletion, 164–67; see also Cultural context

Berbers, 162–63, 166

Biocultural factors, 14; in lactational amenorrhea, 8–9

Birth control, 15, 16, 124–25, 153; intentionality in, 14, 16–17; in Malthus, 151–53; see also Contraception; Population regulation

Birth intervals, 8, 16, 23, 24, 25, 39, 41, 43–44

Birth process, 12, 19, 44

Birth rate, 102, 124, 136; culturally mediated, 34

Births: healthy, 5; illegitimate, 90; live, 101–02; premature, 7
Birthweight, 7, 165
Black Death, 92
"Blaming the victim," 148, 171
Borneo, 143
Bourgeoisie, 95
Brazil, 169, 171, 178–79
Breast-feeding, 8, 24–25, 41–42, 49, 147, 162; vs. infanticide, 33–35; sedentarism and, 38, 39
Breast milk, 7, 8, 9
Bristol, 108
Buddhism, 84

Calories, 23, 24, 49, 164
Cambridge Group, 102
Capital, colonies as source of, 107–08, 109, 138
Capital accumulation, 105, 106
Capitalism, 19, 40, 88, 103, 104, 105; ideological rationalization of, in Malthus, 148–51; and "surplus" population, 138; Third World, 178–79; and underdevelopment, 175
Caribbean, 106, 107, 109, 127, 145
Cattle, 160–61
Celebes, 143
Celibacy, 11, 46, 79, 88, 137; in Christianity, 85, 86
Ceramic containers, 38, 39
Cheshire, 111, 112T
Chiefdoms, 4, 51
Chieftancies, 74, 81
Childbearing, costs of, 166–67; *see also* Birth process
Child care, 5–7, 44, 78, 92
Child labor, 41, 101, 116, 147; in England, 117–18; hunter-gatherer societies, 39–40; and mortality control, 156, 157; value of, 109–13, 120–21, 147, 172–75
Child labor laws, 117
Child mortality, 93, 94, 110, 113; in agricultural economies, 41, 42; ethnoeugenics in, 169–71; medical selective neglect and, 167–68, 171
Child rearing, *see* Costs/benefits of child rearing

Children, 5–7, 16, 101; economic value of, 109–13, 136, 172–75; survivorship of, 159–60, 162; unwanted, 16, 91, 171; wage labor opportunities for, 100
Children's Employment Commission (England), 111
China, 3, 74, 78, 103, 177; infanticide, 97–98, 99, 157; population growth, 77
Christianity, 84–86
Circum-Mediterranean area, 45
City-state(s), 53, 75, 81
Class: and the demographic transition, 116–22; and population regulation, 19; in rise of state, 77; and sexual mores, 122–25; and standard of living, 76
Climatic change, 37, 75
Cocamilla Indians, 52
Coital abstinence, 9, 10, 16, 17, 66–67, 69, 147
Coital frequence and scheduling, 5, 9–10, 78
Coitus interruptus, 9, 122
Colonialism, 18, 103–53; effects on demographic processes, 105–09, 125–38; India, 138–43; and Third World population policy, 177–78
Communism, 151n
Competition, 25–26, 54, 57, 60–61
Concubinage, 86, 90–91, 99
Connacht (province, Ireland), 131, 132, 138
Conscious intent (population regulation), 13–15, 16, 17, 31, 104–5
Contraception, 8, 16, 89, 151, 181; Christianity and, 84, 86; among middle class, 122, 123; modern, 18, 171, 182
Corvée, 74, 89
Costs/benefits of child rearing, 10–13, 73, 100, 182; in agricultural modes of production, 41, 43–44; carrying infants and toddlers, 22, 39, 41; class-based differences in, 120–21, 124; conscious decisions about, 13–15, 16, 17, 31, 104–05; development and, 171–75; and EFM, 157; to females, 56, 60, 167; and fertility rate (England), 117–19; among human foragers, 34–35; in Ireland, 130; and medical selective ne-

glect, 167–68; and optimal family size, 98; recipients of, 18–19, 42–44, 60–61, 69, 89; sedentarism and, 39; in specific circumstances, 51; Third World, 176–77

Cottage industry, 106, 117, 119, 131

Cotton industry, 106–7, 131, 137

Crowding (urban), 76

Cultural anthropology, 2

Cultural context, 1, 2, 10, 11; in abortion, 27–28; in birth and death rates, 34–35; and demographic effects of warfare, 55–56; of infanticide, 29, 30, 31, 32; of intensive economies, 71; intentionality in/and, 16–17; in mortality control, 156; in sex-biased diet, 162–63, 164–67; in sexual response, 66–67; and stress, 66

Cultural evolution, 2, 19–20, 43

Cultural materialism (research strategy), 1–2, 3

Culture, and nature, 2, 4

"Culture System" (Dutch), 143–48

Custom, 102

Danube River valley, 47

Death control. *See* Mortality control

Death rates. *See* Mortality rates

Defense, 11–12, 61

Deforestation, 47, 64, 75, 92

Delphi, 80

Demographic change: conditions of, 176–83

Demographics, 103, 106; Europe, 95–96; "free market," 180–82; of hunting-dependent agricultural societies, 37, 53–55; Neolithic, 40–44; optimizing rationalizations in, 19–20; Third World, 177; warfare in, 55–62

Demographic theory: weaknesses in, 13–14, 15

Demographic transition (the), 100, 124, 155; class and, 116–22; conditions underlying, 176–83; development and, 174–75; historical processes and, 103–5; infant mortality control and, 100–2; poverty/fertility relationship in, 136–38; Third World, 181

Derbyshire, 111, 112T

Development: in colonies, 138, 145; and costs of children, 171–75; and the demographic transition, 174–75; and population regulation, 155–83; *see also* Economic development

Diarrhea, 118, 168

Diet, 38, 41–42, 43, 62, 93, 120, 179; in colonies, 141, 146; infant, 49; Paleolithic, 23; in pastoral societies, 45; and population growth, 49–50; pregnancy, perinatal, lactation, 5, 164–67; and reproduction, 26–27; sex-biased, 42, 69–71, 162–64; *see also* Nutrition

Disease, 41, 60, 92, 93–94, 106, 115, 118, 140; density-dependent, 75–76; as natural fertility control, 151, 152

Division of labor, 22–23, 39, 70

Divorce, 86

Dobe !Kung, 23–24

Domestication, 21, 41, 43, 44, 47*n*; *see also* Animal domesticants

Domestic economy, 111–12

Domestic service, 122

Dowry, 160

Early Holocene, 37

East Africa, 45

East India Company, 139, 141, 142, 144

Ecological conditions: and population regulation, 34–35, 37; and settlement patterns, 40–41

Ecological periodicity, 52

Economic change, 87, 94, 104, 149–50

Economic development, 103, 175; and population policy: Third World, 176–80; *see also* Development

Economic intensification, 71, 110–11

Economic organization, 70, 74

Economy: broad spectrum, 37–38, 39, 40, 41; coercive, 73

Ecuador, 161

Education, 117, 173, 174, 175

EFM, *see* Excess female mortality (EFM)

Egypt, 77, 176–77

Eichstätt, Germany, 96

Elvira, council of, 84–85

Emigration: Ireland, 133, 136

Empire(s), 51, 55–56, 74, 75, 78–79

Employment opportunity, 94, 174–75

Enga (people), 64

England, 166, 172; colonialism: Ireland, 125–38; commercialization of agriculture, 95; demographic rewards of colonialism in, 105–9; EFM, 156; population growth, 93, 100, 102, 105, 109–10, 115, 136, 142, 147–48; urban centers, 113–15; witchcraft, 96–97; working class, 163

Environment, 66, 69; depletion of, 13, 64, 75, 92; infanticide and, 60–61; and productivity/reproductivity relationship, 52–53

Epidemics, 88, 142, 151

Eskimos, 22–23, 32

Estrogen, 26

Ethno-eugenics, 169–71, 182

Etoro (people), 67

Europe, 95; agriculture in, 47, 48; capitalism in, 103, 104; failure of pronatalism in, 92–94; infant mortality control in, 90–92; population growth in, 100–02

European Antiquity: pronatalist policy in, 78–79

Evolution, 14, 21; cultural, 2, 19–20, 43

Excess female mortality (EFM), 156–57, 171; means of achieving, 161–64; in medical selective neglect, 167–68; in South Asia, 157–61

Exploitation, 19, 50, 71

Export crops: India, 141–42; Ireland, 128, 129, 130, 133–34, 136, 138; Java, 143, 144, 145, 146

Export-oriented economies, Third World, 178, 180

Factories, 111, 117, 123

Factory legislation, 120

Factory system, 106, 113, 119

Family organization, 88, 124

Family planning programs, 172, 182–83

Family size, 153, 172; optimized, 94, 98–99; and price of labor, 112–13; prosperity and, 136–38; Third World, 176

Famine(s), 95–96, 138; India, 139, 141–42; Java, 146; as natural population control, 139, 141, 151, 152; *see also* Great Potato Famine (the)

Female children: at risk, 42; *see also* Female infanticide

Female labor: class-based differences in value of, 122–23; value of, 109–13, 132, 156, 157, 159; *see also* Workload, female

Female sexuality: dichotomous ideology of, 123–24; fear of, 96

Female infanticide, 32–33, 34, 92, 97–99, 155–56, 157; warfare and, 55–62

Fertility, 1, 11, 41, 121; controlled, 16, 104; effect of foraging life-style on, 23–25; effect of nutritional deprivation on, 7–8; effect of poverty on, 136–38; malevolent, 97; and women as polluting, 68; *see also* Natural fertility

Fertility control, 13, 16, 17, 55, 94; in ancient Greece and Rome, 80; in Asia, 99; breast-feeding as means of, 33–35; development and, 174–75; in Europe, 100–01; infanticide in, 30; late feudal, 88–89; in Malthus, 151–53; in Paleolithic, 28; physical mechanisms of, 78; rational, 104; U.S. policy and, 181–82; among working class, 124–25

Fertility curves: age-specific, 16, 18

Fertility rates, 5, 10, 33, 176; cultural factors in, 1, 10; in England, 116–17; and female workload, 23; among human foragers, 22; in Java, 147; lactation and, 8–9

Feticide, *see* Abortion (feticide)

Fetuses, 5–7

Feudalism, 84, 87; fertility control in, 88–89

Flax, 131–32, 137

Food distribution, 59–61; within households, 155, 161–64

Food shortages, 42, 76

Food storage, 39, 41, 42

Food supply, 54–55, 58–59, 61–62

Foraging, 21, 22; physiological effects of, 23–25

Fore (people), 69

Foster's Corn Law (England), 130

Foundling homes, 91

Game depletion, 58–59, 61–62

Gathering, 23, 27

Girls, care of, 5, 7–8

Gonadotrophic hormones, 8

Grains, 73; root crops vs., 47–50; exports: Ireland to England, 128, 130
Great Potato Famine (the), 125, 126, 133, 134, 135, 136, 137, 138
Greece, 47, 79–80, 81–84
Guatemala, 40, 161, 178
Gujarat (India), 97

Habitat, carrying capacity of, 13
Hagen (people), 68
Han Dynasty, 77
Health care, 175; *see also* Medical care
Herbaceous plants, 47–48
Herd management, 45
Hewa (people), 69
Hinduism, 84, 161
Hippocratic oath, 80
History, 3–4; and the demographic transition, 103–05
Homicide, 7
Homosexuality, 9, 14, 66–67, 68; in ancient Greece and Rome, 81–84; Christianity and, 84
Hormonal levels, 26
Household: value of child labor in, 111, 117
Household production, 70
Housing, 113, 118, 120
Huallaga River floodplain, 52
Human foragers, 21–35
Human life, as continuum, 29, 182
Hunter-agriculturalists, 94
Hunter-gatherers, 3–4, 21, 68, 70; infanticide among, 56, 94; modern, 34; in Paleolithic-Neolithic transitions, 37–40
Hunting, 22–23, 37–38, 40, 41, 49, 56; and agricultural modes of production, 53–55; in New Guinea, 63, 64; among Yanomamo, 58, 59, 60–62
Hwa Ho River valley, 51, 77
Hypergyny, 99

Illegitimacy, 88–89, 90
Immigration: centripetal, 75; to urban centers, 76, 116
Incest prohibitions, 11
India, 43, 74, 136, 161, 170–71, 173–74; capitalism in, 103; colonialism in, 109, 133, 138–43; development in, 175;

EFM, 156–61; infanticide, 97, 99; population growth in, 77, 177; selective medical neglect in, 168; sex-biased diet in, 163; textile industry in, 107, 139–40
Indonesia, 145
Industrial capitalism, 71, 101, 115; *see also* Capitalism
Industrial employment, 100
Industrialization, 138, 146, 156; in England, 106–08, 113, 115–17, 127–28; and productivity/reproductivity tension, 117–19; and value of child labor, 172, 174
Industrial revolution, 100, 103, 108, 110, 120, 122, 148
Infanticide, 6, 7, 10, 15, 69, 119, 151, 182, 183; in ancient Greece and Rome, 80, 83; in Asia, 97–99; breast-feeding vs., 33–35; Christianity and, 85; deferred, 156; diminution of, 100, 101; and environmental stress, 60–61; in Europe, 90–92; among human foragers, 29–31; among !Kung, 34; and standard of living, 94; suppression of, 124, 157; *see also* Female infanticide
Infant mortality, 34, 41, 93, 94, 110, 136; capitalist development and (Third World), 178–79, 180; culturally controlled, 18; ethno-eugenics in, 169–71; industrialization and, 118–19; medical selective neglect and, 167–68, 171
Infant mortality control, 88, 90–92; in Asia, 97–99; and the demographic transition, 100–2
Infants: care of, 5–7, 78
Infrastructural determinism (principle), 2, 3, 160, 177
Infrastructure, 1–4, 19, 55, 145
Innocent VIII, pope, 96
Intentionality: in behavior, 16–17; in population regulation, 13–15, 16, 17, 31, 104–5
International Monetary Fund (IMF), 178, 179, 180
International Planned Parenthood Federation (IPPF), 181
Iran, 3
Ireland, 82n, 125–27, 161, 172, 177; colonizing effects of English market on,

Ireland (*Continued*)
  127–38, 139; economic redundancy of people of, 132–36; food exports to England, 128, 129, 130, 133–34, 136, 138; political economy of population growth in, 129–32
Irish linen, 131–32
Islam, 143

Japan, 101–2, 157; infanticide, 97, 98–99
Java, 143–48, 172
Jericho (town), 47

Kalahari !Kung, 31
Kalahari San, 24, 26, 39
Kenya, 45–46
!Kung, 29, 33–34, 68

Labor, 48–49, 138, 149; aristocracy of, 12n; demand for, 87, 130, 140–47; forced, 145
Labor conscription, 73, 74, 77, 89
Labor intensification, 53, 64
Labor market, laissez-faire, 149–50
Labor relations, in colonialism, 105, 106, 107, 138
Labor reserve, 89, 109, 145; children as, 110–12
Labor supply, 74, 124, 153
Labor value of children, 109–13, 120–21, 147, 172–75
Labor value of women, 109–13, 132; and EFM, 156, 157, 159
Lactation, 19, 34, 119; dietary deprivation during, 164–67; frequency and scheduling of, 5, 8–9, 78; prolonged, 16, 17, 49; *see also* Amenorrhea, lactational
Laissez-faire, 142, 149–50
Lancashire, 111, 112, 114T, 115, 116, 119
Land, control of, 138
Land tenure, 140
Land use, Ireland, 128–29, 134–35, 137
Latin America, 163, 170, 178–79
Less-developed countries: EFM in, 157–62; modes of reproduction in, 155; population-regulating mechanisms in, 171–72; sex-biased nutritional deprivation in, 165; *see also* Third World
Libido, 8

Life expectancy, 8, 42–43, 119–20, 157
Liverpool, 108, 111, 114, 115, 116
Living conditions: middle class, 120; working class, 113–15, 116, 119–20; *see also* Standard of living
Longevity, 41, 74, 120
Lower class: child-rearing responsibilities of, 94; rationalization of poverty of, 148–50, 152–53

Machiguenga Indians, 48
Maize, 52–53
Male robustness, 56
Males: fertility, 8; food distribution to, 42, 59; and infanticide, 29–30; status of, 61
Malleus Maleficarum ("The Hammer of Witches"), 96
Malnutrition, 7, 8, 78, 167, 168, 179; *see also* Undernutrition
Malthusianism, 126, 129, 132, 133, 135, 136, 137–38, 139
Mammals, 54–55
Manioc (root crop), 52, 58
Manufacturing technology, 106, 107
Marital exchange, 11, 88, 160
Markets: colonies as, 138
Marriage, 10, 83, 88, 89; Christianity and, 85–86; deferred, 120, 137, 151, 152, 175; industrial revolution and, 112–13
Masturbation, 9
Matlab Food and Nutrition Study, 164, 168
Mature states: population growth, 76–78
Mayas, 76–77
Mbuti Pygmies, 39
Meat (in diet), 23, 45, 59, 65, 66, 70, 134
Medical care: selective neglect in, 155, 167–68, 171; Third World, 179
Mediterranean, 74
Menarche: age at, 7, 24, 34; postponed, 23–24, 119
Menopause, 23, 34, 161
Menstrual blood, 68
Menstruation, 24, 68
Mercantilism, 95, 108
Mesoamerica, 40, 48, 49, 74
Mesolithic period, 38, 42

Mexico, 178–79
Middle Ages: Church in, 85–86; demographic theology in, 86–87
Middle class, 120, 122–23, 124
Middle East, 41, 47
Midwives, 97, 168
Militarism, 73
Milk, 49, 118; rationing of, 155, 161–62
Miscarriage, 5; *see also* Abortion, spontaneous
Miseration (misery), 13, 117, 148; index of, 101; as natural fertility control, 151, 152
Misogyny, 96
Miyanmin (people), 63
Modernization, 104
Modes of production, 5, 10, 37–38, 44; changes in, 43; and fertility control, 172, 182; hunting-gathering, 34; marital exchange in, 160; and productivity/reproductivity relationship, 51; and value of child labor, 40, 172, 174
Modes of reproduction, 2, 5–10, 19–20, 44, 172; child labor and, 40; cultural/biological pressures in, 1, 2, 10; death control as, 155; effect of employment opportunities on, 174–75; marital exchanges in, 160; systems and, 14–15
Moral restraint, as method of birth control, 151, 152, 153, 183
Morbidity, men, 8
Mortality: age-specific, 1, 34; in agricultural modes of production, 41; class-determined (England), 120, 121; decline in, 100; effects of nutritional stress on, 7–8; female, 55; infant, 165; juvenile, 76; male, 8; urban, 113, 115–16; working-class (England), 119–20; *see also* Natural mortality
Mortality control, 13, 15, 55, 182; ancient Greece and Rome, 80; culturally mediated, 156; effect of colonialism on, 110; infant, child, 94; infanticide in, 30; intentionality in, 14, 17–18; relationship of birth control to, 153; sex-neutral, 169–71; sex-specific, 155–68; systemic, 155, 157; unconscious decisions in, 161; working-class (England), 119

Mortality rates, 5, 10, 93, 102; cultural factors in, 1, 10, 34; EFM in, 156; fluctuation in, 33; infant, child (England), 110T; sex-specific, 44, 157, 158, 168; women, 162; among Yanomamo, 60
Mothers: deprived, 12; and infanticide, 30; mobility, 22, 23
Muslim religion, 158–59

Napoleonic Wars, 130, 137, 144
Natural fertility, 15–18, 31, 33, 35, 104
Natural mortality, 15–18, 31, 35
Nature: culture and, 2; in environmental depletion, 75; laws of, 151–52
Neglect, 92, 119, 168, 171
Neolithic period, 50, 51, 110, 113; demographic aspects of, 40–44; population growth in, 41, 63, 64, 74, 76
Nepal, 161, 172
New Guinea, 62–66, 94; institutionalized male homosexuality, 66–67; women as polluting, 68–69
Nile River valley, 51, 77
Noncoital heterosexual techniques, 9, 151
North America, EFM in, 157
North Sea Canal, 146
Northern Provinces (India), 97
Nursing, 6, 49; *see also* Breast-feeding
Nurturance (of children), 6, 100, 102, 113, 175, 182; rationing of, 155, 167, 168
Nutrition, 92, 155, 175; and abortion, 28–29; of children, 101, 118; in EFM, 155, 161–64; and fertility, 23–25, 119; sex-biased, 165, 166, 167, 168; in women, 5, 7–8, 9; of working class (England), 134; *see also* Diet

Optimal: vs. optimizing, 19–20
Optimizing rationalities, 1, 5, 14, 19, 155, 171
Optimum population level (proposed), 79
Overlaying, 17–18, 90
Overpopulation, 79, 148; myth of, 148–53
Ovulation, 24, 25

Paleolithic period, 42; population regulation in, 21, 23, 28, 32; reading forward from, 3–4
Paleolithic-Neolithic transitions, 37–40
Paleopathology, 42
Panglossian functionalism, 19
Pastoralism, 39–40, 45–46, 70
Pauline letters, 84
Peasantry, 87, 92; ancient Rome, 82; in capitalist development, 148; dispossession of, 95; fertility of, 19; in India, 140; infanticide, 99; Ireland, 126, 129, 133–34, 137, 138; Java, 144, 146; reproductive potential of, 74, 78; revolts by, 95; standard of living, 76
Pedicide, 182, 183; sex-biased, 155–56
Perimenopausal fertility decline, 7
Peru, 74
Pessaries, 122
Physiology, human, adaptability of, 167, 171
Pig husbandry, 63–66, 69–70
Plague (the), 93
Plantations, 109, 138
Plassey, battle of, 107–08
Pleistocene period, 34, 37, 104
Political authority, 86
Political economy(ies): exploitative, 148–51; of Irish population growth, 129–32
Political upheavals: in rise of state, 77–78
Politico-economic systems, 51; complex, 44; warfare and, 56
Politics in command, 3, 4, 177
Pollution (women), 67–69
Polygyny, 8, 10, 86
Poor laws, 149–50, 152
Poor relief, 111, 126, 149–50
Population: optimum, 79; pristine states, 73–76; ratio of, to productive resources, 13; surplus, 125, 137–38, 150–52
Population densities, 4, 37, 38, 44, 70; in agricultural modes of production, 41, 49, 55; New Guinea, 63–66; prehistory, 13; pristine states, 75; tropical forest systems, 51; urban England, 114–15

Population growth: in agricultural modes of production, 41, 49–50, 53; cotton imports and, 109T; in England, 93, 100, 102, 105, 109–10, 115, 136, 142, 147–48; in Europe, 86–87, 92; in India, 139, 142–43; in Ireland, 129–32, 137; in Java, 143–48; Malthusian means of controlling, 148–53; myth of irrational, 134, 137, 143, 146, 148–53; and price of labor, 112–13; and quality of life, 43–44; in pastoralist societies, 45–46; rates of, 1, 13, 21–22, 75T; sedentarism and, 38–39; subject to systematic controls, 153; urban (England), 113, 114
Population growth curve, 76
Population loss, Europe, 93–94
Population policy, 155; state-formulated, 74; Third World, 176–83
Population pressure: defined, 33n; Ireland, 138
Population regulation, 5–10, 15, 19–20; in age of colonialism, 103–53; and agricultural modes of production, 37–71; conscious, 13–15, 16, 17, 31, 104–5; and the development process, 155–83; among early human foragers, 21–35; homosexuality in, 14; in Malthus, 151–53; infant mortality in, 102; late feudal, 88–89; mechanisms of, 171–72; through natural fertility, 15–18, 31, 33, 35, 104; optimal vs. optimizing, 19–20; by peasants, 78; in preindustrial societies, 182–83; recipients of benefits of, 18–19; and rise of state, 73–102; sex-specific costs of, 19; warfare as component of, 55–62; witchcraft and, 68–69
Pornography, 123
Portuguese, 143
Potato, claim of Irish reliance on, 125–26, 127, 128, 129–30, 131, 132, 133
Poverty, 92, 118, 183; effect of development on, 166–67; effect on fertility, 136–38; and mortality control, 171–72; as natural response to overpopulation, 125, 150–52; and sexual relations, 123–24; Third World, 179–80; working-class (England), 115, 117, 119, 123

Predation, 37–38, 49, 55
Pregnancy, 117, 175; costs of, 18–19; dietary deprivation during, 164–67; illicit, 88–89; nutrition in, 28–29
Prehistory, 3–4; abortion in, 25–26; population densities/growth rates, 13, 34–35
Preindustrial societies: abortion in, 28; conscious decisions about child rearing in, 14, 18; costs/benefits of child rearing in, 11–13; death control in, 155; homosexuality in, 67; infanticide in, 29, 32, 97; population regulating systems in, 1, 10, 19; premarital conceptions in, 9–10; sex-biased nutritional deprivation in, 165, 166, 167; warfare in, 56
Prestate societies: homosexuality in, 81; warfare in, 56
Prey species, 62, 64; *see also* Game depletion
Primates: abortion, 25–26; homosexuality, 66; infanticide, 29–30
Pristine states, 73–76
Private property, 150, 151
Procreation: Christianity and, 85–87
Production, 116; intensification of, 73; and reproductive behavior, 138; *see also* Modes of production
Productivity, 4, 87; sex-role specialization, 22; of women, 49–50
Productivity rate, and reproductivity rate, 13, 20, 25
Productivity/reproductivity tension, 20, 56–57, 70, 117–19, 166–67; in Malthus, 152–53; in tropical fruit systems, 51
Prolactin, 24–25
Proletariat, European, 95
Pronatalism, 74, 92–94, 97; Christian, 85–86; defied by peasants, 78; in European Antiquity, 78–79; and homosexuality, 67; of Irish landlords, 128–29; in Japan, 98
Property relations, 105, 138
Prostitution, 83, 123, 151
Protein, 41–42, 58, 155, 162–64
Protestant ethic, 104
Public assistance, 153
Public sector spending, Third World, 178, 179

Public works, 73
Punjab (India), 97
"Putting out" system, 117

Quality of life, in agricultural societies, 42–43

Rainfall, 42, 47
Rationality, 15; conscious, 103, 104–5
Raw materials, 108, 109, 138, 141
Reagan administration, 181
Religion in command, 3, 4
Rendille (people), 45–46
Rents, 138, 140, 141; raising of, by landlords, 87, 126, 128–29
Reproduction: in capitalist development, 148; costs/benefits in, 10–13; effects of diet, workload, stress on, 26–27; incentives/disincentives to, 176–77; industrialization and, 116–17; myth of imprudent (Ireland), 125–27, 132–55; productivity and, 49–50; *see also* Productivity/reproductivity tension
Reproductive coital sex, 9–10
Reproductive physiology, effect of foraging on, 23–25
Reproductive pressure, 33, 73; coital abstinence and, 66–67; and witchcraft, 67–69, 94–97
Reproductive success: male status and, 61
Reproductivity rate, productivity rate and, 13, 20, 25
Resource availability: and infanticide, 30–31; and population growth, 34; warfare and, 55; scarcity in, 34, 53, 69, 95–96
Resource base, Greek city states, 79
Resource distribution, 70
Resources: control of strategic, 138, 139
Roads, 73, 145
Rome: anti-natalist behavior, 79–80; Christianity and, 85; homosexuality, 81–84; pronatalist policy, 78–79, 81–82, 83–84
Root crops, 47–50, 62–63
Ruling class(es), 19, 73, 77, 79, 129; and ideological rationalization of poverty,

Ruling class(es) (*Continued*)
148–50, 152–53; pronatalist policy of, 74, 78, 89
Rural sector: India, 140–42; Java, 146–47

Sanitation, 41, 76
Scarcity, 34, 53, 69, 95–96
Secondary states: defined, 77; population growth, 76–78
Sedentarism, 4, 37, 40–44, 46–47; demographic consequences of, 42–43, 53–55; and disease transmission, 75; and female workload, 50; pastoralism and, 46; and population growth, 38–39; and sex-associated dietary variation, 70; tropical forests and, 51–53; among Yanomamo, 58
Selection: for survival or marginal diets, 164, 171
Semen, 67, 147
Sentimental satisfactions: child rearing, 10–11
Settlement patterns, 37
Settlement size, 44, 55, 59
Sex: extramarital, 9; nonreproductive, 9
Sex ratios, 32, 92, 156; India, 157–58, 160–61; juvenile, 56, 57–58, 97, 98
Sexual hierarchies, 18–19, 71
Sexual mores, class and, 122–25
Sexual taboos, 9, 49, 67, 88
Sh'ite fundamentalism, 3
Skilled workers, 121*n*
Slave trade, 108, 114
Slavery, 82, 84
Sloths, 55
Social change, 4, 94, 149–51
Social conflict, 55, 59, 69
Social order: ancient Rome, 83, 84; capitalism as, 151
Social services, 175
Social status: and costs of population regulation, 18–19; and food distribution, 59, 61; and rise of state, 73; *see also* Class
Social system, 66, 116; class in, 122; economic advantage of children in, 136–37; global, 105
Sociocultural evolution, 14
Sociocultural systems, 1–2, 304
Sociopolitical evolution, 53

South Asia, EFM in, 157–61
Southeast Asia, 74
Spain, colonialism, 106, 108
Sparta, 79
Sperm motility, 8
Standard of living, 43, 101; and EFM, 156; in Europe, 95–96; family size and, 172; and infanticide rates, 94; in Java, 143, 146, 147; and population growth, 93, 98; social class and, 76
Starvation, 6, 151
State(s), 4, 19, 51, 75; and population regulation, 73–102; warfare in, 55–56
Stature: social class and, 76–77
Stress: abortion and, 25–26, 28; economic, ecological, 76; environmental, 68; nutritional, 69; pregnant, lactating women, 8; reproductive, 54–55; resource, 34; seasonal, 41
Structure, 1–4, 55
Subsistence: Java, 146, 147; India, 140; population and, 148
Subsistence activities, 38; broad spectrum, 39, 40–41
Suckling, 24–25
Suez Canal, 142
Sumatra, 143
Superstructure, 1–4
Sweden, 156, 163, 168
Sweet potato, 63–64, 70
Systems, population-regulating, 14–15

Taboos: pregnancy, lactation, 28, 165–67; sex, 9, 49, 67, 88
Taiwan, 161
Taxation, 73, 74, 77, 89, 138, 141; in kind, 143–44
Technoeconomic restraints, 4
Techno-environmental circumstances, 5
Technology, 38, 86–87; and costs/benefits of rearing children, 34–35; manufacturing, 106, 107
Textile industry, 107–08, 109, 131, 139–40
Theology, demographic: Middle Ages, 86–87
Third World: population policy, 176–83
Tikal (Mayan city), 76
Time frame(s), 3, 4

Trade, 73, 87; colonizing effects of English, 106–7, 127–38
Trade deficits, 178
Trade unions, 121*n*, 128
Treaty of Utrecht, 108
Tropical forests, 47–48, 54, 56, 62; Amazon Basin, 51–53
Tuberculosis, 115, 168
Tuscany, 88

Underdevelopment, 139, 148, 175
Undernutrition, 78, 118, 164, 167
Unemployment, 95, 111, 153
United East India Company (V.O.C.), 143–44
United Nations Fund for Population Activities (UNFPA), 181
United Nations International Conference on Population, Mexico City, 1984, 176
United States, 178; Civil War, 118–19; fertility rates, 117; and Third World population policy, 176, 177, 180–82
Unwed motherhood, 9
Upper class(es), 99, 122; *see also* Ruling class(es)
Urban centers, 75–76, 113–16
Urbanization, 87, 92–93, 156; and value of child labor, 172, 174

Veracruz, 40
Village economy: Java, 145, 146–47
Villages, 4, 41, 53, 62; warfare and, 55–56, 73; fissioning, 59, 60T
Virgin Mary, cult of, 94

Wage labor, 100
Wages, 116, 153, 167
Warfare, 55, 65, 66, 73; as component in population regulation, 55–62, 151; labor supply and, 74, 81–82; among Yanomamo, 61–62
War of the Spanish Succession, 108
Wealth, 83, 88, 106
Weaning, 6, 41, 161–62
Welfare service, 175
West Africa, 41–42
West Indies, 108, 109
Wet nurses, 90–91
White-collar employment, 173, 174
Witchcraft, 67–69, 94–97
Witches: fear of, 94–97; killed, 69, 96, 97; women regarded as, 67, 96, 98
Women: attitudes toward, 67–69, 80, 94–95; bearing costs of lowering fertility/mortality rates, 17–18; care of, 5, 7–8; economic redundancy of, 122–23; in labor force, 117–19, 147, 175 (*see also* Labor value of women; Workload, female); nutritional status, 60, 69; productive role of, 22; status of, 44, 50, 70, 176; *see also* Costs/benefits of child rearing; Productivity/reproductivity tension
Woolen industry, 107, 131
Workhouses, 111, 149
Working class, 113, 130, 134, 149–50, 163; in capitalist development, 148, 152; fertility rates, 117–19; poverty, 115, 123; public assistance to, 153; women in, 122–24
Workload, female, 26, 28, 42, 50, 72; in agricultural societies, 43–44; effect on female infanticide, 56; and fertility, 23–25, 119; and infanticide, 31; during pregnancy and lactation, 5, 165, 166–67
World Bank, 178, 179, 180

Yangtzee River valley, 51
Yanomamo (people), 6, 28, 57–62